The Legacy of Zion

INTERTESTAMENTAL
TEXTS RELATED TO THE
NEW TESTAMENT

Henry R. Moeller,
EDITOR

BAKER BOOK HOUSE/Grand Rapids, Michigan

PHOTOLITHOPRINTED BY CUSHING - MALLOY, INC.
ANN ARBOR, MICHIGAN, UNITED STATES OF AMERICA
1977

In memoriam
William H. Rossell, Ph.D.,
preceptor in Semitics, and friend
and
In gratitude to
James Muilenburg, Ph.D.,
scholar and teacher extraordinary

List of Abbreviations

Ant.	Josephus, *Antiquities of the Jews*
Jub.	*Jubilees*
M.	Mishnah
Man. Disc.	*Manual of Discipline/Community Rule*
Ps. Sol.	*Psalm of Solomon*
T.	*Testament*
War	Josephus, *History of the Jewish War*
Zad. Doc.	*Zadokite Document*

Preface

Two things, principally, inspired the preparation of this book of readings from Judaic documents of the intertestamental era. First was a long-held conviction that in order to understand the New Testament, more is to be gained from the thought-world of the intertestamental documents than from a great deal found in the later talmudic materials. Comparison of those works usually classed as "apocrypha" and "pseudepigrapha" (including the Qumran documents) with the New Testament as well as with the Old has confirmed this conviction, as has much recent scholarship. The non-specialist can at least be sure that more of this material is either clearly prior to, or contemporary with, Jesus and the apostles than is much that is found in the Talmud and Midrash.

Next in importance was the discovery made several years ago during a period of research into Johannine backgrounds that there is available to students no handbook of source readings devoted to those documents that often illuminate most vividly the relationship of New Testament christology to its background of Judaic messianism. R. H. Charles' two-volume *Apocrypha and Pseudepigrapha,* besides being unwieldy and, in some respects, outdated, is too expensive for most Bible-school and seminary students to own. Editions of the separate documents in translation are either old, difficult to obtain, or nonexistent. Because of the breadth of its range, C. K. Barrett's otherwise excellent source book, *The New Testament Background,* omits materials which are of great value for illuminating the background of the New Testament. The same must be said of Howard Clark Kee's recently published *The Origins of Christianity: Sources and Documents.*

If "one picture is worth a thousand words," original documents relevant to a field of study are often worth entire books of discussion. This truth was instilled into my thinking by the first of the two men to whom this work is dedicated. It would be heartily approved by the second. It has certainly proved true in my own experience.

However, students need incentive and guidance if they are to derive the maximum benefit from such documents. A book of selected source readings, in which the general historical relationships of the materials are at least to some extent indicated, and in which thought relationships are pointed to by cross references and notes, seemed to be called for. My purpose, then, was to provide such a reader. Students at my own school were foremost in my mind. A few years ago, using text editions then available, I began to prepare for them annotated selections of several of the documents which form the core of this reader.

A faculty colleague used these selections with his students in the New Testament introduction course. More recently, some have been used in the Biblical Theology course, to illustrate how the Israelite religion developed into Judaism and how great Old Testament themes were carried through the intertestamental era into the New Testament period. Many students have testified to finding these materials enlightening for their biblical studies.

A recent sabbatical made it possible for me to begin expanding that nucleus of readings according to the present plan and format. In the meantime, new editions of important documents have become available, and I have been glad to make use of them. Among these are the Greek texts of the *Testaments of the Twelve Patriarchs,* the *Testament of Job,* important fragments of *I Enoch,* and the *Exodus* of Ezekiel the "Tragedian."

This manual is not intended to supplant C. K. Barrett's work nor that of Howard Clark Kee, noted above, although a small overlap with both may be found. Rather, since it focuses exclusively on Judaic materials, this reader complements and supplements the selections of Judaica to be found in them. Further, since the standard Apocrypha and the Qumran Scrolls documents are so readily available in editions both good and inexpensive, I have drawn most sparingly from them, although they are cross-referenced wherever appropriate.

This is not intended to be a work for specialists, who might wish to raise questions at various points. All that is claimed is reasonable accuracy, both as to the translations and as to the historical interpretations. Understandably I have drawn on the labors of others too numerous to mention here or even in the limited bibliography provided for the guidance of students, although some are acknowledged in the notes to the special Extended Notes in Part Three. All have my profound gratitude.

The contents of this manual represent the results of historical study, and they are intended to foster historical study. Yet it has been my observation that students of a conservative Christian background tend to become uneasy if an author deals with such matters as the person of Jesus, the New Testament scriptures, or Christian beginnings in the objective way that historical studies require; or if he seems to suggest that the New Testament writers did not receive all that they wrote by direct revelation. Let me assure my readers that I am a practicing churchman, and that my faith is centered just where that of the whole Church has been since its beginning: in the revelation of God's love and saving grace through His Son, Jesus Christ.

But He, during His ministry, and His disciples lived and spoke *in* and *from,* as well as *to,* their times. They drew upon their rich religious heritage in Judaism, centralized in their scriptures, in order to communicate God's new Reality present in Jesus. Their success indicates the effectiveness of their communication, and it can teach us something about communicating the gospel in this day. If this work will in any way serve toward that end, its author will be amply repaid.

An expression of sincere gratitude is in order to the Board and Administration of Central Baptist Theological Seminary for granting the sabbatical a few years ago that made possible intensive beginning work on this project; to my colleagues in Bible who, by using many of these materials with students in an earlier format, tested their usefulness and who also carried some of my teaching duties during my sabbatical; and to the late Dr. Charles F. Pfeiffer, who (among other kindnesses), as representative for Baker Book House, encouraged me to produce a manuscript for publication. Finally, I owe appreciation to my publishers without whose patience and expertise this work, in its present form, would not have seen the light of day.

Henry R. Moeller
Central Baptist Theological Seminary
Kansas City, Kansas
September, 1976

Contents

Index of Readings

PART ONE

General Introduction

This reader has been designed mainly to help students in seminary or Bible school to understand more fully the religious background of New Testament thought. It will therefore be to the distinct advantage of the student to read this Introduction in its entirety before making use of Part Two, which is the heart of this manual of source readings.

I. General Purpose and Plan

A. Purpose

Three interrelated aims are in view: First, to help the student gain a sense of the history of Judaism during the period just prior to the times of Jesus and the apostles, in a way not achieved quite so well by textbook discussions alone. The Historical Sketch at the beginning of each major section of Readings contributes to this aim. So do shorter notes and comments interspersed throughout the Readings for explanatory purposes.

Second, to facilitate immediate contact with the Judaic thought-world of the intertestamental period through translated selections from significant documents of the era, especially those not so readily available to most students and laymen. These selections, it is hoped, will encourage the student to read more widely in the source documents of this era. Many of these are currently available in the handy Revised Standard Version of the Apocrypha and in English translations of the Qumran (Dead Sea) scriptures.

Third, to illustrate the importance of the entire corpus of the intertestamental literature for New Testament studies by (a) noting thought relationships between this literature and both Old and New Testaments; (b) highlighting the continuity and development of the great religious themes of the Old Testament during this period as a background for the New Testament; (c) noting the appearance of new doctrines significant for New Testament theology; (d) drawing attention to motifs and terminology in the literature which reappear in the New Testament; and (e) illustrating attitudes toward and the usage of the Old Testament scriptures during this period.

The topical arrangement of the Readings will be the main method of achieving this aim. Marginal cross references, introductions and comments, and the longer discussions of Part Three will also contribute.

B. Plan

PART ONE: General Introduction. This should be read before use is made of Parts Two and Three.

PART TWO: The Documents. This part is divided into three main sections. Each section opens with a Historical Sketch provided by relevant excerpts from Josephus' *Jewish War*. This is followed, in each section, by one or two main subsections, containing Readings arranged in a topical scheme. To enhance understanding, introductory statements are placed before the Readings, and there are special explanatory comments following them.

Wherever appropriate or feasible, cross references in the outer margin indicate further reading in the sources, as well as thought relationships with either the scriptures or other intertestamental documents. Brief explanations of textual points, marked by asterisks, also appear in the outer margin.

PART THREE: Extended Notes. Notes too long to be inserted as comments are included in this part. They are literary-historical and christological in import. It is believed that these discussions will be valuable to the student.

C. A Recommendation

In addition to reading the remainder of this General Introduction, it will greatly augment the student's understanding if he reads a history of the intertestamental times, as well as general introductions to the documents from which the source readings herein are drawn. For the history, *Between the Testaments* by Charles F. Pfeiffer is excellent, as is *Between the Testaments* by D. S. Russell. For general introductions to the documents, *An Introduction to the Apocryphal Books of the Old and New Testaments* by H. T. Andrews is good. If this is unobtainable, *An Introduction to the Apocrypha* by Bruce M. Metzger (dealing only with the books of the Apocrypha) is recommended. Russell's book contains a valuable brief discussion of the apocalyptic materials, but C. C. Torrey's *The Apocryphal Literature* is still the best compendium of introductions to the pseudepigraphical works for the student. It is unhappily out of print. Publication facts for the books mentioned are given in the Bibliography.

II. Intertestamental Literature and New Testament Interpretation

A by-product of the finds at Qumran in 1946-47 and later was a general revival of interest in the intertestamental period and its literature. This was due in part to the discovery that some works long known to scholars (e.g., *I Enoch*, the *Testaments*, and the *Zadokite Document*) were possessed by the Qumran group. Also, ideas found in the documents peculiar to this sect are closely related to ideas already known from many of the previously available works coming from this period.

Without the intertestamental literature at our disposal, we would lack data for historical understanding in many significant areas of study, in Jewish religious history as well as in the study of Christian beginnings. The Qumran literature, most of it from the pre-Christian era, added a large chapter to our knowledge of Judaic religious thought and practice at the dawn of the Christian era. But the rest of the intertestamental literature, to which the average student of the New Testament has too little recourse, is equally important.

The intertestamental period is commonly thought of as the era from about 400 B.C. to the advent of Jesus Christ. It was in this period that the Judaism out of which Christianity emerged developed. However, from the viewpoint of Jewish and Christian *literary* history, the intertestamental period could be considered to overlap most of the first Christian century. This is because (1) significant Jewish writings were produced in the apostolic era (e.g., II Esdras/IV Ezra, the *Book of the Secrets of Enoch*, and the Syriac *Apocalypse of Baruch*) and were made use of by Christian groups; and (2) most of the New Testament writings did not begin to appear much earlier than about A.D. 50-60. But all of the latter show that their authors (Paul, authors of the Gospels, et al.) were under the strong influence of their Jewish backgrounds. The upper limits of the period, from the literary-historical standpoint, can be placed at about 300 B.C., when the dream of Alexander the Great to unite the civilized world by means of the spread of hellenic culture was beginning to be realized through the policies of his successors.

The most stimulating events, from the standpoint of Jewish literary production, were those relating to the struggle of pious Jews against foreign domination and enforced hellenization. In the last two centuries B.C., especially, those zealous for the Law and the traditions of their fathers struggled to the death against hellenizers within and without. It was in the course of this struggle that Judea passed from the shifting control of Egypt and Syria into the iron grip of Rome about 63 B.C. And it was in a Judea groaning under the Roman boot that Jesus was born two generations later.

It was in those times of struggle and suffering that belief in the resurrection of the body appeared as a religious doctrine, and that the messianic hope became a living flame. Both were based on Moses and the prophets;

and both were nourished amid conflict by hasidic pietist, fervent apocalyptist and militant zealot. The messianic era, which seemed about to materialize in the early years of John Hyrcanus I, was rudely pushed into the future again by the harsh realities of foreign interference and internecine rivalries. The hope seemed destined never to be fulfilled. Yet, after John the Baptist, Jesus proclaimed its presence and its coming; and the first Christians were zealous in claiming, after their Pentecost experience, that Jesus was Israel's true Messiah. Moreover, they proclaimed that He was also the "first fruits" of resurrection and the assurance of resurrection to everyone who believed.

In the intertestamental literature, whose bulk exceeds that of the New Testament, we can trace those struggles and hopes, and sometimes get the "feel" of them. We can see how the great ideas of the Hebrew scriptures (the Christian "Old Testament") were preserved and transmitted in a living stream of religious tradition. We can see how some ideas which were implicit in the Old Testament became explicit under the pressure of religious need. Further, although most of the New Testament phraseology derives from the Old Testament (from both its original and Septuagint form), some significant New Testament terms and ideas made their first appearance in this literature. Herein, the scope of the extant literature will be briefly surveyed; and its general importance for the student of New Testament times and thought will be discussed. Then attention will focus on the background that it provides to the Christian claim that the true Messiah and Savior expected by pious Jews in the time of Herod the Tetrarch and Pontius Pilate was none other than Jesus of Nazareth, who was born in the days of Augustus and Herod the Great.

A. The Literature

1. ITS SCOPE

This literature began to appear in the century following the conquests and death of Alexander the Great (ca. 323 B.C.). The Greek translation of the Hebrew scriptures, called the *Septuagint* (and abbreviated LXX), began to be made about 250 B.C. with the translation of the Pentateuch. The apocryphal I Esdras (III Ezra) was possibly produced earlier. But most of the works seem to have been put forth during the Maccabean and Hasmonean periods (ca. 170-63 B.C.), while a few writings come from the Roman era (ca. 63 B.C. and later). Influential pseudepigraphs were produced during the first Christian century. Many of these writings show that the authors were familiar with the Hebrew Bible in its Septuagint form.

The best known are those which appear in the standard editions of the Apocrypha, which used to be, and now again can be found, published in the Bible with the canonical scriptures. In its entirety, the corpus is comprised of a number of types of writing. The most significant works can be catalogued under several broad categories, although some include more than one literary type. In the following, works which appear in the standard

Apocrypha are named first. Other works of a similar type are named following the double colon.

   a. Historical and quasi-historical (including romance and legend): I Esdras (III Ezra); Tobit; Judith; I Maccabees; II Maccabees:: *III Maccabees; Lives of the Prophets;* Josephus' *Antiquities* and *Jewish War;* Pseudo-Philo's *Biblical Antiquities.*

   b. Wisdom and rabbinic: Sirach (Ecclesiasticus); Wisdom of Solomon : : Jerusalem Targum; *Aboth.*

   c. Midrashic homilies and discourses: Baruch : : *Jubilees; Testaments of the Twelve Patriarchs; Testament of Job; IV Maccabees.*

   d. Psalms and prayers: The Prayer of Azariah and Song of the Three Men; the Prayer of Manasseh : : *The Psalms of Solomon;* the Hymn in Sirach 51 (Hebrew version); the *Shemoneh Esreh* ("Eighteen Benedictions").

   e. Apocalyptic and prophetic: II Esdras (IV Ezra) : : *I* (Ethiopic) *Enoch; Assumption of Moses; Secrets of Enoch;* the Syriac *Apocalypse of Baruch.*

2. GENERAL IMPORTANCE

This is a rich and varied literature. It discloses a Judaism which, while holding to the Law and the Prophets as the basis of its faith, was many-faceted. As literature that was written and used within the last two centuries B.C. and in the first century A.D., it witnesses to religious ideas current in Judaism in the early decades of the Christian movement in Palestine. The fact that *Christians* preserved the bulk of this literature (except for that produced in the rabbinic schools and at Qumran) and incorporated much of it into the editions of the Septuagint used by the Church indicates how congenial to the early Christian outlook much of it was. Writings of early Fathers of the Church are witnesses that some of these writings were popular well into the third or fourth Christian centuries. With but slight emendations and additions (as in the *Testaments of the Twelve Patriarchs*) some of it could be, and obviously was, used for moral instruction and as Christian messianic propaganda.

This literature has been called the "bridge between the testaments," and it is surely that. First, it is a continuation of the literary traditions of the Old Testament period, as a survey of the contents of the Apocrypha will show. I Esdras, for example, is a variant version (with a notable addition in 3:1—5:6) of the canonical Ezra. The story of Judith has literary parallels with the biblical Esther, and a similar purpose. The Wisdom of Solomon and Sirach have affinities with Proverbs and Ecclesiastes, although Wisdom is obviously of Alexandrian origin. First Maccabees is an account somewhat in the style of the biblical historical materials, and the list could go on.

   Secondly, and most important, the literature upholds and promotes the ideals of faith and religious duty found in the Old Testament. A prophetic voice of protest against apostasy from the faith of Israel in either practice or belief is heard therein. For those undergoing tribulation in their faith, bright hopes for God's triumphant vindication of His people are offered.

These themes are strong in Judith, the Wisdom of Solomon, I and II Maccabees, and in the psalms and prayers as well as in the apocalypses and testaments. Judaism was conscious of being without an officially accredited prophet (I Macc. 4:45-46; 9:27). Yet this literature became the medium through which the voices of the great prophets of the past spoke in contemporary accents with a message in season for those who would listen.

The subjugated condition of the Jews, when any sign of messianic agitation might be interpreted as revolt by their overlords, made it unsafe to prophesy publicly. But by adopting the role of ancient heroes (e.g., Enoch, Ezra), by relating "prophecies" given by the ancients (the Patriarchs, Moses), or even by writing anonymously, the prophetic word could be circulated *in written form*—perhaps to be read by some literate person in secret meetings—for the great encouragement of the pious. And this the authors of our literature evidently did.

These considerations make such writings primary sources for the study of Christian backgrounds. At the beginning of the Christian movement, the Bible of Judaism was also the Bible of the early Christians: the Hebrew scriptures, our current "Old Testament." However, the canon of Jewish scriptures does not seem to have been officially stabilized until well after A.D. 70. There is evidence that Jewish Christians made use of a number of these works which are now held to be noncanonical. Some in the predominantly Gentile churches did likewise.

꠸ Since the intertestamental authors were all dependent in one way or another on the Jewish scriptures, a study of their writings often indicates how the Old Testament was interpreted by Judaism in the late pre-Christian and early Christian eras. This in turn helps one to understand how the early Christian evangelists and apologists interpreted and used their Bibles, since they followed methods common to their times. The intertestamental writings become the means by which we can understand the general religious climate in which Christianity was born and developed, within which the first Christians put forth their claims concerning Jesus. ꠸

꠸ They are an excellent help to our sensing the heartbeat of Jewish piety at the outset of the Christian era. They open doors through which we are allowed to see Judaism in its many expressions. We meet the popular religion of Tobit, with a strong emphasis on Torah piety mingled with a heavy element of folk superstition. There is the burning nationalism of Judith, in whose story faith in God's sure response to His people's repentance and prayer is so eloquently expressed. We enter the Sage's house of study and hear his wise maxims: "To fear the Lord is the beginning of wisdom"; and we are assured that if we fear the Lord and keep His teachings we shall have length of days and immortality. This Torah (teaching) and wisdom were from eternity with God; they were given from heaven by God to His people; and they were the life and delight of the pious.

Through the prayers and psalms we share in private devotions, or enter the place of meeting to join with the worshipers in praise to the living God, and in prayer that He will soon redeem His people from sins and from oppression. We visit the conventicles of the sectaries where we learn the mysteries concerning the origin and doom of evil, the signs of the coming New Age, the manner of Messiah's appearing, and where we view scenes from the Final War and the Judgment.

The great themes of Jewish faith appear over and over, either explicitly or implicitly: the unity of God and His creative power and activity. He entered into binding covenant with the patriarchs, with His people at Sinai, with the Aaronic priesthood, and with David. The covenants form the basis of the people's solidarity, and of their hope that God will act for them in His own time.

God gave His Torah to Moses, and it has been passed on by an unbroken chain of authorized teachers to its present interpreters. True piety means living according to the Torah as these expositors interpret it. The Torah is a well of living waters, a fountain of life and light. Its precepts are food and light and life for the soul.

While God punishes sin, He readily forgives the truly repentant; but the arrogant sinner will have no share in the life to come. God will, in the Last Day, judge all men, and assign them their eternal lot in keeping with their faith and works. The unrepentant will depart into darkness and fire, but the pious will inherit eternal life and share in the resurrection of the righteous. Before the Last Judgment, however, God will send the Messiah to fulfill the program of the prophets.

Further, our literature permits significant glimpses of the religious party divisions within Judaism and of its main religious institutions. The centrality of the Temple for Jewish religious life stands out most clearly, as does the importance attached to circumcision and strict Sabbath observance. The "sanhedrin" mentioned in the Gospels seems to have developed from the "council of elders" and "senate" mentioned in Judith and I and II Maccabees.

In addition, there appear details of the order and work of the priesthood, glimpses of the rabbinic schools and of their methods of interpreting the Torah, and the claims and ideas of dissident groups. With supplementation by data from the New Testament and Josephus' writings, a fairly complete picture of Jewish religious life emerges. At the same time, the intertestamental materials support, in a general way, the veracity of the New Testament's representation of these matters.

These materials are also primary sources for studying the *immediate* background of New Testament theological concepts and terminology. Much comes ultimately, as mentioned, from the Old Testament. The doctrines of resurrection and eternal life are clearly expressed in a number of these writings, yet they appear in the Hebrew scriptures with real clarity only in Daniel 12. The Septuagint translation of Isaiah 26:19 (followed by the RSV), however, reflects belief in resurrection. (Job 19:25-26 is beset by textual problems that the LXX did not solve.)

The background of the New Testament angelology and demonology shows up clearly in this literature. The origin of evil and calamity among men is often attributed to the fallen angels (cf. Gen. 6). These beliefs reappear in the New Testament in the attribution of disease and mental disorder to the activities of the demons who were released by the deaths of the offspring of the Fallen Ones.

Nearer to the New Testament views regarding moral evil is the doctrine of the two spirits or "inclinations" with which each man is born. The good, or holy, spirit leads to good actions, the evil inclination leads to corrupt deeds; and the two are in tension within him. Each struggles for mastery over him, and it is every man's responsibility to choose which shall be his master. One thinks immediately of Paul's discussion in Romans 7.

This doctrine leads on to another closely related to it, namely, that of the "Two Ways": righteousness or light, and evil or darkness. It is not difficult to relate such ideas to the "flesh-spirit" contrast of Paul, or to the "light-darkness" and "truth-error" contrasts of John. Yet the ultimate background of it all is found in the canonical scriptures, from Deuteronomy onward. It is interesting to note that the doctrine, even though implicit in much New Testament exhortation, emerges again explicitly in the later *Didachē* and *Epistle of Barnabas,* in forms obviously intended for convert instruction.

The foregoing suggests some of the contributions which the intertestamental literature makes toward understanding the thought-world in which the Judeo-Christian authors of our New Testament scriptures lived and worked. One will be convinced of these contributions if he keeps his New Testament (or whole Bible) in hand while reading through a number of the major intertestamental writings. Mark each passage which has verbal or ideational echoes in the New Testament (as well as each which has strong Old Testament rootage). Such an exercise should prove one thing: that the New Testament authors were men of Judaic religious background who were proclaiming Jesus as Christ in fulfillment of God's promises to Israel (cf. Rom. 15:8ff.), and were doing so in essentially *Jewish* terms. What this implies is that the Christian interpreter needs to understand as well as possible the original Judaic background of his New Testament, and that the study of the intertestamental documents will give him invaluable help in this undertaking.

B. Judaic and New Testament Messianism

Careful study of our literature regarding the Judaic messianic hope will disclose two things. First, as it appears in the Gospels and Acts, that hope was developed in the intertestamental period. True, the New Testament writers nearly always appeal directly to the Old Testament for their proofs that Jesus is the Messiah. But they are applying to Jesus and His career the details of a messianic belief which, in the main, had already been developed by Jewish interpreters before them. And these interpreters had used similar appeals to the Old Testament in developing the doctrine.

Second, while there are certain broad motifs common to the expression of the hope, divergences appear in the details and emphases. *All* aspects of the hope were built on the prophetic promises of the Old Testament, but not all groups in Judaism envisaged the Messiah or the details of the messianic program in exactly the same way. One has only to read *I Enoch* XXXVII—LXIX, the *Testament of Levi* XVIII, the *Testament of Judah* XXIV—XXV, and *Psalm of Solomon* XVII to become aware of some differences of outlook (cf. John 7:26ff.).

The climate of expectations to which these writings attest raised the problem for the first Christians: In what ways did Jesus fulfill these various expectations (cf. John 1:19ff.)? How could such different characters and functions be combined in one personality—or were they? The New Testament shows *how* solutions were reached. The intertestamental literature shows us some of the reasons *why* the New Testament writers and the witnesses who preceded them took the approaches that they did to prove that Jesus is indeed the Messiah promised by the prophets.

Since the messianic mission and achievement of Jesus is a principal theme of the New Testament, it will be well to highlight the dominant factors in Judaic messianism. These were (1) the controlling covenants, (2) the messianic program, and (3) the expected personages.

1. THE CONTROLLING COVENANTS

Jewish religious thought was dominated by the notion that God had made certain inviolable covenants with Israel, which He would eventually fulfill. In the two and a half centuries before Jesus' birth, the hopes of the pious fastened tenaciously upon these covenants, expecting their imminent fulfillment. They were:

a. *The patriarchal covenant:* the promise of a posterity to Abraham and his descendants that would become a people through whom God would bless other nations, along with the promise of Palestine as their national home (cf. Gen. 12:1-3; 15; 17:1-21; 22:15-19, and elsewhere).

b. *The Sinaitic covenant:* the people were constituted a nation peculiar to God, with the Mosaic legislation as the basis of their national life (Exod. 19—20). This, with its additions, was known as the "Law of Moses" (Deut. 33:4-5; Mal. 4:4).

c. *The covenant promising a priestly dynasty* to the lineage of Phinehas (Num. 25:10-13; I Chron. 6:4-15; Ezek. 44:15-16; Sirach 45:23-24).

d. *The Davidic covenant:* a continuing dynasty was promised to David's successors (II Sam. 7; Ps. 89:19ff.; Isa. 11:1ff.; Jer. 33:10-18).

e. *The "new covenant":* the preceding covenants were to be reaffirmed when God brought His people back from the Babylonian Captivity. The people would be regathered in peace in their own land under a Davidic king and the Zadokite priesthood, and would obey from the heart the Law of Moses (Jer. 31:31ff.; Ezek. 36:22-28; 37:21-28).

Numerous references and allusions to these covenants occur in this literature; and the Qumran authors, too, show that the covenants were of great importance to them. Prior to the Maccabean revolt, ben Sira' the Sage prayed to God to fulfill His promises in a way that would reflect the covenants (cf. Sirach 36:1-17). Mattathias, who raised the revolt, charged his sons to give their lives for the covenants (I Macc. 2:49-57). Judith cried out to God that the enemy "have planned cruel things against thy covenant," against the priesthood and Temple, the Davidic dynasty, and Israel's tenure of the land (Judith 9:13).

In the *Testaments,* the "patriarchs" have to "prophesy" about things later than the times of Jacob and themselves. The Sinaitic covenant, with the giving of the Law, is implicit in the *Testament of Levi* XIV.4; and the moral teachings of the Law are both assumed and inculcated in all these works. Likewise the covenants of priesthood to Phinehas' lineage and of the Davidic dynasty are implicit in a number of passages (*T. Joseph* XIX.11; *T. Simeon* VII.2; *T. Naphtali* VIII.2; *T. Gad* VIII.1).

Finally, references to the basic covenants appear in the psalms and prayers. In the Prayer of Azariah, a petition for God to honor the covenants occurs in verses 11-13. The *Psalms of Solomon* contain several such references (IX.8-10; X.4; XVII.4, 21). The litany in the Hebrew version of Sirach 51 mentions the dynasty of David and the priesthood of Zadok. The petitions of the "Eighteen Benedictions" are based on the covenants.

Clearly, the religious hopes of Judaism at the dawn of the New Testament era were bound to these great Old Testament covenants, and many were looking for them to be literally fulfilled. It is, moreover, unmistakable that the Judaic religious background and the hopes of the pious are faithfully indicated in such passages as Luke 1:54-55; 67-75; Acts 2:29-31; 3:25-26; Galatians 3:15-18; and in the Epistle to the Hebrews. Paul, in Romans 15:8-9, was writing in full awareness of these things. The New Testament message is based on these covenants, and this is a principal factor in the unity of the Testaments.

2. THE MESSIANIC PROGRAM

The New Testament claims Jesus to be the Messiah whose coming inaugurated the messianic program which Judaism was awaiting. By comparing relevant portions of the New Testament with the major Old Testament prophecies, it is possible to reconstruct in general the messianic beliefs in Jesus' day. It is helpful, however, to find this program set forth in our literature as witness to the lively hopes held by the people of those times. This makes it easier to compare the New Testament data with their authentic background and to note the many agreements, one of which is the similarity of the Old Testament passages that were appealed to by both intertestamental and New Testament writers. One is also enabled to see more clearly those points at which New Testament interpretations and applications of the common scriptures diverged significantly from the Judaic expectations based on them.

The main elements of the messianic program seem to have been: (1) a period of national affliction, leading to the repentance of the faithful and separation of a righteous remnant from the sinners in the nation (Isa. 10:20ff.; 64—66; Jer. 23:3-4; Amos 9:9-10; (2) the appearance of Messiah, who would further purge God's people by judgment, restore the land to Israelite control, and regather the dispersed of Israel from surrounding countries; (3) a time of universal peace, when the blessings of the messianic reign would be extended to righteous Gentiles.

Finally, at the end of a long, but indefinite period, God would usher in the Final Judgment and the New Age. Especially prominent in this program was the insistence that national repentance was a prerequisite for the advent of Messiah. This emphasis was faithfully reflected in the preaching both of John the Baptist and of Jesus (Matt. 3:1-3; 4:17).

The outline, or nucleus, for this program appears in Isaiah 11. Messiah was to be a scion of David. Further details as to the person of Messiah and concerning the messianic program were drawn from numerous, now well-known messianic passages in the Prophets and the Psalms. And in one way or another, the major outline and its more salient details appear explicitly or implicitly at almost every turn in our literature, as the Readings will illustrate. Some striking expressions occur also in the *Zadokite*, or *Damascus*, *Document*, the *Manual of Discipline/Community Rule*, and the *Thanksgiving Hymns* from Qumran, which should not be overlooked.

3. THE MESSIANIC PERSONAGES

The Gospel of John cites a popular belief that a certain prophet—*the* prophet—would come forth in the messianic era, along with Elijah (John 1:21; 6:14; 7:40). The expectation of these personages is also attested by the other Gospels (Matt. 16:14; Mark 8:28). Our literature supports the Gospel witness. Besides such passages as I Maccabees 4:46 and 14:41, the Qumran *Manual of Discipline* says: "But let them conform to the ancient decrees . . . until the coming of a prophet and the anointed ones of Aaron and Israel" (X.10-11). In II Esdras 2:18 one reads: "I will send you help, my servants Isaiah and Jeremiah" (cf. Mark 8:27-28). A catena of "testimony" passages found in Qumran Cave 4 contains Deuteronomy 18:18-19. It helped confirm what had already suspected, namely, that Deuteronomy 18:15-19 was the Old Testament basis for the expectation of a messianic prophet (in addition to the fact that in the Judean court from David's time onward a prophet to the throne seems to have become a major functionary).

As for Elijah, his coming was prophesied in Malachi 4:5. A mishnaic tradition which had its origin in pre-Christian times witnesses to the fact that the coming of Elijah was taken seriously by many (cf. Reading 67, *Eduyoth* 8.7). Elijah was exalted to exceptional proportions and was made the chief personage of the messianic time by the later rabbis. But the process had already begun in pre-Christian times, as Sirach 48:1-11 shows.

Concerning Messiah himself, it is impossible to do full justice here to the relationship of the New Testament christology with the intertestamental expressions of the messianic hope and the Old Testament roots of both.

Illustrative passages appear in the Readings, and more extended discussions are given in Part Three. At the apex of Hasmonean power and popularity, the priest-king was the model for the messianic vision (*T. Levi* VIII.11-15; XVIII.1-3). Others expected the restoration of the Davidic monarchy, with king, high-priest, and prophet to the throne as the national leaders, as in Old Testament times (*T. Judah* XXI.1-5). This was, of course, the biblical view.

After the decline of the Hasmoneans and the nation's subjection to Rome, the hope for a Davidic Messiah seemed to burn still more brightly. *Psalm of Solomon* XVII.22-42 gives a vivid expression of this hope, while *Psalm of Solomon* XVIII voices the confidence that God will fulfill His covenant promises in "the coming generation" (v.6). If the last of these psalms were composed about 40 B.C., as some scholars believe, then this was accurate prophecy from the Christian point of view. Did the aged Simeon belong to a group in his youth among whom these psalms were composed, or read (cf. Luke 2:25ff.)?

The student of the New Testament readily hears in the language of such passages the background of many ideas which, in the New Testament, are associated closely with Jesus. But the total picture, in each case, is that of one who displays the splendor of a Hasmonean high priest at the apex of political power, or the regal glory of a Davidic monarch. When the visions of the transcendent glory of the Enochian "Elect One/Son of Man" add to the dazzlement, Messiah is viewed as well-nigh superhuman in his power and splendor. With such pictures before their eyes, it is no wonder that so few were able to see their Messiah in the humble Jesus. Rather, the marvel is that so many did, and remained faithful to what they saw (cf. John 1:14; 6:66-69).

SUMMARY

The proposition just advanced is that a working knowledge of the intertestamental literature is invaluable for the serious student and interpreter of the New Testament. Some of the documents have been cited to support the contention that many ideas with which one has to deal in the New Testament were part of the living religious tradition of that Judaism from which Christianity itself emerged. They help us to understand better the climate of ideas in which Jesus and His disciples put forth their message. They help us to understand more clearly, too, what the New Testament is actually saying, and why its message comes in the form in which we find it.

Finally, the intertestamental literature enables us to assess with greater clarity the real uniqueness of the achievement of Jesus and the early Christians vis-à-vis Judaism. In one sense, the early Jesus movement was simply another of many similar reforming movements within Judaism. But it differed in two major points from the contemporary orthodoxy which, after the Roman destruction of the Temple in A.D. 70, solidified gradually into "normative" (i.e., rabbinic) Judaism. First, where the Judaism of the

Pharisaic teachers (as well as of the ultra-orthodox Essenes) put the Torah at the center of life and hope, Jesus (followed by the Church) offered Himself as the living Word of God and saving revelation. Second, where Judaism in its messianic hope envisioned a political messiah who would rule a liberated nation-state, Jesus assumed the character of the "Servant of the Lord" who would set men free from spiritual bondage everywhere through His obedient suffering.

He fulfilled this role in such a way that, according to the New Testament witnesses, the other messianic roles were also fulfilled *as to their spiritual intent.* But in so doing, Jesus transformed the idea of the Kingdom of God from that of a theocracy centered in Jerusalem (cf. Isa. 2; Mic. 4; Zech. 14:9ff.) into that of a spiritual realm of universal scope (John 4:19-24). What Judaism hoped for, and what some in the nation had prepared themselves for by repentance and loyalty to the Torah, Jesus brought—so the New Testament claims; and the Christian movement took it to the whole wide world.

The Kingdom was not thereby divorced from its Judaic rootage, as some have apparently wished it could be. But it was released from the restrictions of national boundaries, from the personal ambitions of political leaders hungry for power and acclaim, and from expression by the exclusive norms and symbols of one national tradition and cult. Thus, the dream of the prophets, as well as the hope of those *hasidim* ("pious") who shared Isaiah's larger vision (viz., that the blessing of Abraham might come to all the Gentiles through the Messiah), was realized. And we are the recipients of those blessings through the gospel.

PART TWO

The Documents

Introduction: Concerning the Historical Sketches and Readings

To give a broader basis for understanding the intertestamental era and to provide needed points of historical relationship for the documents, some kind of historical orientation is desirable. Accordingly, selections from Josephus' *History of the Jewish War Against the Romans* (commonly cited as *Jewish War*) are used. To encourage reading necessary to fill out this somewhat abbreviated account, marginal references are given to his voluminous *Antiquities of the Jews* and, where appropriate, to Daniel and to I and II Maccabees. The text used is that given in the Loeb Classical Library Series: JOSEPHUS, Volume II, *The Jewish War*, Books I — III, edited by H. St. John Thackeray (N.Y.: G. P. Putnam's Sons, 1927). Section numbers are those of the text. Those given in parentheses are in agreement with the older editions, such as those of Whiston. The *Antiquities* is cited by book and section number as given in the Loeb Classical Library edition.

The Readings are intended to be illustrative only. Hence, they tend to be rather brief. However, extensive portions from a number of works which, though frequently quoted by scholars in discussions of the background of the New Testament, are not easily available to the student have been used. This is especially true of the *Psalms of Solomon*, the *Testaments of the Twelve Patriarchs*, the *Testament of Job*, the Greek fragments of *I Enoch* (complete only in Ethiopic), and the *Lives of the Prophets*. Readings from such better-known and more easily available works as the standard *Apocrypha* (from I and II Maccabees, Judith and Sirach) and the Qumran, or Dead Sea, Scrolls (from *Manual of Discipline* and the *Zadokite*, or *Damascus, Document*) were included both to illustrate points historical and religious and to encourage further reading in these collections. Such selections have been held to a minimum. However, although it was not in the original plan to do so, this part concludes with rather extensive citations from the Mishnah, particularly the tractate *Aboth*. It was deemed that without some introduction to the illustrative value of the Mishnah and an introduction to the rabbinic mind, the work would be lacking completeness.

The marginal references to both canonical and noncanonical literature are to make it possible for the student to follow up related ideas and themes in the biblical and extrabiblical materials. Introductions, marginal explanatory notes (marked by asterisks) and concluding comments are designed to clarify matters that might otherwise be unclear to the reader. For further information concerning the texts and the author's handling of them, the reader is referred to the Literary-Historical Notes of Part Three.

I. The Maccabean Freedom Struggle

A. Historical Sketch

(Sources: Josephus' *Jewish Antiquities*, Books XII — XIII.vi; *The Jewish War*, Book I; I and II Maccabees; cf. also Dan. 8:1-22 and ch. 11)

1. BEFORE ANTIOCHUS IV EPIPHANES (ca. 325-176 B.C.)

After conquering the Persian Empire, Alexander the Great died in 323 B.C., and his leading generals divided his territories. Ptolemy I Lagos claimed Egypt and founded a dynasty that endured until about 30 B.C. Seleucus I Nicator claimed Babylonia, finally securing his control over it as well as Syria by about 312 B.C. The successors in his dynasty took regnal names alternating between Seleucus and either Demetrius or Antiochus. In accordance with the dream of Alexander, both Ptolemy and Seleucus and their successors actively promoted the spread of Greek culture throughout their dominions, so that this has become known as the Hellenistic Era in Near Eastern history.

During the Persian period (ca. 538-333 B.C.), the tiny "county" of Judea, which had been settled by returnees from the Exile with Jerusalem as its center (cf. Ezra-Nehemiah), was subject to the Persian-appointed governor of Samaria. All of Palestine, as well as Syria to the north, was included in the satrapy known as "Beyond the River (i.e., west of the Euphrates). With the breakup of the empire, Palestine became a buffer zone between the territories of Seleucus and Ptolemy, thus reverting to its old pre-Persian status.

From time immemorial, Palestine had been important as the land bridge between Egypt and Asia. Whoever held Palestine controlled the trade routes that traversed it, to great economic advantage. It was inevitable, then, that the great powers should struggle over it, with little regard for its inhabitants. Ptolemy I secured Palestine for Egypt in about 301, and his dynasty held it for about a century, in spite of attempts made to wrest it from him. But in 200-198 B.C., Antiochus III the Great won strategic battles that gave him and his successors virtually undisputed rule over Palestine, including Judea.

The Jews generally welcomed the change from Ptolemaic to Seleucid rule, even fighting against the Egyptian garrisons on behalf of Antiochus. In gratitude, Antiochus confirmed their ancient privileges of living as a separate people according to their Law, provided for state support of the Temple cult, ordered a general remission of taxes for three years, and exempted certain functionaries from paying any taxes. Yet this favorable status was short-lived. In 190, Antiochus contested the might of Rome. He lost, and was placed under heavy tribute. Seleucus IV, who succeeded Antiochus in 187, inherited this burden of tribute. When a disgruntled and ambitious Jew told him of enormous treasure in the Temple of the Jews, he sent

Heliodorus to seize it (cf. II Macc. 3). This act alienated most of the Jews
from Seleucus.

During the Hellenistic Era, Greek influence rapidly pervaded the Near
East with the encouragement of both Ptolemies and Seleucids. Greek col-
onies were planted all over Syria and Palestine, including the Trans-Jordan
area. Greek customs, religion, philosophy and art filtered into Palestine
through many channels, and the Greek language became the trade language
of the entire Mediterranean world. Jews of the Diaspora were the first and
most directly affected. The majority became exclusively Greek-speaking, as
in Alexandria and Antioch.

For such Jews the Greek translation of the Hebrew Bible (known as the
Septuagint, or LXX) was made, beginning about 250 B.C. In the Diaspora,
often for propagandistic purposes, Jewish writers produced histories of the
Jews and other religious writings in Greek literary styles. While such
activities were apparently discouraged in Judea, where Hebrew or Aramaic
was officially sanctioned, translations of edifying works such as the "Wisdom" of Joshua ben Sira' were made for Jews of the Diaspora. As long as the
adoption of Greek ideas did not contradict or lead to the abandonment of
the Law of Moses and the essentials of the Jewish way of life, little an-
tagonism was aroused. But as many "liberal" Jews, particularly those of the
upper classes, became hellenized and abandoned the stricter tenets of
Judaism, the opposition of the pious and their leaders was kindled. This
growing opposition, along with political rivalries and faction among the
priestly aristocracy and other powerful families, developed a potentially
explosive atmosphere in Judea. Antiochus IV Epiphanes, who succeeded
Seleucus IV in about 175 B.C., set the flame to the fuse.

2. TO THE DEATH OF MATTATHIAS, ABOUT 175-166 (JEWISH WAR I.31-37)

I Macc.
1:10-19.
II Macc. 4:7 ff.
Ant. XII.
235ff.

*Here, and below.
Jerusalem.

31 (i.1). Strife arose among the Jewish aristocracy just when
Antiochus, called Epiphanes, was at odds with Ptolemy VI
about control of Syria. . . .Onias, one of the chief priests,
gained control and expelled Tobias' sons from the *city.

I Macc. 1:20ff.
II Macc. 5.

Ant.
XII.242-47.

Dan. 7:7-8;
8:8-14;
9:26-27;
11:21-39;
12:11.

32. Fleeing to Antiochus, they begged him to use them as
leaders for an invasion of Judea. Having long contemplated
such a notion, the king was persuaded. Setting out with a
huge army, he took the city by storm and slew multitudes of
those loyal to Ptolemy. He let his soldiers pillage without
restraint. He himself plundered the Temple, causing the daily
perpetual sacrifices to cease for three years and six
months. . . .

I Macc.   Ant.
1:41-53.   XI.248-56.
I Macc.   II Macc.
1:54-61.   6:1-11.

Dan. 9:27;
11:31.

34 (2). Antiochus . . . moved by his ungoverned passions and
the memory of what he had suffered in the siege, compelled
the Jews to abrogate their native laws, to keep their infants
uncircumcised, and to sacrifice a hog on the altar.

35. Everyone disobeyed these orders, and the most notable people were slain. Bacchides, sent by Antiochus as garrison-commander, took these ungodly orders as license for his natural bestiality, and perpetrated every excess of wickedness. Torturing person after distinguished person, he gave proof daily and publicly to the city of its captivity. Finally, by the excesses of his crimes he provoked the sufferers to dare to take vengeance.

I Macc.
1:58-64;
II Macc.
6:12—7:42.
Ant.
XII.255-56; cf.
I Macc. 2:15ff.;
II Macc. 6:1ff.;
I Macc. 7:8, 9.

36 (3). Thus Matthias, son of Hasmoneus, one of the priests of the village Modein, formed his family of five sons into an armed band; and he slew Bacchides with altar-knives. He fled into the hills immediately, since he feared the garrison forces.

I Macc. 2:1-27.
Ant.
XII.265-75.

37. But when many from the people joined him, he was encouraged. He came down and fought the generals of Antiochus, whom he both defeated and drove out of Judea. He thus passed from success to sovereignty. Because he had expelled the foreigners, his own people were willing for him to be their ruler. When he died, he left the leadership to Juda, his eldest son.

I Macc. 2:42;
Dan. 11:33-34.

I Macc.
2:42-48; Ant.
XII.276-78.
I Macc.
2:49—3:2;
Ant.
XII.279-86.

Comment:

For related literature typical of the spirit of these times, the student should read the Book of Judith and the messianic passage in Sirach 36, in the standard Apocrypha.

3. JUDA MACCABEUS TO SIMON'S DEATH ABOUT 166-134 (WAR I.38-54)

38 (4). Now Juda, suspecting that Antiochus would not remain quiet, got together a native force, and made a treaty of friendship—the first—with the Romans. So when Epiphanes again invaded the country, Juda struck him a severe blow and repulsed him.

I Macc.
3:1—4:35; II
Macc. 8; 14:6.
I Macc.
8:17-31; Ant.
XII.414-19.
Ant.
XII.287-315.

39. Fresh from this achievement, he moved quickly against the garrison in the city, for it had not yet been cut off. Expelling the troops from the upper city, he confined them to the lower, to the section called *Akra*. He gained control of the Temple-area, cleansed its precincts and walled it around. He had prepared and brought into the sanctuary new vessels for the services, since the former ones were defiled. He built another altar and commenced the sacrifices again.

I Macc.
4:36-61.

Ant.
XII.316-26; II
Macc. 10:1ff.
I Macc. 4:59; II
Macc. 10:8; cf.
John 10:22.

The Jews' feast of *Hanukkah* commemorates this event.

I Macc. 6:1-16;
II Macc.
9:1-29.
40. Now the city was just recovering its condition of sanctity when Antiochus died. His son Antiochus inherited both his kingdom and his enmity toward the Jews.

Antiochus V, with a large army including 80 elephants, invaded Judea and defeated Juda's forces. Juda's brother Eleazar was killed trying to bring down one of the elephants on which he thought the king was mounted. Antiochus then withdrew into Syria for the winter.

I Macc.
6:18—7:50.
II Macc.
10:10—15:37.
Ant.
XII.379-412.

I Macc. 9:1-22;
Ant.
XII.420-34.
I Macc.
9:23-26.
47 (i.6). When the king withdrew, Juda did not remain idle. He combined the many who joined him from the people with those who had come through the recent combat, and fought Antiochus' generals at the village of Akedasa. And after showing himself bravest in the fight, having killed many of the enemy, he was himself slain. After a few days, his brother John met death in a plot laid against him by Antiochus' partisans.

I Macc.
9:62—12:4.
48 (ii.1). His brother Jonathan succeeded him. Among other things, as a safeguard for himself against his countrymen, he strengthened his authority by making an alliance with the Romans. He also made a truce with the young Antiochus. Yet none of these things proved sufficient for his safety.

Antiochus' guardian Trypho, who was plotting to seize power, managed to imprison Jonathan and attacked Judea. When repulsed by Jewish forces led by Simon, Trypho killed Jonathan. Simon pressed the conflict. He captured Gazara, Joppa and Jamnia, overpowered the Syrian garrison in Jerusalem and razed the hated Citadel. However, in spite of an alliance made with Simon against Trypho, Antiochus perfidiously sent an invasion force into Judea to attempt to reduce Simon to vassalage. Simon reacted vigorously.

I Macc.
13:1-40,
43-53; 15:10ff.
Ant.
XIII.201-13.
52. He, though indeed old, directed the conflict with youthful vigor. He sent his sons forward with the ablest troops; then he himself took a division of the army and attacked another front.

53. Having set many ambushes here and there in the hills, he prevailed in every engagement. After brilliant victory, he was appointed high priest. He had freed the Jews from the Macedonian domination of one hundred and seventy years' duration.
I Macc.   41-49; Ant.
14:25-27. XIII.213-14.
I Macc.
13:41-42.

I Macc.
16:14-17.
Ant.
XIII.228-29.
54 (3). He, too, died as the victim of a plot, slain at a banquet by his son-in-law Ptolemy.

B. The Atmosphere of the Times

1. BEFORE THE RISE OF MACCABEAN/HASMONEAN POWER

READING 1: A nationalistic litany (from the Hebrew version of Sirach 51; cf. Sirach 36)

1. *Praise the Lord, for He is good;
for His mercy endures for ever.

*Or, "give thanks to": Ps. 136:1ff.

2. Give thanks to the God of praises;
for His mercy endures for ever.

Ps. 18:3; 22:3; 96:4.

3. Praise Him who guards Israel;
for His mercy endures for ever.

Ps. 121:4.

4. Praise Him who formed all things;
for His mercy endures for ever.

Ps. 104; Isa. 42:5; 45:7; Jer. 10:12ff.

5. Praise the Redeemer of Israel;
for His mercy endures for ever.

Isa. 41:14; 44:6, 24; 63:16.

6. Praise Him who gathers the exiles of Israel;
for His mercy endures for ever.

Ps. 147:2; Isa. 11:12; 27:13; 56:8.

7. Praise Him who builds His city and His sanctuary;
for His mercy endures for ever.

Ps. 102:16; 147:2; Isa. 44:28; Amos 9:11.

8. Praise Him who makes a horn to sprout for the house of David;
for His mercy endures for ever.

Ps. 132:1, 17; Ezek. 29:21; Luke 1:69.

9. Praise Him who has chosen the sons of Zadok for the priesthood;
for His mercy endures for ever.

I Chron. 6:4, 12; 24:3. Neh. 11:10-11; Ezek. 45:15; 48:11.

10. Praise the Shield of Abraham;
for His mercy endures for ever.

Gen. 15:1; Deut. 33:29; Ps. 33:20.

11. Praise the Rock of Isaac;
for His mercy endures for ever.

Deut. 32:18; Ps. 18:2; 71:3.

12. Praise the Mighty One of Jacob;
for His mercy endures for ever.

Gen. 49:24; Ps. 132:2, 5; Isa. 49:26; 60:16.

13. Praise Him who has chosen Zion;
for His mercy endures for ever.

Ps. 78:68; 132:13; Zech. 1:17; 2:12; 3:2.

14. Praise the King of the kings of kings;
for His mercy endures for ever.

Dan. 2:47; 4:25. Ps. 47:2; 95:3.

<table>
<tr><td>

Ps. 148:14; cf.
Luke 1:69.
*Or, "loyal."

</td><td>

15. And He has lifted up a horn for His people,
for the praise of all His *pious ones,

</td></tr>
<tr><td>

Ps. 148:14.

</td><td>

16. For the children of Israel, a people near to Him.
Hallelu-Yah!

</td></tr>
</table>

Comments:

1. Psalm 136 seems to be the stylistic model for this litany. The ideas are quite similar to Sirach 36 and the *Shemoneh Esreh*: cf. Reading 57. Likewise the emphases in the "Benedictus" of Zacharias, Luke 1:68-79, are very similar.

2. On the basis of verses 8 and 9 the psalm is believed to be pre-Hasmonean. It is not impossible that it comes ultimately from the Restoration period, when hopes seem to have been aroused that Zerubbabel would be able to restore the Davidic monarchy. Since Sirach was translated for the Jews of the Diaspora during the period of Hasmonean popularity, it is not hard to understand why, if this psalm was an original part of ben Sira's book, it was deleted.

2. RELIGIOUS CONFLICT

a. Hellenization and apostasy (excerpts from I and II Maccabees)

READING 2: Antiochus' decree (I Macc. 1:11-15, 41-43, 51b-53)

11. In those days many Law-violators emerged in Israel and seduced many. "Let us go and arrange a covenant with the

Cf. Deut. 32:8.
*Strict piety hindered social and business relations with non-Jews, and aroused ill will.

Gentiles who are around us," they said, "for since we were separated from them, *many ills have overtaken us." (12) This proposal seemed good to them. (13) Some of those who were eager for it went to the king, who gave them authority to observe the ordinances of the Gentiles. (14) So they built an

*gumnasion: where Greek sports were performed naked.
*So as not to seem different from non-Jewish men.

*athletic training center in Jerusalem, according to gentile usage. (15) They then made themselves *as if uncircumcised; apostatized from the holy covenant; married gentile women; and secretly engaged in evil practices. . . .

*Antiochus IV. His promotion of a common religion was to secure political unity within his realm.

41. Then the *king wrote to his whole realm that all must be one people, (42) and each must give up his own ethnic customs. (43) So all the Gentiles accepted everything according to the king's word. Even many from Israel were pleased to adopt his religion; and they sacrificed to idols and profaned the Sabbath. . . .

*Of animals unclean to Jews.

51. . . .And he appointed inspectors over all the people, and he commanded the cities of Judea to offer *sacrifice, city by city. (52) Then many from the people, that is, all who abandoned the Law, were joined to them. (53) They did evil things

in the land; and they sent *Israel into hiding, into each of their places of *refuge.

READING 3: The corrupt Jewish leadership (II Macc. 4:7-15; 6:1-6)

4:7. When Seleucus quit this life and Antiochus, called Epiphanes, received the kingdom, Onias' brother Jason obtained the high priesthood by graft. (8) He promised the king, in a petition, three hundred and sixty talents of silver, and eighty talents from certain other revenues. (9) In addition to these, he promised to underwrite a hundred and fifty more if he were *authorized to establish a gymnasium and a youth club, and to register the men of Jerusalem as citizens of Antioch.

*Required to impart the character of a Greek city to Jerusalem and to obtain the Antiochene franchise for its inhabitants.

10. As soon as the king agreed and Jason had seized control, he immediately moved the people into the hellenistic way of life. (11) The existing royal concessions made to the Jews, which had been obtained by John the father of Eupolemus . . . he set aside. Violating the lawful polity of the people, he initiated new customs contrary to the Law. (12) For he gladly founded an athletic center at the foot of the *Citadel; and he led the youth of the aristocracy in submitting to wear the *Greek hat.

II Macc. 3:1-3.

I Macc. 8:17ff.

*Quarters of the Syrian garrison.
*Symbol of Hermes, patron god of youth and the gymnasium.

13. Hellenizing and the rush to adopt foreign ways reached such a peak through the surpassing impurity of the impious Jason—who was no *high priest—(14) that the priests were no longer attentive to their altar-service. They despised the sanctuary and were heedless of the sacrifices. They hastened to engage in the *exercises in the wrestling school, which were contrary to the Law. . . .(15) They disdained values they had received from their forefathers, while esteeming hellenic honors of supreme worth. . . .

*I.e., not legitimately so.

*They exercised naked. Such exposure was a great offense to Jewish piety.

6:1. Not long afterward the king commissioned *an Athenian senator to compel the Jews to forsake their ancestral laws and to cease to live by the laws of God (2) and, as well, to defile the sanctuary in Jerusalem and to name it for Olympian Zeus. . . .(3) Harsh and totally hateful was the imposition of this evil. (4) For the sacred area was filled with debauchery and carousing by the Gentiles. These amused themselves with courtesans and *lay with women in the sacred precincts. Worse yet, they brought in for the offerings things that were unfit. (5) The altar was kept filled with things utterly forbidden by the *laws. (6) One could neither keep the Sabbath,

*Or, "Geron the Athenian."

*Probably as part of Syrian fertility rites.

*Of Leviticus, concerning offerings and sacrifices.

celebrate the traditional feasts, nor openly confess to being a Jew.

b. Reactions

READING 4: Zeal for the Law (I Macc. 1:62-64; 2:19-28)

Acts 10:9-14ff.
Cf. Dan. 1:8.

1:62. But many in Israel stood firm and were stoutly determined not to eat unclean things. (63) They were ready to die rather than to be defiled by food or to profane the holy covenant; and they *did* die. (64) So very great wrath came upon Israel. . . .

2:19. Then Mattathias replied loudly: "Though all the nations under the king's rule obey him and apostatize from the religions of their fathers by choosing to keep his commands, (20) yet will I and my sons and my brothers walk in the covenant of our fathers. (21) Far be it from us to abandon the Law and ordinances. (22) We will not obey the words of the king to turn aside from our religious duty, either to the right or to the left."

So Mattathias answered the king's envoy who had urged him to set an example for others by obeying the edict. Shortly a Jew came up to make the offering prescribed by the decree.

Num. 25:6-15.

24. When Mattathias saw it, he was fired with zeal, and his emotions were aroused. He displayed wrath according to the verdict of the Law: he ran and slew him upon the altar. (25) At the same time, he killed the king's officer who was trying to compel people to sacrifice, and he tore down the altar. (26) He was zealous for the Law, just as Phinehas was in what he did to Zimri the son of Salom.

Cf. I Macc.
2:51-64.

27. Then Mattathias proclaimed loudly in the town: "Whoever is zealous for the Law and supports the covenant, let him come after me!" (28) And he and his sons fled into the hills, abandoning their possessions in the town.

READING 5: Quietistic withdrawal (I Macc. 2:31-38)

Many who were religious quietists, political pacifists, wished only to practice their religion undisturbed. They did not join in the revolt.

*Judg. 6:2;
I Sam. 13:6.

31. It was reported to the king's officers . . . that those who had disregarded the king's command had gone down into *hiding places in the wilderness. (32) So many hurried after them and came up with them. They encamped facing them,

and prepared to fight them on the Sabbath day. (33) And they said to *them: "This has gone far enough! Come out and do what the king has commanded, and you will live." ·The quietists.

34. But they said, "We will not come out, neither will we obey the king's edict, to profane the Sabbath day." (35) So the others began to attack them right away. (36) But *they neither answered them, nor hurled a stone at them, nor blocked up their *hiding places. (37) They said: "Let us all die in our innocency. Heaven and earth testify on our behalf that you are destroying us without just cause." (38) But the enemy pressed the attack against them on the Sabbath; and they and their wives and children died—as many as a thousand persons, along with their cattle.

Cf. Dan. 3:17-18.
·The quietists.
·Probably caves in hillsides.

READING 6: Separatism (*Zadokite*, or *Damascus*, *Document* I.19—II.1; III.20—IV.4; VI.1-5. References are to columns and lines of the original texts.)

The *Zadokite Document* witnesses to the rise of an early separatist movement in Judaism by hasidic priests zealous for the true interpretation of the Law and its proper observance. Their initial separation was probably related to the struggle against the hellenizing of the puppet priests installed by Antiochus IV. But their animosity was later directed toward the Hasmoneans, in whom they were deeply disappointed. The following excerpts indicate the attitudes of this group.

1.19. For *they . . . justified the wicked and condemned the just. They made people transgress the covenant and violated the ordinance, and they assembled against the life of the righteous. They abhorred all those who walked blamelessly, pursued them with the sword, and stirred up controversy among the people. So the wrath of God was aroused against their party, for the devastation of their multitude, and their works were *rejected from before Him. . . .

·The apostates.
Cf. accounts in I and II Macc.
Cf. Luke 1:6
·As defiled or corrupt.

III.20. Those who hold *it fast are appointed for life eternal, and all the glory of Adam is theirs. For God swore to them through the prophet Ezekiel: "The priests and the Levites and the sons of Zadok who kept the ordinances of My sanctuary when many in Israel strayed from Me, *they shall bring near to Me the fat and the blood." The "priests" are those in Israel who repented, who went out from the land of Judah, and the "Levites" are those who joined them. The "sons of Zadok" are the chosen ones of Israel who shall stand at the end of days. . . .

·The covenant.
Sirach 49:16; Man. Disc. IV.23.
Ezek. 44:15ff.
·This is an abbreviated quotation.
Note the allegorizing interpretation.
Dan. 12:13.

VI.1. But God remembered the covenant of old, and He raised up men of insight from Aaron and wise men from Israel. He got them to listen, and they dug the well:

> The well, the princes dug it,
> nobles of the people delved it
> with the staff.

Num. 21:18.

The "well" is the Law. Those who "dug it" are they of Israel who repented, who went out from the land of Judah to live in the land of Damascus.

READING 7: The *Hasidim* (I Macc. 2:42; 7:12-17)

Other than the Zadokite separatists, whose movement may have begun about this time, only the *hasidim* (Gk., *Hasideans*: "pious ones," "ones loyal to the covenant") are mentioned by name in I Maccabees as a distinct party. They appear to have been of an outlook similar to those pietists who died rather than violate the Sabbath.

2:42. Then an assembly of Hasideans joined them. All were prominent men of Israel who volunteered themselves on behalf of the Law. . . .

*High priest by the Syrian king's appointment.

7:12. Then an assembly of scribes gathered before *Alcimus and Bacchides to seek their rights. (13) The Hasideans were the first of the Israelites to seek peace from them. (14) They said, "A priest of Aaron's line has come with the army, and he will not treat us unjustly." (15) He spoke peaceably with them and swore to them: "We will not harm you or your friends"; (16) and they trusted him. But the same day he seized sixty of them and killed them, according to this word which is writ-

Heb., hasidim.

ten: (17) "The flesh of Your *pious ones with their blood they

Ps. 79:2-3; Ps. Sol. VIII.20.

poured out round about Jerusalem, and no one buried them."

3. HASIDIC SENTIMENT

Most of the poems known as the *Psalms of Solomon* were probably composed somewhat later than this period. Yet the attitudes they express are in harmony with the outlook of I Maccabees, especially that of the poems and poetical fragments that appear in that account. Accordingly, the following selections are included here for illustration.

READING 8: National sin merits judgment (*Ps. Sol.* II.2-22)

II Macc. 4:39; 5:15ff.

2. Alien peoples went up to Your altar; they trampled it down with their feet in arrogancy,

3. because the sons of Jerusalem polluted the holy things of the Lord: they profaned the offerings of God by their lawless deeds.

4. Because of these things He said: "Cast them far away from Me. I have no pleasure in them."

Deut. 28:15, 45ff.; Jer. 7:15; 16:11-13; Mal. 1:10.

5. The beauty of her appearance was despised in God's sight. It was utterly dishonored.

Lam. 1:6; 2:1.

6. Her sons and daughters went into miserable captivity among the Gentiles, their necks in marked collars.

I Macc. 1:32; II Macc. 5:14; Deut. 28:15, 41.

7. According to their sins He did to them, abandoning them to those who overpowered them.

Deut. 28:25-26, 47ff.; Ps. 28:4; 66:11-12; Jer. 17:10; Hos. 12:2.

8. For He turned His face away from pitying them, youth, elder and child, one and all, because they all did evil and did not pay heed (to Him).

Deut. 31:17-18; Jer. 33:5; Ezek. 7:22; 39:23-24; Lam. 2:21. Prov. 1:24; Isa. 65:12; 66:4; Jer. 7:13-14.

9. So Heaven became indignant and the land loathed them; because no one had done such things upon it as they had.

Lev. 18:24-28; Deut. 28:23-24; Jer. 16:12-13.

10. Thus the land shall experience all Your righteous judgments, O God.

Isa. 26:9; 66:15; Ezek. 8:18.

11. The sons of Jerusalem became objects of scorn in return for her harlotries; every passer-by was entering in openly.

I Macc. 1:14-15; II Macc. 4:13ff.; Ezek. 16:15-22.

12. They sported in their forbidden activities, just as *they were used to doing; in broad daylight they disgracefully exposed their wickedness.

*"they" Gentiles, apparently.

13. And the daughters of Jerusalem became defiled, polluting themselves by contaminating *intermixtures, contrary to Your decrees.

*Marrying within the forbidden degrees and with non-Jews.

14. My heart and my feelings are in pain about this.

15. I will justify You, O God, in uprightness of heart, because Your righteousness is in Your judgments, O God;

Ps. 119:137; 129:4; Dan. 9:14.

16. For You requited sinners according to their works and their exceedingly evil sins.

Ps. 62:12; Prov. 24:29; Isa. 59:18; 65:6-7; Lam. 1:8; Rom. 2:6, 8-9.

17. You disclosed their sins so that Your justice might appear. You erased their memory from the land.

18. God is a righteous Judge, and there is no respect of persons with Him.

Deut. 10:17; Acts 10:34; Rom. 2:11; I Peter 1:17.

19. For the Gentiles reproached Jerusalem by trampling her down; her beauty was dragged down from her throne of glory.

Jer. 14:21; Lam. 1:6-7; Hos. 4:7.

Isa. 3:24; Jer.
6:26; Lam.
2:10; Amos
8:10.
Isa. 3:18-23.

20. She put on sackcloth instead of an attractive garment; she put a circlet of rushes about her head instead of a diadem.

Cf. Ezek.
16:10-14.

21. She once wore a splendid waist-sash, which God placed around her. Her beauty is now dishonored, cast off upon the ground.

Ps. 74; 85:4-7;
89:38-51;
Lam. 2:8;
5:1ff.

22. And I saw, and I besought the Lord's face; and I said: "Suffice it, O Lord, for Your hand to be heavy upon Jerusalem by means of the gentile invasion."

READING 9: Exultation and hope (*Ps. Sol.* XI)

Joel 2:1; Isa.
40:9-10;
62:11.
*Dan. 4:13, 17:
angels who
mediate God's
will to men.
Zech. 10:3; cf.
Luke 7:16.

1. Announce in Zion with a trumpet-blast proclamations of the *holy ones, proclaim in Jerusalem with a voice of one publishing good news: "God has shown mercy to Israel by visiting them."

Isa. 11:12;
43:5; 60:4.
Isa. 49:12, 18.

2. Stand, Jerusalem, upon a height and behold your children being gathered all together by the Lord from the east and from the west.

Isa. 43:6.
Isa. 11:11;
60:9.

3. From the north they are coming with the joy of their God; from islands afar God has gathered them.

Isa. 49:11.

4. He brought high mountains low as level places for them; the hills fled from their approach.

Isa. 41:17, 19;
55:12-13; cf.
Ps. 96:12-13.

5. The oakwoods shaded them as they passed by; God caused every fragrant shrub to spring up for them,

Ps. 102:16-17;
Isa. 40:5;
52:9-10.

6. So that Israel might pass by in the visitation of the glory of their God.

Baruch 5:1-2;
Isa. 61:3, 10.

7. Put on, Jerusalem, your glorious garments, make ready your holy robe, because God has decreed good things for Israel for ever and ever.

READING 10: Personal perspective (*Ps. Sol.* XIII)

Superscription: "Encouragement for the righteous"

Ps. 18:35;
108:6; 138:7;
Isa. 51:16;
52:7-10.

1. The right hand of the Lord protected me, the Lord's right hand spared us.

Ezek.
14:12-23.

2. The Lord's arm saved us from the sword that passed through, from famine and the death of sinners.

Jer. 15:2-3.

3. Evil beasts ran upon them, in their teeth they tore their flesh, and with their jaw-teeth they crushed their bones;

4. but out of all these things the Lord saved us.

5. The godly is troubled because of his faults, lest he be taken away with sinners; Cf. Ps. 25; 51:2.

6. for the overthrow of the sinner is terrible, but nothing of all these things will touch the righteous; Ps. 91:7-8.

7. because the chastening of the righteous for inadvertent sins and the overthrow of sinners are not alike. Wisd. Sol. 11:10; 12:22.

8. The righteous is chastised in secret lest the sinner rejoice over the righteous. Cf. Ps. 35:19; 38:16-18; Mic. 7:8-9.

9. For He will admonish the righteous as a beloved son, and His discipline will be as for a first-born, Deut. 8:5; Prov. 3:11-12. Wisd. Sol. 11:9, 10; Heb. 12:5ff.

10. because the Lord will spare His loyal ones, and will take away their faults by chastening. Wisd. Sol. 12:2; Isa. 48:9-11; Dan. 12:10; James 1:12.

11. For the life of the righteous is forever; but sinners will be taken away to destruction, and remembrance of them will be found no more; Ps. 16:10-11; 37:28, 38; 41:12; 92:7. Sirach 12:6.

12. but upon the pious is the Lord's mercy—even upon those who fear Him is His mercy. Ps. 147:11; Lam. 3:22-23. Exod. 20:6.

Comment:

The Greek term translated "loyal/pious ones" is the equivalent of the Hebrew term *hasidim*. It means those who were loyal to the Mosaic covenant and who seriously practiced the Jewish way of life. From these "pious ones" both Pharisees and Essenes emerged.

4. THE APOCALYPTIC TEMPER AND ACTIVITY

The apocalyptic literature was undoubtedly produced in hasidic circles as a contemporary form of prophecy. Explanations for the current troubles and predictions of the future were issued as "revelations" given through visions or angelic visitants. They were popular in some circles of Judaism until the second Jewish revolt against Rome (ca. A.D. 135), as well as among many in the early Church. See the General Introduction above.

READING 11: Enoch's message of blessing (*I Enoch* I.1—V.9)

I.1. The message of the blessing of Enoch, just as he blessed the righteous elect ones who will be alive in the day of anguish that will remove all their enemies, while the righteous will be saved. Isa. 11:4; 13:9-16; 14:1-3; 54:7-17; 65:2-23; Jer. 30:7ff.; Amos 9:9-10. Ps. Sol. XIII.1-4; XVI.5; Prov. 28:18.

2. Enoch (a righteous man to whom a vision of God, of the Holy One and of heaven, was opened) took up his *parable Cf. Ezek. 1:1; Rev. 4:1. *Num. 23—24.

Dan. 8:16;
10:1; Zech.
1:9; Rev. 4:1;
7:13ff.

and said: "He showed me, and I heard holy words from the Holy Ones; and as I heard all things from them, also I understood what I saw.

Cf. Dan. 8:17,
26; 10:14;
Hab. 2:3.

But I understood that it was not for the present generation, but for a future one that I was to speak.

3. So concerning the elect ones I speak and concerning them I

*Literally,
"parable."

take up my *discourse:

Isa. 26:21; Hab. 3:3ff.

My Great Holy One shall come forth from His place, (4) the

Mic. 1:3; Isa.
63:3, 6; Deut. 5:4-5; Ps.
33:2; Judg. 68:7-8.

eternal God shall tread upon the earth, upon Mount Sinai. He

Isa. 42:13;59:17; 63:1ff.;
Zech. 14:3.

shall appear from the place of His tent, He shall appear in the

*Eph. 6:10.

*power of His might from the highest heaven.

Isa. 2:5-21.   *Ethiopic
version:
"quake."

5. Everyone shall fear; and the Watchers shall *believe. Hid-

Ps. 97:2-5; 104:32.

den (fires) will blaze up on all the peaks. All the heights of the

Nah. 1:5-6;   Jer. 4:24.

earth shall be shaken, and trembling and great fear shall seize

Isa. 2:21; 10:10; Zech.
24:17; Jer. 14:13.

them as far as the extremities of the earth.

Isa. 64:3; Mic.
1:4.

6. The lofty mountains shall be shaken, they shall fall and be

Isa. 40:4; Nah.
1:5; Hab. 3:6.

dissolved. The high hills shall be brought low: they shall flow

Amos 9:5;   Ps. 97:5.
Zech. 14:10.

down, melting like wax held close to a flame of fire.

Isa. 24:1,
18b-20; 13:13;
10:23; Jer.
4:23-27; Zeph.
1:1-3, 18.

7. And the earth shall be torn asunder, and all things on the earth shall perish; and judgment shall come upon all men.

Isa. 26:12;
12:1-3; 25:1-4.

8. But He will make peace with the righteous; and for the elect

Ps. 85:8; Isa.   Isa. 54:8; Ezek.
32:18; Exod.   39:25; Zech.
20:6; Deut.7:9. 10:6.

there will be safety and peace: His mercy shall be upon them.

Jer. 24:7;
31:1-3; Isa. 43:1.

They will all belong to God; and He will grant them His good

Ps. 147:11; 16:11;
37:39-40.

favor. He will bless them all and He will grant aid to all.

Isa. 40:30-31; 41:10.

Ps. 36:9;   Isa. 9:1-2;
97:11; 112:4; 26:12.
118:27a.

[And He will rescue us (sic!).] Light shall appear for them, and He will make peace for them.

Deut. 33:2;
Dan. 7:9-10;
Zech. 14:5;
Mal. 3:5; Jude
14; Rev.
19:11, 14.

9. For He is coming with His myriads, even His holy ones, to execute judgment against all men, and He will destroy all the ungodly.

Jude 15; Jer.
25:31; II
Thess. 1:8-11;
Rev. 19—20.

He will convict all flesh concerning all their ungodly deeds

Mal. 3:13; cf.
Dan. 7:25;

which they have done impiously, and of the hard words

11:36; Zeph. 2:10f

which they have spoken, and concerning all things which impious sinners have uttered against Him.

(II.1—V.3. In these brief sections, Enoch calls on the impious to see how all things in nature obey God's decrees. His indictment continues.)

V.4. But you have not been faithful, neither have you done

Mal. 3:13-14;
Ezek. 35:13;
Dan. 7:8;
11:36; Ps.
10:7ff.; 17:10;
36:3; 73:9.

according to His commandments. Instead, you apostatized and spoke great and hard words with an unclean mouth against His majesty.

Because you spoke against (Him) with your lies, O hard-hearted ones, there is no peace for you. *Isa. 57:1-13a.* *Isa. 48:22.*

5. Therefore you shall curse your days, and the years of your life shall perish; and the years of your destruction shall be multiplied in an endless curse, and there will be no mercy or peace for you. *Isa. 66:16-17, 24. Ps. 125:5; Isa. 65:11-12. Isa. 57:21.*

6. Then your names will be an eternal curse for all the righteous. Whoever curses will curse by you, and all the sinners and ungodly will take oath by you. But all the blameless shall be granted favor. *Isa. 65:15. Deut. 28:15, 37, 45; Jer. 29:18. Ps. 37:37-40.*

For them there will be forgiveness of sins, and every kind of mercy, peace, and forbearance. For them there will be salvation, a good light, and they shall inherit the land. *Isa. 32:16-18; 57:17-19; Hos. 54:10; 55:6-7; 14:4. Isa. 9:1-7; 21:4. Ps. 25:7-9; 60:20; 37:29; Matt. Rev. 7:17; 5:5.*

But salvation shall not belong to you sinners. Instead, destruction and a curse shall come upon you all. *Ps. 37:10-11; Isa. 13:9; Amos 9:10.*

7. For the elect there will be light and grace and peace, and they shall inherit the land; but to you, the ungodly, there will be a curse. *Isa. 60:1—61:7; 65:9; Ps. 37:9. Ps. 37:22, 34. Ps. 1:4-5; Isa. 66:24.*

8. Then light and peace shall be given to His elect, and they shall inherit the land. Then wisdom shall be granted to all the elect, and all these shall live. They will never sin again, neither against truth nor by arrogance. *Isa. 60:20-21; 57:13. Ps. 37:28-30; Prov. 2:6-7; Isa. 33:6; Dan. 2:21. Jer. 3:17.*

In an enlightened man there will be light, and in a discerning man there will be understanding. *Prov. 1:5-6; Dan. 2:23; 5:14; Hos. 14:9; Jub. IV.17-19.*

9. They shall never transgress, neither shall they sin all the days of their lives. They shall not die in the heat of (divine) wrath; but they will fill up the allotted days of their lives, and their lives will be prolonged in peace. *Zeph. 3:11-13. Isa. 65:20-23. Amos 9:14-15.*

Their years of joy shall be multiplied in lasting exultation and peace throughout all the days of their lives." *Isa. 35:10; 61:7; 65:13c-14a, 18; Zeph. 3:14-20.*

Comment:

As compared to Charles' rendition of the Ethiopic version, the Greek seems redundant. The Greek redactor seems to have added concordant passages from biblical psalms and prophets, particularly in V.6-9. Psalm 37, with its fourfold reiteration that the righteous/humble/blameless will inherit the land in peace, prosperity, and longevity (while the sinners and wicked will be condemned/cursed and cut off), seems to have provided the nucleus of these additions.

The whole passage above is thematically related to what is the central portion of the Ethiopic version, viz., secs. XXXVII — LXIX, "The Similitudes"—not extant in Greek. The main theme of the three "parables" that comprise those sections is the judgment and punishment of the kings, the mighty and sinners, and the rewarding of the elect and faithful with peace, prosperity, joy, wisdom and longevity at the appearance of the "Son of Man"— cf. Matt. 12:18; Luke 23:35.

READING 12: Doom on the fallen angels; the earth cleansed; messianic blessings (I Enoch X — XI)

Five preceding sections expand the story of Genesis 6:1-4 in great detail: the names and deeds of the angels who defected are recounted. They not only left their heavenly station to take human wives and beget children by them, but they taught mankind the secrets of magic and sorcery, astrology, cosmetic allurements, metallurgy and the arts of making weapons and armor. (Influence from the Greek myths of Prometheus and Pandora seems evident.) Their offspring, the giants, devastated the earth and corrupted themselves. The faithful angels protest to God and ask why He allows it to continue.

*I.e., Noah.

X.1. Then the Most High, the Great Holy One, spoke concerning these things. He commanded and sent Istrael to the *son of Lamech:

Gen. 6:7, 13.

Gen. 6:17.

2. "Tell him in My name: 'Hide yourself.' And show him the coming end: that all the earth is to perish. A deluge is about to come upon the whole earth, and it will destroy all things that are on it.

Gen. 6:14ff.

3. Teach him how he may escape from it, so that his lineage will remain for all generations."

*He taught metallurgy and weaponry to men. Rev. 20:2.

4. Next He said to Raphael: "Bind *Azael foot and hand, and cast him into darkness. Make an opening in the desert in Dudael and cast him therein.

Isa. 14:11, 19; Job 10:21-22. II Peter 2:4; Jude 6.

5. Spread under him rough and pointed rocks, cover him with darkness, and let him stay there forever. Cover his face and do not let him see the light.

Rev. 20:7-10.

6. In the Great Day of Judgment he will be taken away into the place of fire.

7. Then heal the earth which the angels have devastated. Show men a remedy for the earth so that they may heal its calamity, and so that all the sons of men may not perish because of the secrets which the Watchers taught them.

8. For the earth has been desolated, devastated by the deeds of Azael's instruction: indict him for all kinds of sins."

9. Then the Lord said to Gabriel: "Proceed against the giants,

the corrupt ones, the sons of fornication. Destroy the sons of the Watchers from among men. Send them into (self-) destructive conflict. For length of days are not for them;

10. and no request of their fathers concerning them will be granted—for they hoped to live an eternal life, that each would live five hundred years."

Cf. Sec. XIII, Reading 13a.

11. And He told Michael: "Go and bind *Semyaza and the rest of them with him who mingled with the women to become defiled by their uncleanness.

*Their leader in defection: *I Enoch* VI.3.

12. And when their sons have slaughtered themselves, and they have seen the destruction of their beloved ones, then bind them for seventy generations in the valleys of the earth until the day of their judgment and consummation, until the condemnation for an age of ages is completed.

Wisd. Sol. 14:6.
Jub. V.9-11.

13. Then they shall be taken off into the fiery *abyss, to the torment and to the prison of eternal confinement; (14) and whoever is condemned and annihilated from now on will be bound together with them until the completion of the generations.

Rev. 20:10, 14-15. *Gk., *chaos*; cf. *I Enoch* XC.24.

15. Destroy all the spirits of the corrupt ones, even the Watchers' children, because they did wrong to mankind. (16) Also, destroy every kind of wickedness from the earth, make every evil work cease, and let the *plant of righteousness and truth appear forever. With joy it will be planted.

*Cf. *Jub.* VII.34; XVI.26; Ps. 80:14; Isa. 11:1; Jer. 32:41; Ezek. 17:22-23.

17. And now all the righteous shall escape. They will live to beget thousands. They shall fulfill all the days of their youth and their Sabbaths in peace.

Gen. 6:9-21; Ezek. 9:4-6; Ps. *Sol.* XIII.
Isa. 44:4; 54:1-3; 65:20-25.

18. Then the earth will be cultivated in righteousness. Trees shall be planted in it, and it will be full of blessing; (19) and all of the trees of the earth shall exult. They will plant vines, and every vine that they plant will produce jugs of wine. Each measure of seed will yield a thousandfold; and each measure of olives will produce ten *bath of oil.

Jub. VII.34-35. Amos 9:13-14.
Ps. 96:12; Isa. 44:23.
Isa. 65:21; Jer. 31:5.
Ezek. 34:27.
*Heb., *bath* = about 10 gallons.

20. You must cleanse the earth from all uncleanness, wickedness, sin and impiety. Bring to a halt every kind of uncleanness now occurring on earth.

21. Then all the peoples will serve, and bless and worship Me. (22) And the whole land will be clean from defilement and uncleanness, from wrath and affliction. I will not send these against them any more for all the generations of the ages.

Isa. 2:2-3; Jer. 31:34; Zech. 14:5; 9, 16ff.
Gen. 8:21; 9:11.

Deut. 28:12;
Ezek. 34:26;
Mal. 3:10-12;
cf. Isa. 55:10.

XI.1. Then I will open the heavenly storerooms of blessing, to bring them down upon the earth, upon the labor of the sons of men.

Ps. 85:10-11;
Isa. 32:17; Jer.
33:6; Zech.
8:16, 19.

2. And truth and peace will be in partnership together for all the days of the age, even for all the generations of men."

Comment:

Under hellenistic influence, the story of Gen. 6:1-4 was filled out by the addition of elements drawn from Greek mythology, as noted above. This expanded version was well known in some Jewish circles, and circulated in variant forms, as attested in the *I Enoch* anthology. It was known to the author of *Jubilees* as well as to the author of the *Zadokite Document*. The story is alluded to in Judith 16:7; Baruch 3:26-28, and Wisd. Sol. 14:6.

The tradition persisted in Jewish esoteric lore, as well as in the popular religion, as attested in the Synoptic Gospels. Finally, it appears with adaptations in the Judeo-Christian books of II Peter, Jude and Revelation.

READING 13a: Enoch's censure of the Watchers (*I Enoch* XII.1—XIII.5; XIV.1-7)

Charles, in the Introduction to his critical, annotated edition of *I Enoch*, points out numerous verbal parallels to *I Enoch* in the Pauline writings as evidence that this tradition had influenced the apostle's thought. Perhaps his notion that the saints will judge angels (cf. I Cor. 6:3) is related to the following (and similar) passages within the Enoch collection.

XII.1. Before these things, Enoch was taken; yet no one knew where he was taken or what happened to him.

Dan. 4:13, 23.

Jub.
IV.21-23.

2. But his activities concerned the Watchers, and he was spending his days with the holy ones.—

Cf. Dan.
9:20ff.

3. Now as I, Enoch, was standing and blessing the Lord Most High, the King of the Ages, the Watchers of the Great Holy One began calling to me:

*Or,
"teacher"; cf.
Zad. Doc.
I.11.

Gen. 6:2.

II Peter 2:4;
Jude 6;
I Enoch VI.

Cf. I Enoch
X.7-8, Reading
12.

Jub. V.8-11.

4. "Enoch, you *scribe of righteousness, go and tell the heavenly Watchers who abandoned the highest heaven, the eternal sanctity of their station, to defile themselves with women, even those who have done just as men do and have taken wives for themselves: 'You have caused a great devastation on the earth. (5) There will be neither peace nor forgiveness for you.' And inasmuch as they rejoice over their children, (6) they shall see the murder of their children. They will lament and make entreaty for ever over the destruction of their children; but they shall have neither mercy nor peace."

XIII.1. Then Enoch told *Azael: "Begone! You will not have peace. A harsh sentence has been decreed against you, for you to be put in bonds. (2) You will be granted neither forbearance nor any request because of the hurtful things that you showed to men, because of all the ungodly deeds, the wickedness and sins that you secretly taught them." *Cf. *I Enoch* X.4. Reading 12; Lev. 16:8ff.

3. Then I went and spoke to all of them, and they all became afraid: fear and trembling seized them. (4) They asked me to write a petition for them, to the intent that they might receive forgiveness; and they asked me to read the petition for them before the Lord of heaven. (5) For they could speak no more nor lift their eyes to Heaven for shame concerning those sinful deeds for which they had been adjudged guilty.

Enoch wrote their petition, as requested. He went to sit by the "waters of Dan" near the foot of Mt. Hermon and began reading the petition to the Lord. But he received a vision in which he was commanded to censure these Watchers, the "angels that sinned"—II Peter 2:4; Jude 6—and to corroborate the message of doom previously given them.

READING 13b: Enoch's vision of the Glory (*I Enoch* XIV.8—XV.4; XVI.2-4)

XIV.8. Thus was I shown in vision: Lo! in the vision, clouds were inviting me, mists were calling me; stars in their courses urged me on, lightnings cheered me on, and winds in the vision gave me wings. (9) They lifted me up and carried me into heaven. I went in until I drew near great walls built of hailstones surrounded by tongues of fire; and I began to be afraid. (10) Then I entered the tongues of fire and approached a great house built of hailstones. Its walls were as if made of stone slabs, yet were entirely of snow, and the floor was of snow. (11) The ceilings were like the *courses of the stars and lightnings. Amidst them were fiery cherubim, and their heaven (was) water. (12) Flaming fire encircled the walls, and its gates blazed with fire. Judg. 5:20. Ps. 18:11-13. *The constellations in zodiacal arrangement.

13. I entered that house, hot as fire and cold as snow, with nothing in it to sustain life. Fear covered me and trembling seized me. (14) I began shaking and trembling, and I fell down. Ezek. 1:28b.
I saw in my vision, (15) and lo! another door was standing open opposite me, and there was a house larger than this one, built entirely of fiery flames. (16) It so completely excelled in glory and dignity and magnificence that I cannot declare to

you its glory and splendor. (17) Its floor was fire, and its upper parts were lightnings and the courses of the stars, and its ceiling was blazing fire.

Ezek. 1:26;
Dan. 7:9.

18. As I was looking I saw also a lofty throne. Its appearance was like crystal, and its wheels like the shining sun; and I saw cherubim. (19) From beneath the throne proceeded rivers of flaming fire, and I was unable to look at it.

Ezek. 1:5ff.
Dan. 7:10;
Ezek. 1:13.

20. On it was seated the Great Glory. His garments were like the sun, more brilliant and whiter than any snow. (21) No angel was able to enter this house and see His face because of the splendor and glory, nor was any earthly being able to see Him.

Ezek. 1:26-28;
Dan. 7:9; Ps.
104:2; Rev.
4:2.
Isa. 6:2; Rev.
4:3.
I Tim. 6:16.

Exod. 33:20.

22. The flaming fire encircled Him, and a great fire guarded Him, and no one could approach it. Ten thousand times ten thousand stood before Him whose every word was a deed. (23) And the holy angels who were near Him did not withdraw at night nor depart from Him.

Ps. 50:3; 97:3.

Dan. 7:10;
Rev. 5:11.

Gen. 1:3; Ps.
33:9; 148:5.

Rev. 4:8.

24. Now up to this time I had fallen on my face and remained trembling. But the Lord called me by His mouth and said to me: "Approach, Enoch, and hear My word."

Ezek. 2:1; Dan.   Enoch's
8:18. This is   commission
                  from God.

Cf. Acts 22:14.

25. Then one of the Holy Ones came to me. He raised me and stood me up, and led me to the door; but I kept my face bent downward.

Dan. 10:10.

XV.1. And He said to me: "The trustworthy man, man of truth, the scribe" (and I heard His voice), "fear not, Enoch, O trusty man and scribe of truth. Come hither and hear My voice. (2) Go and say to those who sent you: 'It was you who should *intercede for men, and not men for you. (3) Why did you abandon eternal heaven, lofty and holy, to sleep with women, to be defiled with the daughters of men and take wives for yourselves? You did just like sons of earth and fathered children for yourselves, your sons the giants. (4) But though you were holy ones, spirits living eternally, yet you became defiled by women's blood. In fleshly blood you begot children, and like human blood you lusted, just like those of flesh and blood who die and perish.' . . .

Cf. Ezra 7:6,
12.
Ezek. 2:1; Rev.
4:1.

*As the
archangels did,
I Enoch IX.

Gen. 6:1-4;
I Enoch
VI—VII; Jub.
VII.21ff.

XVI.2. And now to the Watchers who sent you to appeal on their behalf . . . say:

*This is
Charles' reading. The
Greek is contradictory.

*Either
wilfulness, lack
of insight, or
obstinacy.

3. 'You were once in heaven, but *not every mystery was revealed to you, and you knew worthless ones. Yet this you betrayed to the women in your *hardness of heart, so that by this mystery women and men multiply evils upon the earth.'

4. Say therefore to them: 'There is no peace.' " Isa. 57:21.

READING 14: History in theriomorphic symbolism (I. *Joseph* XIX)

In this vision, Israelite history is summarized from the early captivities to the author's own times. The actors are presented in the guise of animals.

XIX.1. My children, hear also the things I saw in visions: (2) I saw twelve stags grazing, then nine were separated and dispersed in the earth; likewise the other three. (3) And I saw that the three stags became *three lambs and cried to the Lord, and He led them out into a *verdant and well-watered place—He led them out of darkness into light. *[II Kings 17. II Kings 24—25; II Chron. 36. *Tribes of Judah, Benjamin and Simeon. *The Restoration; cf. Ps. 107:14; 60:1; Isa. 42:16; I Peter 2:9.]*

4. There they cried to the Lord until the nine stags came together with them and they became like twelve sheep. Then after a little time they increased and became many flocks.

*5. Now after these things I looked, and lo! twelve bull-calves sucking one heifer which produced a sea of milk, and the twelve flocks and innumerable herds drank from it. *[*A change of scene and symbolism.]*

6. And the horns of the *fourth ox grew up to heaven and became like a wall for the flocks, and between the two horns there grew out another *horn. *[*Judah, the fourth-born patriarch, and his tribe. *Symbol of a national leader.]*

7. And I saw a young bull which went around them twelve times, and became a great assistance to the cattle. (8) Then I saw in the midst of the horns the other horn become a lamb and, fighting on his right, one as a lion; and all the wild beasts and reptiles were fighting against him. But the lamb conquered them and destroyed them utterly. (9) Then the oxen rejoiced because of him and the heifer was overjoyed together with them. *[I Enoch XC.6ff.]*

10. Now these things must occur in their proper time, in the last days. *[Dan. 8:19; 11:27.]*

11. As for you, my children, honor Levi and Judah, for the salvation of Israel will arise from them. *[Jub. XXXI.16-20.]*

12. For my *kingdom which is among you will come to an end like a field-watcher's booth, which will not be seen after the summer. *[*Or, rule. Job 27:18; Isa. 1:8.]*

Comments:

1. This "vision" is an abbreviated summary of a much longer one recounted in *I Enoch* LXXV—XC, which begins with Adam and recounts biblical history in the theriomorphic mode. The righteous are symbolized

by oxen, sheep, and lambs (or rams); the wicked and the gentile enemies of Israel are symbolized by rapacious beasts, birds and serpents. The story of the angels that fell and their judgment is included.

2. In verses 3 through 8 there are numerous variations in the manuscripts. I have generally followed Charles' text, rather than that of de Jonge, since it keeps closer to the general trend of the Enoch vision and omits the alterations (Pharisaic, Essene or Christian) which are retained in de Jonge's edition.

3. *Lamb* and *lion* (v. 8): The *lion* was the symbol of the tribe of Judah (Gen. 49:9). The *lamb* seems to represent the priestly leader from Levi. This is in agreement with the basic doctrine of the *Testaments,* according to which the national leader comes from Levi and is given support by the tribe of Judah. This was the actual historical situation from the time of the late Restoration period: political power was vested in the high priests. If, as is believed with good reason, this "vision" relates to the Maccabean struggle, then the lamb may symbolize Juda Maccabeus. See the Extended Note on "Lamb of God" in Part Three.

II. The Hasmonean Heyday
(ca. 134-69 B.C.)

A. Historical Sketch
1. JOHN HYRCANUS I TO SALOME ALEXANDRA (Jewish War I.55-112)

John Hyrcanus succeeded his father Simon (I Macc. 16). He dealt first with his treacherous brother-in-law, Ptolemy, and then with the Syrians. He was finally able to pacify the country, establishing his authority. The first of the line of Hasmonean priest-kings, he was immensely popular with the people at the beginning of his rule. Apparently not a few of them felt, at first, that he might be in actuality the long-awaited Messiah. But not all shared this viewpoint.

67 (8). Out of envy at the success of John and his sons sedition arose among his countrymen, and many held conclaves in opposition to them. They did not rest until, having stirred up open conflict, they were defeated. *Ant. XIII.288-96.*

68. For the rest of his life, John enjoyed prosperity. After administering the government in the best way possible for thirty-one full years, he died leaving five sons. *Ant. XIII.299-300.*
He was truly a most favored person, with nothing to complain of against fortune concerning himself. For he alone had possessed the three best offices: as ruler of the nation, high priest, and prophet.

69. For *deity conversed with him so that he was not ignorant of coming events. Thus he foresaw and prophesied that his two older sons would not remain in control of affairs. . . . *Gk., daimon. In Ant. XIII.300, to theion, "the deity."*

70 (iii.1). After his father's death, the oldest son Aristobulus changed the government into a monarchy, the *first to wear a diadem. This was four hundred and seventy-one years and three months from the return of the people into their country after being released from servitude in Babylon. *Ant. XIII.301-19. *i.e., of the Hasmoneans.*

Comment:

Simon and John Hyrcanus I had the *actuality* of monarchy, though not the outward symbols. In adopting a Persian symbol of royalty, Aristobulus both declared his intention to be formally recognized as a monarch and set the style for his successors. That this held some special significance for the people of the time is indicated by the very pointed, if inaccurate, dating of this event.

71. Of his brothers, Antigonus was next. Aristobulus appeared to love him, and held him worthy of equal honor; while he bound and imprisoned the others. He also imprisoned his mother because she quarreled with him about the authority, since John had left her in charge of the realm. He was so cruel as to kill her by starvation in her imprisonment.

72 (2). But retribution overtook Aristobulus through his brother Antigonus, of whom he was fond and who had a share in the government. For Aristobulus killed him, too, on the grounds of slanders made up by evil men among his courtiers. . . .

Aristobulus was made to believe that Antigonus was scheming to try to assassinate him so as to take over the kingship; so he arranged to have Antigonus killed. His own wife was party to the plot. He died of great remorse when he finally learned the truth.

Ant.
XIII.320ff.

*His Hebrew
name was
Jonathan (Gk.
Iannaios)*

85 (iv.1). Aristobulus' wife released his brothers from prison and installed *Alexander as king. He seemed to be of suitable age and to have a moderate disposition. However, when he came to power, he put to death one of his brothers, who was ambitious to be king. The survivor, who preferred to live aloof from public affairs, he held in honor.

Alexander soon began a career of conquest. He first took Gadara and Amathus east of the Jordan, but they were speedily recovered by their overlord, Theodorus. After this defeat Alexander turned to the coastal towns and captured Gaza, Raphia and Anthedon. The pious among his subjects resented his neglect of his high-priestly duties in favor of conquest, and their leaders stirred up trouble for him.

Ant. XIII.372.

88 (3). After he had reduced these towns to servitude, the Jewish people rebelled against him at one of the feasts. . . .And it was thought that he could not have gotten the better of the uprising without the help of his mercenary force.

He continued his forays, however, apparently imagining himself a latter-day David, and tried to recover the territory of the old Judean monarchy.

*Ant.
XIII.375ff.*

90 (4). Next he fought with Obedas, king of the Arabs, who had prepared an ambush beforehand near Gaulane. He ran into it and wasted his whole army. . . .Though he escaped to Jerusalem, the people—who had disliked him for a long time—were aroused to insurrection by the enormity of the disaster.

91. Yet he got the better of them again, and in one fight after

another he slew no less than fifty thousand Jews in the course of six years. However, his victories brought him no satisfaction, while they wasted his realm. So he ceased hostilities and tried to reconcile his subjects by persuasion.

92. Instead, they despised still more his change of mind and inconsistency of temper. When he inquired what he could do to pacify them, they replied: "Die; for scarcely even by death could people be reconciled to anyone who had perpetrated such things." At the same time, they appealed for help to Demetrius, called "the Untimely." He readily agreed, hoping for greater gains; and when he arrived with an army the Jews joined forces with these allies at Sichem.

Demetrius' army won the battle and drove Alexander into the hills. At this, the sympathies of large numbers of the Jews changed, about 6,000 deserting Demetrius for Alexander. Demetrius withdrew his army in fear and disgust.

96 (6). Yet the remainder of the multitude did not drop their quarrel when their allies departed. They kept up the struggle against Alexander until he had killed a great many, and the remainder he drove into the town Bemesilis. When he had subdued it, he took the people captive to Jerusalem. *Ant. XIII.380-83*

97. He was in such an excess of rage that his savagery was carried to ungodly lengths. He impaled eight hundred of his captives in the city and slew their wives and children before their eyes, while he looked on, drinking and lounging with his concubines.

98. The people were struck with such consternation that the next night eight thousand of the resistance party fled beyond Judean borders; and their exile ended only with Alexander's death. Having brought tranquillity at last and with difficulty to the realm, he rested from conflict.

But Alexander was not to rest. He had to repulse an incursion by the Syrian, Antiochus Dionysus. After this he was defeated by Aretas, king of Coele-Syria, who made a treaty with him and withdrew. Then he campaigned successfully in Trans-Jordan, taking several cities and their territories.

105. . . .Alexander returned to Judea after three full years of campaigning. He was gladly received by the nation on account of his success. But he got the beginning of disease along with rest from war.

106. Troubled by an intermittent fever, he thought he could *Ant. XIII.398*

drive the malady away by becoming active in affairs again. So he involved himself in some ill-timed campaigns. He forced his body beyond its ability, so that his energies gave out. Thus he died in the midst of troubles after a reign of twenty-seven years.

Ant.
XIII.399-406.

*Her Hebrew name was Salome, "peace."

107 (v.1). He left the kingdom to his wife Alexandra in confidence that the Jews would much rather obey her (than anyone else). Since *she completely lacked his cruelty and had opposed his iniquities, the populace held her in their good will.

108. He was not mistaken in this hope: this little woman kept a firm grasp on the government by her reputation for piety. For, indeed, she observed most strictly the traditional customs of the nation, and would remove from power any who offended against the sacred laws.

Ant.
XIII.407ff.

109. Of her two sons by Alexander, she appointed Hyrcanus, the older, as high priest. She did so in view of his seniority as well as because he was too lethargic to be bothered about public matters. She restricted the younger, Aristobulus, to private life because he was so impulsive.

110 (2). Now growing up into authority alongside Alexandra were the Pharisees. These were a certain society of Jews reputedly more pious than others and more accurate expositors of the laws.

Matt. 16:19;
18:18; John
20:23.

Ant.
XIII.410ff.

111. To these Alexandra paid overmuch heed out of her devotion to God. So they, gradually, took advantage of her naiveté and in time became managers of everything, both banishing and recalling, both loosing and binding. In short, the advantages of the kingdom were theirs, while the expenses and difficulties were Alexandra's. (112) Nevertheless, she administered the larger matters. By constant recruiting she doubled the size of the army and collected not a few mercenaries. Thus, she not only strengthened her own nation, but was feared by foreign rulers. Yet, if she ruled over all the others, the Pharisees ruled her.

2. THE "THREE SECTS" OF THE JEWS (Ant. XIII.171-73)

*Of Jonathan,
ca. 155 B.C.;
cf. I Macc.
9—12, and
below.

171 (9). Now about *this time there were three sects among the Jews, differing in their views regarding human affairs. The first were called "Pharisees," the next, "Sadducees," and the third, "Essenes."

* Gk.,
heimarmēn;
cf. Isa. 5:11.

172. The Pharisees say that some things are the work of *destiny, yet not everything. It depends on us whether certain other events occur or not.

173. The Essenes, however, declare that destiny controls all
things, and that nothing comes to men but what it decrees. *Man. Disc. III.15-17.*
But the Sadducees oppose the notion of destiny, considering
it nonexistent and that human affairs are not subject to its
decrees. Rather, all things depend on us, so that we are re- *Cf. Zeph. 1:12c.*
sponsible for our own good, and what is bad we get through
our own lack of forethought.

Comments:

1. Josephus inserts this brief account of the three sects in his history of
Jonathan, successor to Juda Maccabeus. Whether the Pharisees and the
Essenes had separated this early into such well-marked sects is problema-
tic, although possible.

2. "Destiny": Josephus' term had acquired the popular meaning of
"fate," especially as astrologically determined. Both Christianity and, later,
Gnosticism offered ways of escape from the implacable decrees of fate thus
conceived. However, Josephus is here apparently adapting the notion of
"divine providence," or the "will of God," to the understanding of his
non-Jewish readers.

a. The Pharisees
(1) Doctrines and way of life (*Ant.* XVIII.12ff.; *War* II.162, 166a)

Since Josephus' account in the *Antiquities* includes details not given in the
War, the former is also used in regard to the Jewish "sects."

Ant. XVIII.12. The Pharisees keep their way of living simple
and do not give in to indulgence. They follow the way of those
things which their *teaching has selected and handed down as *Gk., logos.
good, considering worthy of defense the observance of *those *Their doctrine.
things which it was customary to enjoin. Out of honor for
their seniors, they hear them first and defer to them; nor do
they make bold to contradict anything which they propose. *I Tim. 5:1, 17; I Peter 5:5.*

13. They hold that all things are brought about by providence;
yet they do not deny to human will the impulse to do them. *Sirach 15:11-17.*
For they say it pleased God that a blending should occur, *T. Judah XX.1-3, Reading 32.*
namely, that into the council chamber of providence He was
willing for men with both good and bad intentions to enter.

14. They hold souls to have the power of immortality and that *Acts 23:6-8.*
under the earth there are both punishments and honors to
those who, respectively, followed a life either of ill-doing or of *Rom. 2:5-11.*
virtue. The first will be handed over to eternal imprisonment,
while the good will have an easy return to life. *Matt. 25:46; II Macc. 7:9; Acts 24:15.*

War II.162 (14). Now of the first two, the Pharisees are considered to interpret the laws accurately, and they are the leading

*To do good

*John 5:29,
Gk.; Mark
9:47-48.

sect. They attribute all things to providence and to God. They hold that to practice righteousness or not is mainly one's responsibility, but in each case providence *assists. Each soul is indestructible, indeed; but to pass into another body is for the *good alone, while the souls of the *depraved are chastised with unending punishment. . . .

166. The Pharisees are friendly to each other, and maintain harmonious relations with the public.

Comment:

Josephus' accounts of Pharisaic teaching about the relation between the divine will and human responsibility, on the one hand, and about the resurrection, on the other, are undoubtedly adapted to appeal to non-Jewish readers. On the first subject, the statement in *War* II.162 is clearer. But even in *Ant.* XVIII.13, it is possible to detect the notion of the good vs. the evil "impulse" or "inclination," which was a common dogma of pietistic Palestinian Judaism.

(2) Pharisaic influence; Hyrcanus' disaffection (*Ant.* XVIII.15; XIII.288ff.)

Matt. 23:2-3.

XVIII.15. Because of these teachings they have become most influential among the populace. Vows to God and sacred rites are generally performed according to their interpretation. By following the best in their way of life and doctrines, the people of the towns have testified to the greatness of their merit.

XIII.288. Jewish envy was aroused against Hyrcanus over the success of himself and his sons. The Pharisees were especially hostile to him. . . .And so great is their power over the multitude that if they say anything against king or high priest they are believed immediately.

289. Now Hyrcanus was once one of their disciples, and was held in great affection by them. Once he invited them to a banquet and entertained them hospitably. When he saw that they were enjoying themselves a great deal, he began to speak to them: "You know how I desire to be righteous, and that I do everything in such a way as may be pleasing to God and to you. . . . (290) At the same time, if you see me doing anything wrong or turning aside from the way of righteousness, lead me back into it and correct me." Then, when they testified that he was virtuous in everything, he enjoyed their praises.

However, a contentious Pharisee told Hyrcanus that he ought to relinquish the high-priesthood and retain only the governorship, and cast aspersions on his legitimacy. This brought the bad feelings to the fore, which a wily Sadducee took care to keep stirred up. When the Pharisees, on being asked what punishment their slanderous brother deserved, suggested something less than capital punishment, Hyrcanus was persuaded that they all believed the same way. In his anger, he joined the Sadducees, and abolished many Pharisaic regulations. The Pharisees were out of favor with the government until the days of Salome Alexandra.

(3) The oral tradition of the Pharisees (*Ant.* XIII.297-98)

297. At the moment I want to point out that the Pharisees had delivered to the people certain ordinances from the successions of the fathers which are not found written in the Laws of Moses. Because of this, the Sadducees reject them. They say that the ordinances that are written are to be considered binding, but the traditions of the fathers are not to be followed. (298) Between the two parties, controversies and great differences arose about these things.

Cf. Gal. 1:14.

Cf. Mark 7:6;
9:12; Luke 4:4;
Rom. 1:17.
Mark 7:5-13.

Comment:

What was written had supreme authority for the Pharisees, too, of course. Paul, the ex-Pharisee, uses the formula "it is written" repeatedly to establish points which he wishes to make. However, the oral tradition was of equal authority for the Pharisees. What the "successions of the fathers" and their traditions were is set out in the Mishnah tractate *Aboth*. Chapters 1 and 2 are of special importance. The "chain of tradition" that they traced back to Moses enabled them to claim the same authority for their oral traditions that the written scriptures possessed. Cf. Reading 67. Jesus seems to have rejected a great deal of this tradition, although probably not all of it.

b. The Sadducees

Josephus gives little detail concerning the Sadducees, and what he offers is mostly brief contrasts with the doctrines and influence of the Pharisees.

(1) Their teachings (*War* II.164-65; *Ant.* XVIII.16-17a)

War II.164. As for the Sadducees, the second of the orders, they reject the notion of *providence completely. They place God beyond either the doing or the seeing of any kind of wrong. (165) They say that the choice of good or of evil lies before a man and it is according to his own judgment which of the two he will follow. As for the ideas of the soul's perpetuity and of punishments and rewards in Hades, they reject them.

*Cf. the
Pharisaic
doctrines,
above.
Hab. 1:13; to
the contrary, see Amos 3:6.
Sirach
15:14-17;   Deut. 30:19;
cf. James
Mark 12:18. 1:13ff.
Acts 23:7-8.

Ant. XVIII.16 (4). The Sadducees hold the doctrine that souls perish along with the bodies. They accept nothing other than the laws by way of observance. For they count it a virtue to debate with their teachers of wisdom, after which they follow.

Luke 20:27-38.

17. There are only a few men who have come to this doctrine, but these are men of foremost rank.

(2) Their lack of influence (*Ant.* XIII.298b; XVIII.17b; *War* II.166)

Ant. XIII.298b. Now the Sadducees have the confidence only of the wealthy, having no following among the common people. But the Pharisees have the multitude for allies. . . .

XVIII.17b. They achieve, however, nothing worth speaking of. For whenever they get into a place of authority, they submit under pressure, they yield to what the Pharisees say. The people would not put up with them otherwise.

War II.166. The Sadducees are rather rude in their manners toward each other, as harsh in their dealings with their own kind as they are to foreigners.

Comment:

The Sadducees seem to have emerged as a distinct party in the era of hellenizing agitation, after ca. 200 B.C., as those who favored the modern trends. The core of the party was probably the leading families of priests who claimed descent from Zadok, whence the name: cf. II Sam. 20:25; I Chron. 29:22; Neh. 11:1-11; Ezek. 40:46 and related references. They accepted only the Pentateuch as authoritative scripture, rejecting the Prophets and Writings as secondary, and the Pharisaic oral traditions *in toto*. Because they controlled the Temple and its revenues they became wealthy and politically powerful, as I and II Maccabees and Josephus make clear. Members of the nonpriestly aristocracy and others of wealth and power were their allies. But they did not command the affections of the people, nor the allegiance of all the priests and Levites, many of whom belonged to those hasidic, or pietistic, groups that later formed themselves into the Pharisees and the Essenes.

c. The Essenes

Josephus claims to have spent time with the Essenes and to have passed through three stages of Essene initiation. In addition to the Qumran Scrolls, which contain some Essene writings, Josephus' descriptions, which have the interest of an eyewitness account, are still a major source of information concerning them.

(1) General description (*War* II.119b-127)

119b. But those called Essenes have a reputation for developing gravity of character. Although Jews, too, they display greater mutual friendship than others.

Heb. 13:1.

120. They turn from pleasures as bad, while they consider self-control and resistance to passions as virtue. They hold marriage in disdain, but they adopt other people's children

Titus 2:12; II
Peter 1:5-6.

while they are teachable. They consider these to be their own kin and mold their characters in accordance with Essene ways.

121. Marriage and the issue from it they do not reject entirely; but they desire to protect themselves from the wantonness of women, since they are persuaded that none of them keeps her troth to a man.

Cf. Sirach 9:1-9; 25:24; T. Reuben V.1—VI.4.

122. They do not esteem the value of riches, and their community of goods is remarkable: you will find none exceeding another in property. For their rule is that those entering the order must give their goods into the possession of the order. Thus, neither humiliating poverty nor overabundant wealth is seen among them anywhere. But the possessions of each are put together into one fund and, like brothers, they all have a share.

I Tim. 6:9-10; Heb. 13:5.

Man. Disc. I.11-13; VI.18-23.

Acts 2:44-46; 4:34ff.

123. . . .They think it important . . . always to be dressed in white. Those who are *elected take care of the community's affairs, and they are chosen to attend to everything with a view to the needs of all of them severally.

Rev. 3:4-5; 7:9; 19:14.

*By show of hands; cf. II Cor. 8:19. Gk.

Acts 6:2ff.

124 (4). They do not belong to one city only, but many settle in each town. To those of their sect who come from elsewhere they throw open everything as if they belonged there; and they go in to those whom they have not seen before as if they were intimates.

Rom. 12:13; Heb. 13:2; I Peter 4:9.

125. Thus, when they make a journey they carry nothing with them except arms for fear of robbers. In each town one is specially appointed to be responsible for entertaining strangers, providing them *clothing and necessaries. . . .

Mark 6:7-9.

Matt. 10:11.

*Cf. Sec. 129, below.

127. They neither buy nor sell to each other; but each gives to another what he needs, in exchange for something he finds useful. Yet even apart from exchanges, they are free to take from their fellows whatever they may desire.

Tobit 4:8; Matt. 5:42.

Comment:

Josephus does not mention a monastic order of Essenes, indicating above that they were scattered throughout the towns of Palestine. However, the Roman historian Pliny the Elder described briefly a group whose residence was on the west side of the Dead Sea, north of En-gedi. This is probably a reference to the ancient monastic community which we know as Qumran, the producers and preservers of the Dead Sea Scrolls.

(2) The form of their piety (*War* II.128-36)

128. Their reverence toward the deity takes a form peculiar to

Cf. *Man.*
Disc. X.1ff.

*The sun.

*Cf. Sec. 123,
above.

*Cf. Sec. 129,
above.

*Members of
the order from
elsewhere, cf.
Sec. 124,
above.

Man. Disc.
VI.10-12.

*Or, alms.

Zad. Doc.
VI.20—VII.1.
Rom. 12:13;
Gal. 6:10; Heb.
13:16.

Eph. 4:26-27;
James
1:19-20.

Col. 3:12-15.

Matt. 5:33-37.

themselves. Before sunrise, they utter nothing of a "worldly" nature, but offer certain traditional prayers, as though entreating *it to rise.

129. Afterwards they are dismissed by the *overseers to the crafts in which each is skilled. They work diligently until the fifth hour, when they again gather into one place. After girding themselves in linen clothing, they wash themselves off in cold water. Following this purification, they assemble in a private room, into which no heterodox person has ever been allowed to enter. Now cleansed, they pass into the refectory as into some holy sanctuary.

130. When they have sat down, the baker sets bread beside each in order, and the cook sets for each a plate of one kind of food.

131. The priest offers thanks before the meal, and it is forbidden to taste anything before the prayer. He offers prayer again after breakfast. Thus both when beginning and when ending the meal they pay respect to God as the provider of life. Then they take off their *robes as though they were sacred, and go back to work until evening.

132. When they return, they take supper in a similar way, and *strangers are seated with them, if any happen to have come. No outcry or disturbance profanes their house; but speaking each in turn, they yield to one another.

133. To outsiders, the silence of the residence seems like some dreadful mystery. But, in fact, it is due to their constant sobriety and the allotment of their food and drink to a measure just sufficient to satisfy their bodily needs.

134. In other things, they do nothing except by the arrangement of the overseers. Two things alone are at their discretion: giving aid and extending *mercy. They are permitted to help the worthy, if asked, and to supply food to the destitute, on their own. But they are not allowed to make gifts to relatives without the consent of the custodians.

135. Righteous masters over wrath, they keep their tempers in check; leaders in fidelity, they are servants of peace. Indeed, anything spoken by them has more weight than an oath. Yet oath-taking they avoid and consider it worse than perjury. For they say that anyone who cannot be believed apart from an oath is already condemned.

136. They show unusual eagerness regarding the writings of the ancients, choosing especially those which relate to the

welfare of soul and body. In such books they make investiga-
tions concerning medicinal roots and the properties of stones
for the healing of ills.

Comment:

Josephus' description continues through Sec. 161, but the preceding is
sufficient to give the general idea. There are remarkable agreements between the details concerning the Qumran sect which appear in their major
documents and those which appear in Josephus' account. The serious
student would be well advised to read the latter in its entirety and to
compare it with such Dead Sea literature as the *Zadokite Document* and the
Manual of Discipline.

B. Literature of the Times (about 150-60 B.C.)

Of the nine or ten major works contained in the standard Apocrypha,
three were produced in Palestine and three in Alexandria, Egypt, during
this period. Of the so-called pseudepigrapha, it is probable that these were
also written about this time: *Jubilees*, the original edition of the *Testaments
of the Twelve Patriarchs*, major sections of the *Enoch* collection, the *Testament of Job* (although possibly a little later). In addition, several of the major
Qumran works were probably produced at this time.

The older works were in circulation, too. Interestingly, a Hebrew text of
Sirach (written about 180 B.C.) was found in Qumran Cave II, indicating
that his wisdom had found favor with that sect. Ben Sirach's grandson took
the book to Alexandria, translating it into Greek about 130 B.C. for the use
of the large Greek-speaking Jewish community there. To this we owe its
preservation and inclusion in the Church's scriptures.

1. IN SUPPORT OF THE HASMONEAN REGIME

READING 15: Divine accreditation in vision (*T. Levi* II.9b-12; IV.1—V.7;
VIII.1-19)

In the introductory section, Levi is represented as being disturbed about
all the evil which he sees around him. He is therefore granted a vision of the
seven heavens, and receives an angelic declaration of the ministry to which
he is to be called.

II.9b. And the angel said to me: "Do not marvel at *those, for *The three heavens he has
you will see four other heavens, more brilliant and incompar- seen.
able, when you go up there; Cf. II Cor. 12:2-4.

10. because you will stand very close to the Lord, and you will Num. 3:5-10.

Mal. 2:4-6. *Cf. Mark 4:11; Eph. 3:3.
Cf. Luke 24:21.
be His minister. You will announce His *mysteries to men; and you will make proclamation concerning the one who is about to redeem Israel.

Zeph. 3:15-17.
Cf. Isa. 40:5 in Luke 3:6; Isa. 42:6ff.
11. Also, through you and Judah the Lord will be seen among men, saving every family of mankind.

Num. 18:8-23.
12. Your livelihood shall be from the Lord's portion, and He will be your field, vineyard, fruits, gold and silver. . . .

IV.1. Now then, know that the Lord is going to execute judgment upon the sons of men. . . .

Cf. War I.68 in the Historical Sketch, above.
Deut. 33:8, 10a; II Chron. 17:7-9; 30:22; 35:3a; Ezek. 44:23ff.
*Literally, "seed."
2. So the Most High has heeded your prayer, to separate you from wickedness so that you may become for Him a son, a royal servant and a minister of His Presence. (3) You will make the light of knowledge shine as a lamp in Jacob, and you will be as the sun to all the *offspring of Israel.

Num. 6:22-27.
Isa. 11:10; 42:1, 6; 49:1, 6.
4. And a blessing will be given to you and all your seed, until the Lord shall visit all the nations in the compassions of His son for ever.

5. Therefore counsel and insight have been granted you so that you may instruct your sons concerning him,

Gen. 12:3.
6. because whoever blesses him will be blessed, and those cursing him will be destroyed."

Cf. Rev. 4:1.
V.1. Then he opened for me the gates of heaven, and I saw the holy sanctuary, and the Most High on a glorious throne. (2) And He said to me: "Levi, the blessings of the priesthood have I given to you until I come to dwell in the midst of Israel."

Ezek. 37:24-28; 43:7, 9; Zeph. 3:15-17; Zech. 2:5, 10-11.
3. Then the angel led me to earth. He gave me armor and a sword, and said: "Take vengeance on Shechem for Dinah's sake. I will be with you, because the Lord sent me."

Cf. Gen. 34.

Cf. Jub. XXX.
(4. So at that time I made an end to the sons of Hamor, as it is written in the heavenly tablets.)

5. I said to him: "I pray, lord, tell me your name so that I may call on you in a day of trouble."

Dan. 12:1; cf. Rev. 12:7.
6. He replied: "I am the angel who intercedes for the race of Israel so that they may not be completely beaten down, because every evil spirit is attacking them." (7) Then after these things, when I awoke, I blessed the Most High and the angel who intercedes for Israel's tribes and all the righteous. . . .

Comment:

In IV.2, above, it is announced to Levi that he is to become "a son, a royal servant and a minister of His Presence." There is little in the O. T. background to justify this ascription, either for priest or Levite. It is too obviously the combining of the titles of Davidic royalty—the king is God's "son" and "servant," cf. II Sam. 7:8, 14—with the high priesthood. If Josephus is to be trusted, John Hyrcanus I did not openly claim kingship, even though he enjoyed royal power. But an eager apologist might not hesitate to ascribe it to him. At any rate, his sons Aristobulus and Alexander claimed the regal estate openly.

VIII.1. And there again, after seventy days passed, I saw a *vision, just as at the first:

*Literally, "matter"; cf. Ezek. 9:2; *I Enoch* XX. *Jub.* XXXII.

2. I saw seven men in white clothing who said to me: "Stand up and put on the priestly vestments, even the crown of righteousness, the breast-piece of discernment, the robe of truth, the *frontlet of faithfulness, the *turban of preeminence, and the ephod of *prophecy." (3) Then each brought a piece and put it on me, and they said: "From now on you are the Lord's priest, you and your descendants for ever."

Exod. 28:4-39; 39:1-29; Sirach 45:6-13; *Ant.* III.152-78.

*Exod. 28:36-37. *Or, "the sign" (of chief rank).

*Cf. I Sam. 23:9-11.

4. The first anointed me with holy oil and gave me a *staff of judgment.

Exod. 29:7; Lev. 8:12; 21:10; Sirach 45:15.

*Literally, "rod"; cf. Exod. 4:17-20; Ps. 2:9; Exod. 40:12-13, 30-32; *T. Levi* IX.11.

5. The second washed me with clean water, and fed me *bread and wine, most holy, and put a holy and splendid vestment on me. (6) The third put a linen garment on me, like an ephod. (7) The fourth put a purple sash around me. (8) The fifth gave me an olive branch. (9) The sixth put a crown on my head. (10) The seventh put the diadem of priesthood on my head, and filled my hands with an odorous offering so that I could be a priest to the Lord.

*Possibly part of the ritual in the author's time.

Cf. Zech. 4.

Lev. 8:25-28.

11. Then they said to me: "Levi, your offspring will be divided into three branches, as a sign of the glory of the Lord who is to come. (12) Now *he who was faithful shall be first. No portion shall be greater than his. (13) The second shall be in the priesthood. (14) And the third shall be called by a new name, because a king will arise out of *Judah who will set up a new priesthood after the gentile pattern, for all the nations. (15) And his appearance will be marvelous, as a prophet of the Most High from our father Abraham's lineage. (16) Every desirable thing in Israel will be for you and your line. You will eat everything pleasant to the sight, and your sons will share the table of the Lord. (17) From them will come *chief priests, judges and scribes; for by their mouth that which is holy shall be guarded.

Exod. 40:34-35; Lev. 9:22-23. *Probably Moses; cf. Num. 12:7.

*I.e., the territory of Judah.

Cf. Ps. 110:4. Isa. 42:6.

Cf. *War* I.68 in the Historical Sketch, above.

Num. 18:12-14; Gen. 3:6.

*E.g., Aaron, Samuel, Ezra, Ezek. 44:23-24; Lev. 10:11; Num. 1:52-53; 3:5-10; 4:4ff.; Hag. 2:11; Mal. 2:1-7.

Cf. Gen. 37:9;
41:5, 25   18. When I awoke I realized that this dream was like the first
one. (19) So I hid this in my heart also, and did not disclose it
to any living person.

Comments:

1. The literary technique of these passages is *apocalyptic:* a revelation of
the future granted through a dream or vision, with an angel or angels
assisting in the action or interpretation of the vision. Cf. Dan. 8:15ff.;
9:21ff.; Zech. 1:8—6:8.

2. The garments with which Levi was invested are those peculiar to the
high priest. They agree, in general, with those described in Exod. 28 and 39,
in Sirach 45:6-13, and in Josephus, *Ant.* III.152-78. The clearly implied
emphasis of these dreams, along with a dream of Jacob to the same intent
reported in Sec. IX, is that since the office of priest, and particularly that of
high priest, was granted Levi centuries before the high priesthood was
settled on Aaron and his line, *any* descendant of Levi could legitimately so
serve, even if not in the Zadokite line. Paul uses the same kind of argument,
though on firmer scriptural ground, when arguing for justification apart
from circumcision; cf. Rom. 4:9ff.

3. Vv. 14-15 above give the clue that the author has the Hasmonean
hierarchy in view, and most likely John Hyrcanus I.

a. The "new priesthood after the gentile pattern": from time immemorial
in the Near East, except in Israel, the monarch had also served as high
priest. This is what "after the order of Melchizedek" means in Ps. 110:4.
Melchizedek was both king and high priest of Salem (Gen. 14:18-20). In the
Israelite monarchy the powers were separated. Yet the high priesthood was
historically the older, and it survived as the center of authority after the
Captivities and Restoration. But until Israel was freed from foreign domination, no high priest could dare to assume openly the independent control of
the government or the symbols thereof. This passage reflects the new
situation of independence as a result of the Maccabean struggle (cf. I Macc.
14ff.)

b. V. 15: Of all the Hasmoneans, the gift of prophecy was attributed only
to John Hyrcanus I, as far as we know. "A prophet . . . from our father
Abraham's lineage" probably is intended to be reminiscent of Deut. 18:15.
The patriarchs, especially Abraham, were considered to have been
prophets; and any Israelite—since all were children of Abraham—might
qualify, if granted the inspiration (Joel 2:28). Why not the high priest as
well, the one seemingly most favored by God?

READING 16: Admonitions to support and obey (*T. Reuben* VI.8-12; *T.
Simeon* V.4-6; VII.1-3; *T. Judah* XXI.1-5)

T. Reuben VI.8. Therefore I command you to obey Levi, since he will know the Law of the Lord and will give orders for judgment and sacrifices on behalf of all Israel, until the *completion of the times of the anointed high priest, about which the Lord spoke. ^{T. Levi II.10; IV.3, Reading 15.} ^{*Dan. 8:19; Matt. 13:39; T. Benjamin XI.3; Zad. Doc. IV.8-9.}

9. I adjure you by the God of heaven that each of you do truth toward his neighbor; ^{Zech. 8:16-17; John 3:21; I John 1:6; T. Dan V.2; Man. Disc. I.5.}

10. And draw near to Levi in humility of heart, so that you may receive a blessing out of his mouth; ^{Num. 6:22-27.}

11. for it is he who will bless Israel and Judah, for by him the Lord has chosen to rule over all the people.

12. So bow down before his seed, because he will die on our behalf in struggles visible and invisible; and he will be among you as a *king of ages. ^{*I.e., as a dynasty; cf. Ps. 110:4.}

T. Simeon V.4. For I have seen it inscribed in a *writing of Enoch that your sons after you will be corrupted by fornication, and they will do injury to Levi with the sword. (5) But they will not prevail against Levi, because he will fight the war of the Lord and will overcome every one of your *encampments. (6) And they will be but few, divided among Levi and Judah; and none from among you will govern, even as my father Jacob prophesied in the Blessings. . . . ^{*Not in extant editions.} ^{Cf. Num. 25:6-8, 14.} ^{*Or, armies.} ^{Cf. Gen. 49:5-7; Josh. 19:1; 21:4.}

VII.1. And now, my sons, obey Levi; and by Judah you will be *redeemed. Do not rebel against these two tribes, because from them will God's *deliverance *arise for you. (2) For the Lord will raise up one from Levi as high priest, and one from Judah as king. Thus He will *save all the nations and the race of Israel. (3) Therefore I am enjoining all these things so that you may instruct your children, so that they will observe these things in their generations. ^{*Or, delivered.} ^{*sōterion, "salvation."} ^{*Used of the sun and of leaders.} ^{*Form of sōzō, "save, deliver"; this is messianic doctrine.}

T. Judah XXI.1. And now, children, love Levi, so that you may endure; and do not exalt yourselves against him lest you be completely destroyed. (2) For the Lord gave the kingdom to me, and the priesthood to him, and subordinated the kingdom to the priesthood. (3) To me He gave the things upon earth, to him the things in heaven. (4) As the heaven is higher than the earth, so the priesthood of God is higher than the earthly kingdom. (5) For the Lord chose Levi to draw near to Him on your behalf, and to eat at His table, even the first fruits of the choice things of the sons of Israel. ^{II Chron. 26:16-20 may be the basis for this.} ^{Cf. Jer. 33:14-18.} ^{Cf. T. Levi VIII.16, Reading 15.}

Comments:

1. These readings are so obviously propagandistic, so thoroughly Jewish

and partisan in concern, that it is hard to see how scholars can attribute these testaments to Christian, even *Judeo*-Christian, authorship in the first or second centuries A.D., as some have. Such propaganda was scarcely relevant in Jesus' day and, with the destruction of the Temple in A.D. 70, well-nigh unthinkable. But it was most apropos in support of the Hasmonean regime which began to fall into disfavor with many in the latter part of John Hyrcanus I's rule. It is even possible, according to Philonenko's contention, that this was propaganda of the schismatic Zadokites in favor of their Righteous Teacher—although there are considerations against this view. Charles' view that these documents, produced at least in part in support of the Hasmoneans, were reworked by a hasidic editor to bring them into line with biblical messianism still holds water.

2. "In struggles visible and invisible" (*T. Reuben* VI.12): this may well refer to the struggles of the Maccabeans and Hasmoneans, both on the battlefield and against secret plots against their lives. Cf. I Maccabees, especially 14:29-32 and Josephus, *Ant.* XII—XIII.

3. "Obey Levi; and by Judah you will be redeemed" (*T. Simeon* VII.1); "For the Lord . . . subordinated the kingdom to the priesthood" (*T. Judah* XXI.2): this is essentially a *priestly* point of view. It may have found its scriptural support in II Chron. 26:16-20, and in the observation that Ezekiel, in his visions of the Restoration, has very little to say about the role of the Prince (cf. chs. 45—46). The *de facto* historical situation in the time of the Maccabees and Hasmoneans was that leadership was vested in the hierarchy, but the Judean populace supplied the fighting forces. So this "prophecy" could be considered to have been fulfilled. However, from the biblical messianic viewpoint, the *king* had to be a Davidic scion (Isa. 11; Jer. 33:14-18; *Ps. Sol.* XVII), and *he* would bring the deliverance. Our author reveals his bias in the way in which he uses prophecy to fit the *status quo*.

2. PRAYER AND PRAISE IN ISRAEL

READING 17a: Prayer for guidance and strength against an enemy (Judith 9:2-14)

Cf. Gen. 34
with *Jub.*
XXX.1ff.

Gen. 34:7.

*Of their circumcision and subsequent execution.

2. O Lord, God of Simeon my forefather to whom you gave a sword for vengeance on the foreigners who unbound the virgin's girdle to defile her, stripped bare her thigh to her shame and polluted her womb to her disgrace—for You had said, "It must not be done"; yet they did it. (3) Therefore you appointed their rulers to slaughter, and their couch (which was ashamed of their deceit) was met by *their blood; for You struck down slaves with the chiefs and the chiefs on their thrones. (4) You gave up their women for booty and their daughters for captives, and all their spoils for division among

the sons beloved by You. They were zealous for You, and they abhorred the defilement of *their blood, so they called on You for help—O God, my God, also hearken to me, a widow!

*I.e., of their family through Dinah's rape.

5. For You did the former things as well as these; and the things that followed, things that are now, and things to come You planned. Whatever You intended occurred, (6) and whatever You purposed came forth and said: "Lo, here we are," for all Your ways are prepared and Your judgment is with foreknowledge.

Isa. 37:26; 46:8-10; 41:4; 42:9; 48:3-7; 44:24;

Ps. 115:3; 135:6ff.

Isa. 40:26; Job 38:35; Baruch 3:34.

7. For look! the Assyrians have increased in their might: haughty are their cavalry and they flaunt the strength of their infantry. They hope in shield and javelin, in bow and sling, and do not recognize that You are the Lord who shatters wars: *Lord is Your name.

Cf. Hab. 1:6-11.

Ps. 46:9; 76:1-3; cf. Exod. 15:3; II Macc. 12:28.

*I.e., Yahweh.

8. Break in pieces their strength by Your might and strike down their power in Your anger; for they plan to pollute Your holy things, to defile the tabernacle where Your glorious Name resides, and to demolish the horn of Your altar with the sword. (9) Look at their arrogance! Send Your wrath upon their heads! Grant to the hand of me, the widow, the strength to do what is purposed. (10) Strike down slave with chief and chief with attendant by the guile of my lips, shatter their high-mightiness by a female hand!

Cf. II Macc. 8:18; 9:5-8; 2:4-5.

Cf. Judg. 4:17-21; 5:24-27.

11. For Your power is not in a multitude, nor Your rule by means of those who are strong; but You are the God of the humble, Helper of the lowly, Support of the weak, Protector of the rejected, Savior of those who are without hope.

Cf. Judg. 7:4-7; I Sam. 14:6; II Chron. 14:11; 20:5-15ff.; I Macc. 4:8.

Cf. I Sam. 2:6-8; Ps. 149:4.

12. O God! God of my father and God of Israel's inheritance, Owner of heaven and earth, Creator of the waters, King of all Your creation, hearken to my prayer (13) and grant my deceitful word to be their wound and bruise—for they have planned *cruel things against Your holy house, against Your covenant and the crest of Zion, even against the house belonging to Your sons. (14) And cause all nations and every tribe to recognize and to understand that You are God, God of all might and power, and that there is no one else who protects the race of Israel but You alone.

*Literally, "hard/harsh."

Cf. II Macc. 2:17-18; 7:6.

I Macc. 4:8-11; II Macc. 8:36.

Comment:

To appreciate the main request of Judith's prayer, the preceding chapters must be consulted. In the situation as described, there are parallels both with Esther and the story of Sisera and Jael in Judges 4. What Judith proposes to do is to play up to the general of the enemy army, enticing him to try to seduce her. This will justify her killing him, on grounds similar to those on which Levi and Simeon slaughtered the Shechemites, the son of whose chieftain had raped their sister Dinah.

As a tract for the times of the Maccabean struggle, Judith reflects the popular theology and biblical interpretation of that era. With this should be compared the petitions for help of Mordecai and Esther, in The Additions to Esther, and the petitions for help found in I and II Maccabees—all in the RSV edition of the Apocrypha.

READING 17b: Prayer for self-discipline (Sirach 22:27—23:6)

Ps. 141:3;
Prov. 13:3;
23:9.

22:27. Who will set a guard upon my mouth, and upon my lips a seal of prudence,

*Prudence; cf. James 3:1-12;
Sirach   Prov. 10:14.
28:25-26.

lest I fall away from *it, and my tongue destroy me?

*Literally,
"counsel."

23:1. Lord, Father and Master of my life, do not abandon me to their *wish,

Prov. 13:3;
18:7.

do not let me fall by means of them.

Ps. 139:23-24; Prov. 2:1-5;
Prov. 12:1   3:11-12;
                Sirach 4:17.

2. Who will set scourges upon my intentions, and over my heart the discipline of wisdom?—

*Unintentional Deut. 8:5; Ps.
sins.   94:12; Heb.
                12:5-6.

so that they will not spare my *errors, and not at all pass by my sins;

*Sins of
ignorance.

3. so that my *mistakes may not be multiplied, and that my sins may not abound,

Ps. 7:3-5;
Prov. 16:7;
25:28.

lest I fall before those who oppose me, and my enemy rejoices over me.

Prov. 6:16-17;
21:4.

4. Lord, Father and God of my life, do not give me supercilious eyes,

Ps. 119:36;
Prov. 15:27;
28:16.

5. and turn lust away from me.

Prov. 23:20-2;
6:24ff.

6. Do not let gluttony or lust seize me, and do not hand me over to a shameless soul.

Cf. Rom.
1:24ff.

Comment:

The prayer is cast in the personal mode, and may have been originally a genuine and sincere prayer of the author. As it stands in the present text, however, it introduces a series of wisdom homilies dealing in turn with swearing and foul talk, incest and adultery, and the character of the adulteress. It may have been given as a model petition for Sirach's disciples.

READING 18a: A sectarian community hymn (*Man. Disc.* X.5-17a)

5. . . .At the beginning of months, on their festivals and holy

days appointed for *remembrance, in their set times, (6) with an *offering of the lips I will bless Him, according to an *ordinance which is engraved for ever; at the beginning of the years and at the return of their *appointed times, at the completion of the ordinances established for the days of His decree, one after the other . . . , the seasons of the years to the seventh of them, (8) and at the beginning of the sevens of years to the *season of liberation. And all my life the engraved ordinance shall be on my tongue as the fruit of praise and the portion offered by my lips.

*Of God's mighty acts in the past. Ps. 50:14; 23; 51:15ff.
*The Mosaic Law concerning the festivals. *Or, "festivals."
*I.e., the Jubilee year; cf. Lev. 25. Isa. 57:18c; Heb. 13:15.

9. I will sing with knowledge and all my music will be for the glory of God: my lyre and harp *attuned to His holy order, and the flute of my lips will I lift up *according to the notes of His justice.

I Cor. 14:15; Eph. 5:19.
*Implied, Ps. Sol. XV.3.
*I.e., as a written musical score.

10. With the entrance of the day and of the night I will enter into the covenant of God, and with the going forth of the evening and the morning I will recite His statutes; and where they are I will set (11) my limits so as not to *turn back. His judgment convicts me according to my perversities, and my transgressions will be before my eyes as an engraved precept. I will say to God: "(You are) my Righteousness," (12) and to the *Most High: "(You are) the Founder of my prosperity, Well of Knowledge, Spring of holiness, Height of glory, and the Almighty One of eternal splendor."
I will choose whatever (13) He *points out to me and I will accept that in which He judges me.
As soon as I stretch hand or foot, I will bless His name; as soon as I go out or come in, (14) sit or stand, or when I lie on my couch, I will sing for joy to Him. I will bless Him with an offering of utterance from my lips, *from among the ranks of men, (15) even before I lift my hands to *eat the delicacies of the earth's produce.
Whenever I am afraid or in terror, or in a place of distress or desolation, (16) I will bless Him for His manifold wonders. On His might I will meditate and upon His mercies will I rely every day.
For I know that in His hand is the judgment of (17) everyone who lives, and all His deeds are truth.

Cf. Deut. 6:1-7; Ps. 5:3; 63:6.
Ps. 55:17; 119:54-55.
Ps. 119:2-5, *I.e., from 30, 102, 133, God's way. 165.
Ps. 51:3; Isa. 59:12. Ps. 4:1; Jer. 23:6.
*Elyon: Gen. 14:19-20.
Deut. 8:18; Ps. 84:11; 85:12; 103:2, 5.
*Or, "teaches." Ps. 119:75; Ps. Sol. III.3.
Deut. 6:7.
Isa. 12:6.
*In assembly at meals.
*Literally, "make myself fat on."
Ps. 27:1-2; 56:3-4.
Job 37:14; Ps. 26:7; 40:5; 72:18; 143:5; Sirach 16:26-30; 18:1-7.
Ps. 106:45; 119:41, 116.
Deut. 32:4; Ps. 33:4.

Comments:

1. This hymn, the first part of which is given above, concludes the *Manual of Discipline* (or, *Community Rule*), a guidebook for the members of the Qumran community. The last section of ordinances specifies that the member is to obey and delight in the words of God, and to bless and praise

the Lord on all occasions. The hymn opens with a vow to follow this precept literally and faithfully.

2. The Pharisaic brotherhoods, also, maintained carefully the daily times of prayer and praise, as well as the scrupulous celebrations of the various festivals specified in the Law. From this we may get an idea of what Paul, the converted Pharisee, had in mind when he admonished the Thessalonian church to "pray without ceasing" (i.e., constantly, or regularly): cf. I Thess. 5:17; Luke 18:1.

READING 18b: Praise for God's help in difficulties (*Qumran Hymns* IV.5-6a; 12b-13; 22-25, 27-29; VII.6-15)

IV.5. I praise You, O Lord, because You enlightened my face regarding Your covenant. . . .

Cf. Prov. 4:18
and Hos. 6:3
together.

6. . . .I seek You; and as bright dawn of perfect light You appeared to me. . . .

Isa. 14:24;
46:10.

12b. . . .For You, O God, reject every design of (13) Belial. It is Your counsel that will stand, and the design of Your heart is fixed for ever. . . .

Ps. 20:9, Heb.

22. . . .As for me, by laying hold on You I am established and I will rise up against those who reject me. My hand will be upon all who scorn me, because (23) they did not reckon with

Cf. Mic. 3:8;
I Cor. 2:4; Gal.
1:15-16.

me up to the time that You showed Your might in me.

*Ps. 27:1.

You have appeared to me in Your power as perfect *light, and You have not daubed with shame the faces of (24) any of those who were sought out by me.

Those who gathered to Your covenant, and those who walked in the way of Your heart hearkened to me, and they made

Cf. Ps. 5:4,
Heb.
Cf. Ps. 99:4;
Isa. 42:3; Matt.
12:20.

preparation for You (25) in the counsel of the holy ones; and judgment went forth for them for victory, and truth went forth for equity. . . .

27. . . .By me You have illumined the faces of many, and You have given help beyond measure, because You made known

II Cor. 12:4;
Eph. 3:4-5.

to me Your secrets of (28) wondrousness, and by Your wonderful counsel You have shown Yourself strong with me, and

Ps. 40:5.

have done wondrously in the presence of many for the sake of Your glory, to make known (29) to all living Your mighty

Ps. 107:8ff.

acts. . . .

Ps. 55:22.
Isa. 40:29-31;
63:11b-13;
Mic. 3:8.

VII.6. I praise You, O Lord, because You sustain me by Your strength, and (7) the spirit of Your holiness You have poured into me lest I stumble.

Ps. 23:5; 27:3;
31:19-20.

You strengthened me in the presence of wicked conflicts, and

amidst all their threats (8) You have not let me be frightened
away from Your covenant.

You have set me like a strong watchtower, like a lofty wall. <small>Ps. 18:2; 61:2-3.</small>
You have founded my house upon a rock (9) with durable <small>Ps. 27:5; 40:2. cf. Matt. 7:24-25.</small>
bases for my foundation, and each of my walls is as a *tested <small>*Cf. Isa. 28:16: "a tested</small>
wall that will not shake. . . . <small>stone"; *Man. Disc.* VIII.8.</small>

12. . . .For all who provoke me to judgment You will pro-
nounce guilty, so as to distinguish by me between righteous
and wicked. (13) For You know every intention of action, and <small>Ps. 139:1-4.</small>
each answer of the tongue You discern. And You order my
heart (14) according to Your teachings and Your truth, to
direct my steps aright in the well-trodden ways of righteous- <small>Ps. 23:3.</small>
ness, to walk before You in the *limits of (15) the righteous—to <small>*Or, "boundary of</small>
paths of glory and life and peace. . . . <small>righteousness."</small>

Comments:

1. The author expresses himself in phrases copiously drawn from the
canonical Psalms, his models for composition, and the Prophets, and uses
the poetical devices common to biblical poetry. It is not easy to convey this
style in idiomatic English, and the translation represents a deliberate com-
promise between smooth English and a literal rendering. The text is from
Eduard Lohse's edition.

2. Some specialists believe that in these psalms we hear the voice of the
founder of the Qumran sect. Along with other literature of the sect, these
hymns testify to religious conflict. Some of the expressions seem to reflect
the struggle between Judaism and hellenism that had exercised the souls of
the pious from before the time of the Maccabees to the times of Jesus and
later.

3. The remarkable claim to divine authority expressed in VII.12-14 should
not be overlooked. The writer claims the direct guidance of God when he is
exercising the office of judge. This guidance is a combination of inner
inspiration, or special insight, and "Your teachings and Your truth," i.e.,
the Torah. Cf. I Cor. 5:3-5; II Cor. 10:5-8.

3. WISDOM AND ESOTERIC KNOWLEDGE

a. Viewpoints of Wisdom

READING 19a: The nature and origin of Wisdom, Palestinian viewpoint
(Sirach 1:1-4, 6, 8-10, 14-20, 25-27)

1. All wisdom is from the Lord, and it is with Him for ever. <small>Prov. 2:6; Wisd. Sol. 9:4.</small>

2. Sand of the seas, drops of rain, and days of an age—who
will count them out? (3) The height of heaven and the breadth

of the earth, the Abyss and Wisdom—who will trace them out?

4. Wisdom was created before all things, and from the beginning, the *understanding of prudence. . . .

6. To whom has the root of Wisdom been revealed? And its resourcefulness, who knows it? . . .

8. The One is wise, He who sits upon His throne: He is greatly to be feared.

9. The Lord Himself created it. He saw and apportioned it. He *poured it out upon all His works, (10) along with all flesh, according to His gift; but He supplied it abundantly *to those who love Him. . . .

14. The *beginning of Wisdom is to fear the Lord. It is created with the faithful in the womb.

15. With men it *put down an enduring foundation; and it will be entrusted with their descendants.

16. To fear the Lord is Wisdom's abundance, and it fills men up with its fruits.

17. It fills all their houses with desirable things, and their storehouses with its produce.

18. The fear of the Lord is the crown of Wisdom, making peace and *health to flourish.

19. And He saw and apportioned it, and rained down knowledge and understanding; and He exalts the reputation of those who take hold of it.

20. To fear the Lord is the root of Wisdom, and its branches are length of days. . . .

25. In the treasuries of Wisdom are parables of knowledge; but to sinners godliness is an abomination.

26. If you desire wisdom, keep the commandments, and the Lord will supply it to you in abundance.

27. For the fear of the Lord is wisdom and discipline; and to be faithful and tractable is His good pleasure.

Comments:

1. Vv. 5 and 7 do not occur in the best mss., and appear to be glosses in those in which they do occur. Vv. 11-13 were omitted as being tangential to the purpose for including this reading.

Marginal references (left column):

Job 38:4ff.; Isa. 40:12ff.

*Cf. Job 28:12, 20, LXX.

Ps. 89:6-7. Job 28:27, Heb. and Gk.

*Prov. 8:23, Heb.

Cf. Wisd. Sol. 7:24ff.   *I.e., to Israel: cf. Baruch 3:36—4:4.

*Or, "first principle," Ps. 111:10; Prov. 1:7; 9:10; 15:33.

*Literally, "built as a nest."

Cf. Prov. 8:18-19.

Prov. 8:19; 24:4.

Prov. 19:23; 4:9.

*Gk., "health of healing."

Cf. v. 9, above.

Prov. 3:16; 4:8, 8:18.

Cf. v. 6, above. Prov. 3:2, 10:27.

Prov. 1:5-7, 13:19.

Cf. v. 10, above.

2. As is evident, this homily on "All wisdom comes from the Lord" is a tissue of reminiscences from wisdom passages, chiefly from Proverbs and Job. Interestingly, ben Sira' evidently took the verb *n-s-k* in Prov. 8:23 in the sense of "pour out"—cf. v. 9, above. This suggests an equating of Wisdom with God's Spirit, which is also said to be "poured out." The verb could also mean "cast metal." The Septuagint apparently took the verb as a metaphorical extension of this idea, translating with a verb meaning "to found or establish." Most of the popular English translations have followed the Septuagint. However, like Sirach the Berkeley Version and The New American Bible render the verb "pour out." In the light of other things which are said about Wisdom in both canonical and extracanonical writings, it seems that Sirach's interpretation of Prov. 8:23 is correct.

3. "He . . . apportioned it," vv. 9 and 19. The Greek verb reflects a Hebrew verb which means "count out, count up, enumerate; recount; assess." I have adopted the RSV rendering as accurately reflecting the intended sense: God "counted out" His Wisdom, so as to give each part of His creation a share. According to the prevailing thought on Wisdom, each aspect of the creation (i.e., the universe) displays God's purposive wisdom, and each embodies some of His creative, or effective, wisdom.

READING 19b: The Alexandrian viewpoint on Wisdom (Wisd. Sol. 6:12, 22; 7:7-14; 7:22—8:1; 9:1-18)

As a literary device, this section of the Wisdom of Solomon is addressed to "kings, judges, and rulers of the earth," as if from their fellow potentate, Solomon. Though the author writes in good contemporary Greek, and his vocabulary is sprinkled with terms and phrases from the popular Greek philosophies, his thought is essentially biblical and orthodox.

6:12. Wisdom is bright and unfading, easily seen by those who love *her and found by those seeking her. . . . [In Gk. and Heb., "Wisdom" is grammatically feminine, making personification easy.]

22. What Wisdom is and how she came into being I will *explain, and will not hide mysteries from you; but I will trace out her way from the beginning and will set knowledge of her in plain sight; and I will not avoid the truth. [*Or, "report," relate."]

"Solomon" tells how he realized that, though a king, he was not different from other men, and needed wisdom for his task.

7:7. Because of this I prayed, and I was granted prudence; I called on the Lord, and the spirit of Wisdom came to me. (8) I [Cf. I Kings 3:4-14; 4:29.] chose her ahead of scepters and thrones; and I esteemed wealth for myself as nothing compared to her. . . . (10) I loved her more than health or handsomeness; and I chose to have her instead of light, because the light of Wisdom is sleepless.

Cf. 7:30,
below.

I Kings 3:12ff.

Cf. 7:27b,
below.
*Or,
"instruction."

(11) All good things came to me together with her, and immeasurable wealth was in her hand. . . . (13b) Her wealth I do
not hide, (14) for it is an unfailing treasure for men. By acquir-
ing it men make themselves ready for friendship with God,
being recommended by the gifts which come out of *discipline. . . .

*Implied   *Isa. 35:6b,
contrast.   LXX.

*Or,
"penetrating."
*I.e.,   Cf. Ps. 11:4;
"anxiety."   Prov. 15:3;
               Zech. 4:10b.
Cf. Wisd. Sol.
1:4.

Cf. Ps. 147:15.

7:22. For there is in Wisdom a spirit which is: keen-witted,
holy, unique *yet multiplex; ethereal, agile, *easily understood, without stain, forthright, harmless, loving the good;
(23) *keen, unhampered, beneficent; philanthropic, firm, unfailing, without *care; all-powerful, all-scrutinizing, pervading all intelligent, pure and most subtle spirits.

Cf. Wisd. Sol.
1:7a; Sirach
24:3b-6.

Sirach 24:3;
Prov. 2:6;
8:22-23.
*By stealth.

24. For Wisdom is more active than any motion, pervading
and permeating through everything because of its purity; (25)
since it is an exhalation of the power of God, a pure effluence
of the glory of the Almighty; therefore nothing defiled can
*gain access to it.

Isa. 60:19-20;
Heb. 1:3.
*eikon,
"image,
likeness."
*I.e., alone; cf.
Sirach 24:5.

Ps. 104:24-30.
Cf. v. 14,
above.

26. Wisdom is the radiance of everlasting light, a spotless
reflection of God's activity, and a *representation of His
goodness. (27) Although being *one Wisdom maintains all
things, and while remaining in herself, she renews all things.
And, in generation after generation, by passing into devout
souls she prepares them to be friends of God and prophets.

28. For God loves no one except him who lives intimately with
Wisdom.

*I.e., the light
of day; cf. John
1:5.

29. For its radiance exceeds the sun, and is beyond that of all
the starry constellations. Compared to light, Wisdom has
precedence: (30) for night succeeds *this; but evil does not
prevail over Wisdom.

*The universe;
Gk., ta panta.

8:1. Wisdom extends robustly from end to end of the world,
and manages *all things effectively. . . .

"Solomon's" prayer for wisdom: Wisd. Sol. 9:1-2, 4, 6, 9-13, 16-18

Cf. Ps. 33:4-9;
104:24; Prov. 3:19-20.

*ta panta,
"the
universe"; cf.
8:1, above.

Gen. 1:26-28.

9:1. O God of the fathers and Lord of mercy, the One who
made *all things by Your word, (2) and in Your wisdom
prepared man that he might, under You, have the mastery
over the creatures who were brought forth. . . .

Cf. Ps. 89:38ff.

4. Grant me the Wisdom which sits by Your throne, and do
not reject me from among Your servants. . . .

6. For even if anyone among men be perfect, yet without the
Wisdom which comes from You he will be accounted as nothing. . . .

9. With You is the Wisdom which knows Your works, who Prov. 8:27-31. was beside You when You made the world, and who understands what is pleasing in Your eyes and what is right by the standard of Your commandments.

10. Dispatch her from Your holy heavens, send her from the throne of Your glory, so that she may labor together beside me, and that I may know what is well-pleasing to You, (11) for Prov. 8:30. she knows and understands all things. She will direct me Cf. Prov. 2:6ff. prudently in my undertakings, and will guard me by her glory. (12) Then my deeds will be acceptable. I will govern Cf. Wisd. Sol. 10:1ff. Your people righteously and will be worthy of my father's throne.

13. For what man can learn the purpose of God, or who can infer what the Lord wills? . . . Cf. I Cor. 2:16.

16. For with difficulty do we reason out the things on earth, and even things at hand do we discover laboriously; but who can trace out the things in heaven? (17) So who can know Your Isa. 55:9. John 3:12. purpose, unless You grant Wisdom and send Your holy spirit *I.e., the heaven of God's throne. from the *highest?

18. But thus, by Wisdom, were the *tribes of those on earth set *Of Israel, as the following chapters show: God's Wisdom is the Savior of His people. right: men were taught the things pleasing to You, and were saved.

Comments:

1. These passages from the Wisdom of Solomon should be compared with the preceding passage from Sirach, and with Sirach 24 *in toto*. A number of key ideas will be found in common with those of Proverbs 1:1—3:20 and ch. 8, especially. It soon becomes evident that, for both ben Sira' and "Solomon," while God's creative wisdom is displayed in the created universe, His moral wisdom (the supreme guide for life) is to be found in the Jewish scriptures: cf. Sirach 1:26; 24:22-23; Wisd. Sol. 9:9.

2. In his praise of Wisdom, ben Sira' likened Wisdom to a delightful and well-tended Oriental paradise copiously yielding all kinds of desirable fruits: Sirach 24:13-21. He was intent on commending both the intellectual pleasure and the practical worth of the pursuit of Wisdom. "Solomon" commends those sides of it, too; but in 7:22-27 he emphasizes the purity of Wisdom's spiritual and moral character and its power to renew the minds and hearts of men as well as to govern the universe. Specialists note that his language in this passage is like that of the Stoic philosophers in their descriptions of the "world-soul," which, for them, was the organizer and sustainer of the universe. "Solomon's" passage, then, contains an implied polemic in behalf of Jewish faith against the popular philosophies.

3. Even in Greek translation, the language of Sirach is much closer to that of the Bible than is the Wisdom of Solomon. This is because Joshua ben Sira'

of Jerusalem apparently taught and wrote in Hebrew for disciples who were familiar with the Hebrew scriptures. Some large Hebrew fragments of Sirach have survived. In his grandson's translation, the Hebrew is often clearly reflected.

"Solomon" wrote contemporary Greek for Jews of Alexandria who heard or read their Bible in the Greek version. Moreover, he was apparently writing for people who were exposed to and affected by all the winds of pagan philosophic opinion which blew through that most cosmopolitan city. Yet in spite of differences in language, the outlook of the two authors was remarkably close in those things which were most central to the Jewish faith. A major difference is that "Solomon" gives no expression to a messianic hope.

For further discussion, cf. "Judaic Wisdom and Wisdom Christology" in the Extended Notes.

b. Natural science and esoteric lore

READING 20a: Knowledge of natural things (Wisd. Sol. 7:15-21)

Solomon's wisdom and knowledge were reputedly vast and wide-ranging—see I Kings 4:29-33. Later legend interpreted verse 33 to mean that he could talk *to* the birds and animals, that is, that he knew their languages. In this passage the author credits his broad knowledge to the instruction given by the divine Wisdom.

*Or, "to make valid inferences from the facts given."	7:15. May God grant me to speak with good judgment, and *to think in a way worthy of the gifts given me; because He is the guide even of Wisdom and the corrector of the wise.
Wisd. Sol. 3:1. Job 12:10; Ps. 31:14-15; Sirach 10:5.	16. For we as well as our words, all our practical wisdom and skill of craftsmanship are in His hand.
	17. It is He who gave me trustworthy knowledge of the things that exist, so that I could know:
Cf. Sirach 42:18-25. *Not in modern sense.	the constitution of the cosmos and the activity of the *elements; (18) the beginning, end and midpoint of time periods; the changes of the sun's course, and the transitions of the seasons; (19) the cycles of the year, and the positions of the stars;
*Or, "winds." *Or, "varieties of."	20. the natures of living beings and the tempers of wild animals; the powers of *spirits and the reasonings of men; the *distinctions among plants and the potencies of roots.
Wisd. Sol. 8:4, 6; 9:9, 17; 14:2; Prov. 8:30.	21. I came to know what is secret and what is unconcealed; for Wisdom, the fashioner of all things, gave me instruction.

Comments:

1. Note the broad range of practical, empirical knowledge which is comprehended in this catalog: astronomy, zoology, meteorology, botany, as well as animal and human psychology. Job 36:24—39:30, though more detailed, includes about the same range of general topics. These were all staples in the equipment of the sage of those times.

2. The author claims, in v. 20 above, that herb lore was part of his panoply of wisdom. Josephus notes, interestingly, that the Essenes gave much attention to the knowledge of medicinal roots; cf. *War* II.136 in the Historical Sketch above.

READING 20b: The secret knowledge (*I Enoch* XVII—XXV)

I Enoch XVII—XXXVI describes Enoch's angel-conducted tours through the unseen regions of the earth and nearer heavens. Among other things, he gets to know some of the things of which Job was ignorant: see Job 37:14-18 and chapters 38—39. Perhaps some of these things were included in the knowledge of "what is secret" mentioned in the Reading above, v. 21. To understand the following, the reader should acquaint himself with the notions which men of that age held concerning the structure of the world and its environing cosmos. (Cf. *Interpreter's Bible Dictionary*, Vol. I, pp. 703ff., for diagram and discussion.)

XVII.1. Taking me up, *they led me to a certain place in which were those who were like flaming fire; and *they appeared as if men whenever they wished. ^{°Angels. Ps. 104:4, LXX.} ^{°Angels; cf. Judg. 6:11-23; 13:2-20.}

2. Then they led me away into a gloomy region and to a mountain whose *peak reached into heaven; (3) and I saw the place of the luminaries, the treasuries of the stars and of the thunders; and I looked into the depth of the air, in which were a fiery bow and arrows with their quiver, and all the lightnings. ^{°Lebanon or Hermon, the two highest peaks in the Palestine-Syria area. Ps. 7:12-13; 18:14; 77:17; 144:6; Hab. 3:11.}

4. Then they took me as far as the living waters and the fire of the west which *produces all the settings of the sun. (5) And we came to the river of fire, in which the fire runs down like water and flows into the great western sea. (6) I saw the great rivers, and I went as far as the *Great River and the Great Darkness, and away to the place where nothing living walks. ^{°I.e., the sunset's fiery appearance.} ^{This from Greek notions of the underworld. Job 38:16-17, 19.} ^{°The earth-girdling Ocean-river.}

7. I saw the *wintry winds of darkness and the outpouring of all waters from the Abyss. (8) I saw the mouth of all earth's rivers, the mouth of the Abyss. ^{°Job 37:9.}

XVIII.1. I saw the treasuries of all the winds. I saw that by ^{Ps. 135:7.}

Ps. 104:27-30.
Job 38:4-6; Ps.
104:3, 5.
them He made preparations for all creatures. I saw the foundations of the earth, (2) and the cornerstones of the earth.

Cf. Dan. 7:2.
I saw the four winds which bear up the firmament of heaven,
(3) and how they stand between earth and heaven. (4) I saw
the winds of the heavens turning and bringing to its end the
*Literally,
"wheel."
Cf. Job 36:29;
37:11-18.
*journey of the sun; (5) the winds of earth rising up in a cloud;
the limits of the earth and the firmament of heaven above it.

Another detail
from Greek
myth.
6. Then I went on and saw a region which burned night and
day, where the seven mountains made from precious stones
were. . . . (9) And I saw a burning fire. Beyond these mountains (10) is the limit of the great earth. There the heavens were
all drawn in together. (11) And I saw a great chasm into which
columns of fire were falling, immeasurable as to depth or
height. (12) Beyond this chasm I saw a region where there was
Cf. Jer.
4:23-28.
neither firmament of heaven above nor firm-founded earth
beneath, neither water under, nor birds above; but it was a
region desolate and terrifying. (13) There I saw seven stars,
like great mountains, burning. When I asked concerning
them (14) the angel said: "This region is the end of heaven and
earth, the prison for the stars and the powers of heaven. (15)
The stars rolling in the fire are those which transgressed the
Lord's arrangement in the beginning of their rising . . . by
Cf. Jude 13.
not appearing in their proper seasons; (16) and He was angry
with them and bound them until the time of the completion of
*Gk. =
10,000.
their punishment, for a *myriad of years."

Cf. I Enoch
X—XI,
Reading 12.
XIX.1. Then Uriel said to me: "The angels who mingled with
women shall stand here, as shall their spirits which, assuming
many forms, are abusing mankind and will lead them astray
Deut. 32:17;
Ps. 106:37.
to sacrifice to demons until the time of the Great Judgment, in
which they will be condemned to destruction. (2) And the
*Mythic sea
nymphs whose
songs drove
sailors mad.
women of the transgressing angels will become *sirens.

3. Now only I, Enoch, saw these sights, the ends of all things;
and no man may ever see as I saw.

Enoch gives the names of the seven archangels: Uriel, Raphael, Raguel,
Michael (who is over the beloved people), Sariel, Gabriel and Remiel; and
he is shown the prison of the fallen angels. This seems to be the beginning
of a second journey, a different angel guiding each stage.

*Uriel.
XXII.1. From there I traveled to another place, and *he showed
me at the west another great and lofty mountain of hard rock.
*Literally,
"hollows."
Cf. biblical
teaching re
Sheol-Hades.
Greek influence
is evident in
this passage.
(2) There were four *ravines in it, deep and very smooth.
Three of them were dark, but one was light and there was a
spring of water in it. And I said: "How smooth are these
ravines, and how very deep and dark in appearance!"

3. Then Raphael, one of the holy angels who was with me, said: "These ravines exist so that the spirits of dead persons may assemble in them. . . . (4) And they made these places to contain them until the days of their judgment, until the time determined in which the Great Judgment upon them takes place."

5. I observed dead men petitioning, and the sound of it went ahead into heaven and made its appeal. (6) So I asked Raphael, the angel who was with me: "Whose spirit is this which is appealing, the voice of which goes up to heaven and makes petition?" (7) And he answered: "This is the spirit which came from Abel whom Cain, his brother, murdered; and Abel appeals concerning this until Cain's seed is destroyed from off the earth and disappears from among men." *Gen. 4:10; cf. Matt. 23:35; Rev. 6:9-11.*

8. Then I asked about the ravines, as to why one was set apart from the others. (9) So he answered me: "These three were made so that the spirits of the dead might be separated. And this one, in which is the spring of water with light, is set apart for the spirits of the righteous. (10) This one was created for sinners who were not judged during their lifetimes, whenever they die and are buried in the earth. (11) Their spirits will be separated here for great torments of scourgings and tortures of the accursed until the Great Day of Judgment. He shall bind them here for ever until the age of retribution on the spirits. *Cf. Job 3:13-19; Eccl. 3:20. In the O.T. view, Sheol seems to have been undivided.* *Cf. I Tim. 5:24*

12. And this one has been set apart for the spirits of those who make their appeal, who are making declaration concerning their loss, whenever they were slain in the days of sinners. (13) And this one was created for the spirits of men who will not be devout but sinners, who were impious and partners of the *lawless. But because they were tormented by *them, and being worse afflicted here, their spirits will not be visited with vengeance on the Day of Judgment; but neither shall they be raised up from here." *Cf. v. 5, above.* *°Cf. I Macc. 1:11, 52. °The "lawless"; cf. II Macc. 6:12-16.*

14. Then I praised the Lord of glory: "Blessed are You, Lord of righteousness, Eternal Ruler!"

Comments:

1. It is not difficult to see how, from such a background of ideas that were widespread in the Graeco-Roman world, the notions of Purgatory and degrees of punishment in Hades got into the ancient Church.

2. Re *I Enoch* XXII, above, the Mishnah tractate *Sanhedrin* 10.1-3 lists those who "have no share in the world to come." Included are the "generation of the Flood" and "the men of Sodom" (ed. Danby, p. 397).

3. Re XXII.13, the Tosephta tractate *Sanhedrin* 13.1-2 records the opinions of three leading rabbis of the late apostolic era: Rabbi Gamaliel II, Rabbi Jehoshua ben Hananiah and Rabbi Eliezer ben Hyrkanos. They conclude that "the children of the wicked of the Gentiles will not live and neither will they be judged" (i.e., in the Age to Come; ed. Zuckermandel, p. 434). This is ostensibly arrived at by a clever, and somewhat arbitrary, interpretation of Malachi 4:1. One somehow feels that a well-known view is being put forth (it is identical with *I Enoch* XXII.13), a view for which the rabbis have developed support by somewhat fanciful exegesis.

Enoch next travels to a number of mountains, on the seventh of which is the Tree of Life prepared for the righteous. The description owes a great deal to popular hellenism.

XXIV.3. The seventh mountain was in the middle of these, and was the tallest, resembling the seat of a throne. Beautiful trees surrounded it. (4) And there was among them a tree which I had never smelled before, and no one had ever enjoyed another, for there was no other like it. Its smell was the most fragrant of all odors, its leaves and flowers and wood never withered, and its fruit resembled the fruit clusters of a date palm.

Cf. Gen. 2:9,
3:22.

5. Then I said: "How is this tree so beautiful and fragrant? How are its leaves and flowers so fair to the sight?" (6) So Michael, leader of the angels who were with me, replied:

XXV.1. "Enoch, why do you ask and why do you wonder at the smell of the tree, and why do you want to know the truth?" (2) And I answered: "I want to know about all things, but most especially about this tree." (3) So he replied: "This high mountain, whose top is like the throne of God, is where the Great Lord, the Holy Glorious One, the Eternal King, sits whenever He comes down to visit the earth with benefits. (4) No one has the right to touch this fragrant tree till the Great Judgment in which there will be vindication for all and the eternal consummation. Then to the righteous and godly will be given (5) its fruit: to those chosen to live it will be for food. And it will be transplanted to the Holy Place beside the temple of God the Eternal King. (6) Then they will make merry joyfully and be glad, and they will enter the Holy Place. Its fragrance will be in their bones, and they shall live long lives on the earth such as your fathers lived. And in their days no torments nor plagues nor *scourges shall touch them."

Cf. Ps.
68:15-18.

Ps. 65:9,
104:13ff.

Cf. T. Levi
XVIII.11; Rev.
2:7, 22:14.

Cf. Isa.
65:18ff.

Isa. 65:20,
22b; cf. Gen. 5

*I.e., diseases
or
misfortunes.

Comments:

1. As suggested by a scholar of an earlier era, and borne out by internal

indications, the author of this section of the Enoch materials seems to have lived in the north of Palestine in the vicinity of ancient Dan, near the foot of Mt. Hermon: cf. *I Enoch* XIII.7 in Reading 13a. It is not impossible that he was either an Essene hermit, or a member of an Essene community located in this area.

Nor is it difficult to see behind his visions actual experiences that he may have had on this mountain's heights: seeing the sun flash from its snow-covered crest, looking down from its heights upon a summer thunderstorm over the valley below, experiencing stormy nights upon its flanks (cf. *I Enoch* XIV.8ff. in Reading 13b), seeing the almost overwhelming array of stars on a clear night, gazing down into the Anti-Lebanon ravines and gorges, or out into the desert wilderness to the east, etc.

2. Such personal observations, combined by a fertile and active imagination with images from well-known biblical passages, could well have provided much of the content of the visions. However, that does not account for all the elements present. Hellenistic influence is evident. Enoch's "journeys" were evidently inspired by the already ancient legends of a hero's journey through the underworld, of which there exist Sumerian, Babylonian, Greek and Roman versions. A popular version of such journeys furnished our author with a model, which he assimilated as much as possible to biblical ideas and adapted to Jewish sensibilities.

The apologetic value of this process should not be overlooked. It represents a chapter in the sustained polemic of Judaism against hellenism which was waged with all means throughout this period. If the Mesopotamians had Gilgamesh and Ishtar, if the Greeks and Romans had Heracles and Aeneas, the Jews had Enoch. Who but such a man—the most righteous of the pre-Flood generation, whom God took up to Himself without death—could have made the journeys through the unseen world, to see regions celestial as well as infernal, and to be given revelations of God and the final things? See further discussion in the Extended Note on "Apocalyptic: Form and Substance."

READING 21a: Heavenly mysteries (*T. Job* XLIX.1—LI.4)

On his deathbed, Job gave each of his daughters a beautiful cord of heavenly workmanship. As each put hers on, her heart was transformed, and she was enabled to sing like angels and archangels and was given supernatural sight.

XLIX.1. And then Kasia put her cord around herself, and had her heart transformed so that she no longer had an inclination for worldly things. (2) And her mouth took up the dialect of the archangels, and she sang praise concerning the work of the Exalted Place; (3) so that if anyone wants to know the

Cf. Rom. 12:1-2; Ezek. 36:26.

Cf. Jer. 17:12.

*The ma ' ma 'asēh
aseh ha-shamayim.
beresñit or

*"Horn of
Plenty"; Heb.,
Keren-happuch

*Divine
attributes.

*Or,
musteria,
"mysteries."

*work of the heavens, he can find it in the Hymns of Kasia.

L.1. Finally, the other daughter named *Amaltheias-keras put hers on; and she began chanting hymns in the dialect of those on high, (2) since her heart was also changed and was withdrawn from worldly things. For she spoke in the dialect of the cherubim, singing praise to the Master of the *excellencies and declaring their glory. (3) He who wishes, then, to come up with a trace of "The Day of Paternal Glory" will find it written in the Prayers of Amaltheias-keras.

LI.1. After the three stopped singing, (2) I Nereios, Job's brother, (3) sat down near Job who was upon his bed. I had heard the marvelous things uttered by my brother's three daughters; (4) and I wrote for myself the entire scroll, full of notations of the hymns of my brother's three daughters; for these things are salvation because they are the great *things of God.

READING 21b: The divine Throne-chariot (4Q S1 40 24: *Serek Shirōt 'Olat Ha-Shabbat*, lines 3-8)

*Heb., kisse'
merkabah.

*Literally, "go,
walk."
*Ezek. 10:13.

*Or, "train,"
as of a gown or
long veil.
*A pale yellow
alloy of gold
and silver.

3. . . .From above the firmament the Cherubim were blessing the form of the *Throne-chariot, (4) and the renown of the firmament of light they were shouting joyously from beneath the seat of His glory. When the wheels *move, the holy angels return and go out. From (5) between the glorious *turning wheels there is the appearance of a fiery *cascade in the likeness of *electrum, and works of (6) brightness, in a many-hued splendor of colors, wonderfully mingled and bright. The spirits of the Living God walk continually with the glory of the (7) wonderful Chariot. And there was a gentle voice of blessing at the noise of their going, and they praise the Holy One when they return on their ways. When it lifts up, they rise wonderfully. And when it rests (8) they stand still.

Comments:

1. From Qumran Cave 4 came fragments in Hebrew that J. Strugnell, who edited them, called "Angelic Liturgies." This one deals with the chariot of Ezekiel's visions and later speculations. Ezekiel 1 and 10 should be closely compared with the above.

2. These esoteric matters were known to the rabbis of the first Christian century, especially the speculations about the "Work of Creation" and the "Work of the Chariot" (*ma 'asēh merkabah*). They tried, however, to discour-

age the cultivation of such lore in favor of "searching the Scriptures," i.e., interpreting the Law. Ezekiel 1 was not to be read in the synagogue as a reading from the prophets—Mishnah tractate *Megillah* 4.10. It was considered unsettling for the simple, and even potentially dangerous for the advanced: " . . . may not be expounded . . . the Story of Creation before two, nor the Chariot before one alone, unless he is a Sage that understands of his own knowledge"—Mishnah tractate *Hagigah* 2.1 (ed. Danby, pp. 212-13). The Tosephta tractate *Hagigah* repeats this, and relates that Rabbi ben Zoma' lost his sanity because he was overly preoccupied with the "Work of Creation" (ed. Zuckermandel, p. 234). Now, it seems, the Essenes also cultivated this lore.

READING 21c: The "mystery of iniquity" ("Livre des Mystères," lines 2-8)

A fragment was found in Qumran Cave 1, the first two intelligible words of which are "secrets-of iniquity." It has ideational affinities with the Enoch material, especially that in Readings 12 and 13. The fragment obviously belongs to a longer piece dealing with this subject.

2. . . .secrets of *iniquity (3) . . . and they do not know the secret of what is to be. They do not consider ancient things, and they do not (4) know what is to come upon them; and their souls will not escape from the mysteries of the future.

*Literally, "rebellion"; cf. II Thess. 2:7.

5. And this is the sign for you that this will be: When the offspring of wickedness are shut up and Wickedness departs before Righteousness as darkness vanishes before (6) light. As smoke clears and is there no more, so Wickedness will depart forever and Righteousness will appear, like the sun, as the order (7) of the world. And all those who *hold the secrets of wonder will be no more. *Knowledge will fill the earth and folly will be no longer therein. (8) The word is certain to come, and the *burden is reliable.

*Cf. I Enoch XVI.3

*Hab. 2:14.

*Prophecy.

Comments:

1. It is possible that this is a homily based on the Flood story, with embellishments drawn from the Enoch lore. The opening lines bring to mind one of Jesus' sayings on the same subject: Matt. 24:36-39. The "mysteries of the future" are probably the details of the coming New Age and the Great Judgment, as revealed to Enoch. Line 5 harks back to a theme already found in the Enoch materials of previous Readings.

2. Line 7, "all those who hold the secrets of wonder" (or, wonderful mysteries"), seems to be an allusion to what is referred to in *I Enoch* XVI.3, Reading 13b. The "secrets of wonder" are what the Watchers knew and passed on to men through their human wives, as detailed in *I Enoch* VIII:

weaponry, metallurgy, gem crafts, cosmetic arts, herb lore, magic and astrology. These are all "wonderful," since they are arts and lore known only to the initiated; but they are also "worthless" since they do not promote righteousness and lead men astray from God. They are part of the wickedness of mankind which must depart to make room for universal righteousness. Therefore, those who possess the secrets of these mysteries, i.e., the initiates in such arts and crafts, are doomed to suffer the same fate as the Watchers who originally taught such things to men.

4. THE PROMOTION OF PIETY

In his Schweich Lectures of 1913, F. C. Burkitt suggested that the *Testaments of the Twelve Patriarchs* were produced as a manual of moral instruction for the people of those territories that John Hyrcanus I had added to his domain. Many of them had been forced to become Jews and to submit to circumcision (*Jewish and Christian Apocalypses*, pp. 34-36). There is considerable plausibility to this theory. That a major concern of the author of the *Testaments* was to promote piety and godly living is beyond doubt.

READING 22: Avoid women and lust (*T. Reuben* III.9-11; IV.1, 6-7, 11; V.1-6; VI.1-4)

III.9. And now, children, love the true and it will guard you. I am instructing you; hearken to Reuben, your father: (10) Don't pay attention to the appearance; don't get alone with another man's wife; don't busy yourself with feminine affairs. (11) For if I had not seen Bilhah bathing herself in a sheltered place, I would not have fallen into great iniquity. . . .

Prov. 6:25ff.

Sirach 9:8-9;
M. Aboth 1.5.

Cf. Gen. 35:22;
II Sam. 11:2.

IV.1. Therefore, do not pay attention to the beauty of women, neither think about their affairs. . . .

T. Issachar
IV.4; Sirach
25:21.

6. For sexual sin is the ruin of the soul. It separates one from God and brings one near to idols; because it leads the mind and the inclination astray, and leads young people down to Hades before their time. (7) For sexual sin has destroyed many: because even if he be old or well-born, it makes him a reproach and a laughingstock to Beliar and his fellow men. . . .

Prov. 5:5;
7:27.

11. If sexual sin does not get power over your mind, then neither can Beliar overpower you. . . .

V.1. Women are corrupt, my children. Because they do not have authority or strength over the man, they use wiles of dress and manner so that he will be attracted to them; (2) so

Eccl. 7:26; Ps.
Sol. XVI.8.

Cf. Prov. 7:6ff.

that the one whom they cannot prevail against by physical power, they yet prevail against by deceit.

3. Moreover, the angel of the Lord told and taught me about them, that women yield to sexual desire more than men. In their hearts they devise schemes against men; through adornment they first lead their inclination astray. Then, by their glances they instil the poison; and finally, through the deed, they take them captive. (4) For a woman cannot take a man by force, but by the manner of a harlot she can beguile him. _{Prov. 6:25} _{Prov. 7:21ff.} _{Prov. 7:6ff.; Sirach 9:8; cf. Gen. 38:12ff.}

5. Therefore, my children, flee sexual sin; and command your wives and daughters not to adorn their heads and their faces, because any woman who resorts to such tricks is reserved for eternal torment. (6) For thus women allured the Watchers before the Flood. . . . _{I Tim. 2:9ff.; I Peter 3:3ff.}

VI.1. Therefore, keep yourselves from sexual sin; and if you want to keep pure in your inclination, guard your senses from every female. (2) Command the women also not to pair off with men so that they, too, may keep pure in thought. (3) For frequent meetings, even if the immoral act is not done, is with them a disease without cure, while for you it is an eternal reproach of Beliar. (4) Because fornication has in itself neither understanding nor godliness, but all jealousy inhabits its desire. _{Tobit 4:12a; Eph. 5:3; Col. 3:5; Cf. I Cor. 7:1}

READING 23: Avoid drunkenness and avarice (*T. Judah* XIII.1-3; XIV.1-4, 7-8; XVI.1—XVII.2)

XIII.1. Now, my children, give heed to your father concerning whatever I command you. Keep all my words so as to perform the Lord's ordinances and obey the commandment of the Lord God. (2) Do not pursue your own lusts or the imaginations of your thoughts in the pride of your heart. Do not boast in your deeds of youthful strength, because this is especially evil in the Lord's eyes. (3) For, since I myself once boasted that in battle no attractive woman's face seduced me, and I reproached my brother Reuben concerning my father's woman, Bilhah, the spirits of jealousy and of fornication arrayed themselves against me so that I fell to Bathshua the Canaanitess, and to Tamar, who had been espoused to my sons. _{Eph. 4:17ff. Cf. Jer. 16:12; 18:12. Prov. 20:29; Jer. 9:23b.} _{Cf. Gen. 35:22; 49:3-4.} _{Cf. Gen. 38}

Judah then tells how the sheikh of Adullam enticed him to take Bathshua for his wife by showing him the gold of her dowry and by plying him with wine. This forms the basis for the following exhortations.

Cf. Eph. 5:18

Prov. 23:29ff.
Cf. Hos.
4:10-12; 5:4;
Isa. 5:11-12.

Cf. Prov. 20:1;
Isa. 28:7-8;
Tobit 4:15.

*asotia: Eph.
5:18; cf. Luke
15:13; Gk.

Cf. Ps. 104:15;
Eccl. 9:7.

*The pronoun
is plural.
Hos. 4:11.

*Greed and
lust.

XIV.1. And now, my children, do not get drunk with wine, because wine turns the mind away from the truth, incites to lustful anger, and leads the eyes into error. (2) For the spirit of fornication has wine for its servant to promote the sensuality of the mind. Because these two, indeed, take away a man's reason. (3) For if anyone drinks wine to the point of intoxication, it confounds his mind with unclean thoughts leading to unchastity and it heats up the body for sexual indulgence; and if the cause of the lust is at hand, one commits the sin and is not ashamed. (4) Such is wine, my children, that he who becomes drunk has no regard for anyone. . . . (7) So the one who drinks wine needs understanding; and this is discretion in regard to winedrinking: one may drink as long as he maintains sobriety. (8) But if he transgresses this limit, the spirit of error invades his mind. It makes the drunkard use foul language and transgress unashamedly, rather even to glory in such dishonor, supposing it to be good. . . .

XVI.1. Therefore, keep a limit for yourselves on the use of wine, my children. For there are in it four evil spirits: of lust, of burning desire, of *profligacy and of a desire for dishonest gain. (2) If you drink wine in gladness, with regard for the reverence of God, you will live. For if you drink heedlessly and put away the fear of God, at last drunkenness occurs and shamelessness comes in. (3) But better you do not drink at all, lest you sin by words of insult and strife, by slander and transgression of God's commands, and so perish before your time.

4. Verily, wine reveals the mysteries of God and of men to strangers, even as I revealed the commands of God and the mysteries of my father Jacob to Bathshua the Canaanitess, to *which people God said not to disclose them. So wine becomes a cause both of conflict and of confusion.

XVII.1. So I am commanding you, children, not to love money, nor to look at women's beauty (because even I was led astray to Bathshua the Canaanitess because of silver and her attractiveness), (2) for I know that because of these two things my tribe will grow wicked. (3) Because these things will make even wise men of my descendants to change for the worse, and the kingdom of Judah—which the Lord gave me for obedience to my father— *they will cause to be diminished.

READING 24: Cultivate simplicity/sincerity (*T. Issachar* IV.1—V.4; VII.1-7)

The theme of the *Testament of Issachar* is *haplotēs,* which has the sense of singleness of purpose (as opposed to deceit or double-dealing), simplicity of life, sincerity and even generosity. This theme is found a number of times in the New Testament epistles (Rom. 12:8; II Cor. 8:2; 9:11-13; 11:3; Eph. 6:5; Col. 3:22).

IV.1. Now hear me, children, and walk in sincerity of heart, because I see in it everything which pleases the Lord. (2) The sincere man does not covet gold, nor take advantage of his neighbor. *He does not long for many kinds of foods, nor desire different kinds of clothes. (3) He does not mark out a long time to live, but waits upon the will of the Lord alone.

Eph. 6:5; Col. 3:22-23.

Exod. 20:17; Luke 12:13-34; Mark 7:21-22; Eph. 5:3-5.
*He is neither a gourmandizer nor a "clothes-horse."
Ps. 27:14; 40:31; Lam. 37:7, 9; Isa. 3:25-26.

4. So, the spirits of error have no power at all against him; for he does not look receptively at feminine beauty, lest his mind be defiled by such distraction. (5) Envy will not invade his meditations; evil influences will not waste his soul away, nor is he greedily anxious for money-getting. (6) For he walks in uprightness of life, and all things he looks at in sincerity, not welcoming with his eyes any wickedness from the error of the world, lest he see any of the commandments of the Lord being perverted.

Prov. 6:25; Sirach 9:8; *Sol.* XVI.7-8; 25:21; *Ps.* Matt. 5:28.
Prov. 14:30; 23:17.
Matt. 6:19.
Luke 12:16ff.; Sirach 31:1.

V.1. Therefore, my children, observe the Law of God, acquire sincerity and walk in guilelessness without busying yourself with your neighbor's affairs.

Ps. 32:2; 34:13; I Thess. 2:3; I Peter 4:15.

2. But love the Lord and your neighbor, and show mercy to the poor and the weak. (3) Bend your back to agriculture and labor at working the land in every kind of husbandry, offering gifts to the Lord with thanksgiving. (4) Because with the first fruits of the earth the Lord blesses you, even as He blessed all the saints from Abel until the present. . . .

Gen. 49:15, LXX: "he bent his shoulder to toil, and became a husbandman/farmer.

VII.1. I am a hundred and twenty-two years old, and I am not conscious of being guilty of any *mortal sin.

*Cf. I John 5:16-17.

2. Other than my wife, I have known no woman; nor have I committed adultery *by raising my eyes. (3) I did not drink wine so as to go astray. No desirable thing of my neighbor did I covet. (4) Guile did not come into my heart, falsehood did not issue from my lips.

Cf. Job 31; Exod. 20:14ff.
*I.e., by the lustful look. Cf. *T. Benjamin* VI.3; and *T. Issachar* IV.4, above.
Ps. 32:2; 34:13; I Peter 3:10.

5. With every man in distress, I joined my lament, and with the poor I shared my bread—I did not eat it alone. Not a *rule did I break; I practiced piety and truth all of my days. (6) I loved the Lord with all my strength; likewise I loved every man as my children.

Sirach 7:34; Rom. 12:15.
Job 31:17. *Literally, "boundary, limit."
Deut. 6:4, 5; Mark Lev. 19:18; 12:30-31.

Ps. 97:10

Job 5:22-23

7. You also, my children, must do these things, and every spirit of Beliar will flee from you, no practice of wicked men will overcome you. You will subdue every wild animal, since you have the God of heaven with you as you walk with men in sincerity of heart.

READING 25: Be compassionate and show mercy (*T. Zebulon* V.1-3; VIII.1-6; *T. Job* XII.1-4; XLV.1-2)

The *Testament of Zebulon* opens with an account of how the "patriarch" disagreed with his brothers' sale of Joseph, and how he had compassion and pity on his unfortunate younger brother.

Cf. Prov.
14:31

Prov. 12:10;
27:23; Sirach
7:22

Ps. 91:1-3.

Ps. 44:21;
139:2. Jer.
12:3

V.1. And now, my children, I am charging you to keep the Lord's commandments, and perform mercy to your neighbor—have compassion towards all, not only men but also animals. (2) For because of these things the Lord blessed me; and when all my brothers became ill, I got by without sickness, for the Lord knows the purposes of each one. (3) So, my children, have mercy in your hearts, because just as anyone treats his neighbor so the Lord will treat him. . . .

Deut. 15:7-11;
Tobit 4:16.
Luke 6:36;
Eph. 4:32

Cf. Isa. 57:15

Cf. Ps.   Matt.
18:24-26; 18:24-35.

Cf. Gen.
43—45

Lev. 19:18

Cf. I Cor.
13:5c

Cf. Eph.
4:31-32

VIII.1. Therefore, my children, have sympathy for every man in mercy, so that the Lord may be merciful to you in His compassion; (2) because even at the last days God will send His mercy upon the earth, and wherever He finds a man of compassionate mercy, He will dwell with him. (3) For as much as a man shows compassion to his neighbor, by so much does the Lord have compassion on him. (4) For when we went down to Egypt, Joseph did not hold a grudge against us; but when he saw me, he was compassionate. (5) To his example take heed and refrain from holding grudges, my children. Love each other and do not keep account of wrong, each against the other, (6) because this separates unity, scatters kindred apart, and troubles the soul. For he who holds grudges does not have a merciful heart.

The *Testament of Job* is a separate document, not one of the "Twelve Patriarchs." In preceding sections Job has told his children how, with his tremendous wealth, he clothed and fed orphans and widows, the destitute and weak; and how he lent money to poor but capable men to trade with upon their agreement that they, too, would use the profits for the benefit of the poor. At the seat of his sheikhdom he maintained a large tent where free food was dispensed daily to the poor.

XII.1. And if, sometimes, a generous-hearted man came to

me, saying: "I don't have the means to assist the poor, yet even so I would like to serve the poor today at your table," (2) then I would consent, and he would serve and then eat. And when evening came I would constrain him to receive something from me, saying: (3) "I think that you are a worker, a man expecting and waiting for your wages. You must receive something." (4) And I did not allow the wage of a laborer to remain with me in my house. . . .

Lev. 19:13;
Deut.
24:14-15;
Tobit 4:14.

XLV.1. And now, my children, I am going to die. Only do not forget the Lord. (2) Do good to the poor; do not disregard the weak. . . .

Tobit 4:5-13;
Sirach 4:1ff.;
cf. Gal. 2:10.

READING 26: Reject anger and falsehood; be truthful (*T. Dan* II.1—III.3; V.1-3; VI.1-4, 8-10)

The theme of the *Testament of Dan* is inordinate anger and falsehood. These are the third and sixth of the "spirits of error" discussed in the *Testament of Reuben*.

II.1. And now, my children, I am dying, and I tell you truly that if you do not carefully keep yourselves from the spirits of falsehood and of anger, and love truth and forbearance, you will perish. (2) For there is a blindness in anger, and no wrathful person sees another as he really is. (3) A father or a mother?—he regards them as enemies. A brother?—he does not know him. A righteous man?—he does not notice him. A friend?—he does not acknowledge him. (4) For the spirit of anger casts around him the nets of deceit and blinds his natural eyes. Through falsehood this spirit darkens his reason and foists on him its own outlook. (5) By what does it cast the net over his eyes? By hatred of heart; and this spirit gives to him its own heart for envy against his brother.

Prov. 19:5, 9,
11, 19; 20:3,
17; 21:6; et
passim.

Prov. 15:1,
LXX: "wrath
destroys even
the prudent."

Cf. I John
2:11.

III.1. Anger is wicked, my children, for when it is in the soul it becomes the soul itself. (2) Even the body of the man of anger it makes its own and gains the mastery over his soul. It supplies the body with its own strength so that it may do every kind of iniquity.

3. And whenever one commits such things, he justifies the deed, since he does not see things rightly. . . .

V.1. Therefore, my children, keep the commandments of the Lord, and observe His Law. Depart from wrath and hate falsehood, so that the Lord may dwell among you and Beliar

Prov. 16:32;
19:11;
22:24-25; Eph.
4:31.

Eph. 4:25; Col.
3:9.

may flee from you. (2) Each must speak truth with his neighbor, and must not fall into sensuality and disorders; but be at peace, holding to the God of peace, and no conflict will overpower you. (3) Love the Lord during your whole life, and

love each other with a true heart. . . .

VI.1. And now, my children, fear the Lord and beware of

Satan and his spirits. (2) But draw near to God and the *angel who intercedes for you, because he is the mediator between

God and man for the peace of Israel. Against the kingdom of the Enemy will he stand up. (3) Therefore the Enemy is eager

to *cause the downfall of all those who worship the Lord. (4) For he knows that on the day that Israel *believes, the kingdom of the Enemy will be finished. . . .

8. Therefore, my children, keep yourselves carefully from every evil work. Reject anger and every falsehood, and love truth and forbearance. (9) The things which you hear from

your father you must pass on to your children so that the *father of nations may receive you. . . . (10) So depart from every iniquity and cling to the Law of the Lord.

READING 27: "Let all be done decently and in order" (T. Naphtali II.2—III.5)

After a brief introductory biographical section, the author moves into a meditation on the relationship between man's physical and psychic constitutions, with emphasis upon the divine origin and the religious desirability of orderliness of life.

II.2. For just as the potter knows how much a vessel is to hold and so brings enough clay to make it, so the Lord makes the body for the likeness of the spirit, and He puts the spirit into

the body to empower it. (3) And the one is adjusted to the other to the third of a hair's-breadth; for the *whole creation of the Most High is created by weight, measure and rule.

4. And just as the potter knows the use for which each vessel is best fitted, so also the Lord knows how far the body will persist in the good, and when it begins to tend toward the

bad; (5) for there is nothing formed and no purpose that the Lord does not know, because He created every man in His

own image.

6. As is his strength, so is a man's work, and as his thought, so is his action; as his preference, so his practice; as his heart, so also his speech; as his eye, so also his sleep; and as his soul, so

also is his discourse, whether in the Law of the Lord or in the law of Beliar. . . . (8) For God made everything good in order: the five senses in the head, the neck joined with the head, and the hair for glory; then the heart for intelligence, the abdomen for discrimination of stomach-contents. . . . `Ps. 1:2; 119:10-11.` `Cf. Gen. 1:31; Eccl. 3:11.` `Cf. I Cor. 11:15.`

9. So then, my children, let yourselves be orderly in good works, and do nothing disorderly in contempt (of the Law) nor out of its appropriate time. (10) For if you tell the eye to hear, it cannot; so neither can you do the works of light while you are in darkness. `Cf. I Cor. 14:40; II Thess. 3:6ff.; Gk.` `Cf. Eccl. 3:1.` `Cf. John 9:4.`

III.1. So then, do not be eager to corrupt your doings by covetousness, or to mislead yourselves by empty words; because by keeping quiet in purity of heart you will be able to hold fast to God's will and to reject the will of the Adversary. `Prov. 1:19; 15:27.`

2. Sun, moon and stars do not change their order; thus also you must not change the Law of God through disorderly actions. (3) The nations were led astray and left the Lord, and changed their order: they went after stocks and stones, after spirits of error. `Jer. 31:36; Sirach 16:26-27; Ps. Sol. XVIII.10-12; I Enoch II.1ff.` `Gen. 6:5; 11:1-9; Jub. V.2; I Enoch VIII.1ff.; Wisd. Sol. 13:1-9; Rom. 1:24-27.`

4. But you, my children, must not be thus, but should recognize, through the firmament, the earth, the sea, and all created things, the Lord who made all these things, so as not to become as Sodom which changed the order of nature. (5) Similarly, the Watchers also changed the order of their nature. These the Lord cursed at the Flood and because of them devastated the earth of inhabitants and fruits. `Ps. 104; Isa. 40:12-26; Rom. 1:19-20.` `Gen. 19:1-8; II Peter 2:6-8; Jude 7.` `Gen. 6:1-7; Jub. V.6ff.; I Enoch VI—XVI.`

READING 28: Reject envy and hatred; be loving (*T. Simeon* IV.5-9; *T. Gad* III.1—VII.7)

The *Testament of Simeon* warns against the spirit of error and envy, admonishing to brotherly love according to Joseph's example.

IV.5. Therefore, my children, guard yourselves from all jealousy and envy. Walk in sincerity of soul and in goodness of heart, taking *your uncle for example, so that God may give you grace and glory and a blessing on your heads, just as you saw happen in his case. `Cf. Gen. 37:11ff.; Gal. 5:19-21.` `Ps. 26:11; Prov. 2:20; 10:9; 14:2.` `*Joseph` `Ps. 8:5; 84:11.` `Gen. 41; Prov. 11:26.`

6. All his days he never reproached us about this matter, but loved us as himself, even above his sons. He honored us and gave riches, cattle and produce to all of us. (7) So then, my beloved children, you must each love your brother with a good heart, and put away from yourselves the spirit of envy, `Gen. 50:15ff.`

Prov. 14:30

Prov. 10:12;
Rom. 13:13.

Cf. Job 7:14ff.;
Ps. Sol. V1.3.

Lev. 19:17; I
John 3:15.

Prov. 10:12;
26:24ff.

Prov. 29:10;
Wisd. Sol.
2:10-20.

Cf. Ps. 31:18;
73:8-9; 94:4;
101:5.

Sirach 1:22;
James 3:14ff.

Ps. Sol.
IV.2-3.

Prov. 27:4.

I John 3:11-15;
Ps. Sol.
IV.2-3.

Wisd. Sol.
2:23-24.

Rom. 13:8-10.

Cf. Gal.
5:19-21.

(8) because it makes the soul cruel and corrupts the body. It makes one's attitude angry and quarrelsome, and it provokes to bloodshed. It leads the reason into distraction, and does not allow men's understanding to take effect. But it even takes sleep away, and brings confusion to the soul and trembling to the body. (9) Because even in sleep some wicked jealousy, appearing in one's dream, devours him and by wicked spirits disturbs his soul and startles his body. His mind is awakened in confusion, and he appears to men as one having a wicked and venomous spirit.

The *Testament of Gad* is concerned with the evil of hatred.

III.1. Listen now, my children, to words of truth, so as to perform righteousness and every law of the Most High, and not to be led astray by the spirit of hatred, because it is an evil in all the actions of men. (2) The hateful person loathes whatever one may do: if one performs the Law of the Lord, he does not applaud; if one reverences the Lord and desires righteous things, he does not esteem him. (3) He finds fault with the truth; he has ill will for the upright; he is eager for slander and loves arrogance—because hatred is blinding his soul, just as I also used to regard Joseph.

IV.1. Therefore, my children, keep yourselves from hatred because it works lawlessness against the Lord Himself. (2) For it does not wish to hear the words of His commandments concerning love of one's neighbor, and it sins against God. (3) For if a brother stumble, right away it wants to announce it to everyone, and is eager for him to be condemned for it and punished with death. . . . (5) For hatred also works by envy against those who prosper: it is always ill at hearing and seeing their success. (6) For just as love wishes to make even the dead alive, and to call back those who are condemned to die; so hatred wishes to kill the living and does not want those who have sinned but a little to live. (7) For the spirit of hatred, through meanheartedness, works together with the Adversary in all things for the death of men; but the spirit of love works together with God's Law, by forbearance, for the salvation of men.

V.1. Hatred is evil because it constantly joins with falsehood, speaking against the truth. It makes small things great, turns darkness into light, and calls sweet bitter. It teaches slander, strife, insolence and every kind of greed for evil things; and it fills the heart with a devilish poison. . . . (3) Righteousness expels hatred and humility destroys it. For the righteous and humble man is ashamed to commit wrongdoing, not because he is condemned by another but by his own heart, because the Lord examines his intentions. (4) He does not defame another man, since his fear of the Most High overcomes hatred; (5) for fearing lest he offend the Lord, he will generally not do wrong to any man, even in thought.

Cf. Sirach 14:1; I John 3:19-21.
I Sam. 16:7; 139:23-24; Ps. Ps. 44:21; Sol. XIV.8.
Exod. 23:1-2.

6. These things I recognized at last, after I repented concerning Joseph. (7) For true repentance in a godly way destroys disobedience and banishes darkness. It enlightens the eyes, supplies knowledge to the soul, and directs one's inclination toward salvation. (8) And those things which it did not learn from men, it perceives through repentance. (9) For God brought on me a disease of the liver, and except for the prayers of my father Jacob it would soon have called my spirit from me. (10) For through whatever things a man transgresses, by those things is he chastised. (11) Since, therefore, my liver was mercilessly hostile toward Joseph, I was judged for eleven months by suffering mercilessly in the liver, for just as long a time as I held a grudge against Joseph until the time when he was sold.

II Cor. 7:9-11.
Cf. Exod. Sol. 11:16; 21:24; Wisd. Gal. 6:7; Col. 3:25.

VI.1. And now, my children, love your brother, each of you, and put away hatred out of your hearts, loving each other in deed and word and inward thought. (2) For in front of our father I used to speak peaceably to Joseph; but when I went outside the spirit of hatred darkened my mind and my soul was stirred up to kill him.

I John 3:11-18
John 13:34-35.
Prov. 10:18; 26:24; T. Dan II.4-5.

3. Therefore, love each other from the heart; and if anyone sins against you, tell him in peace, banishing the poison of hatred, and in your soul do not retain guile. And if he repents after confessing, forgive him.

I Peter 1:22
Matt. 18:15f.; Luke 17:3-4.
Matt. 6:12-15; Gal. 6:1.

4. But if he denies it, do not quarrel with him lest when he takes an oath you sin doubly, since he has received the poison from you. . . . (6) But if he denies it, yet is ashamed when reproved and is calm, do not excite him. For the one who denies (may yet) repent so as to offend you no longer. Rather, he may even honor you and be peaceable. (7) Yet even if he is without shame and persists in his wickedness, forgive him even so from the heart, and leave the vindication to God.

Cf. Sirach 8:10.
Deut. Sirach 28:2ff.; 32:35-36. Matt. 18:35; Rom. 12:19.

VII.1. If anyone is more prosperous than you, do not be offended; but instead pray for him that he may be fully prosperous, for this profits you as well. (2) And even if he is further promoted, do not be envious, remembering that all flesh will die. (3) Rather, offer praise to the Lord who provides good and

Ps. 73:2ff.
Ps. 103:15-16; I Tim. 6:6-8. Isa. 40:6-7.

Ps. 147.

Ps. 1:1-2;
119:14-16.

useful things for all men. Scrutinize the ordinances of the Lord, and your inclination will be at rest.

Ps. 37:1;   Sol. 5:15ff.;
73:1ff.; Prov. Sirach 9:11;
23:17; Wisd. 11:22.

Ps. 73:18-20.

Ps. 86:5.

II Peter 2:9.

I Thess. 5:18.

Ps. 37:7-16;
Prov. 10:22;
Ps. Sol. XII.5;
I Tim. 6:6.

4. And even if one becomes wealthy by base means, as my uncle Esau, do not be jealous, for you are awaiting the end (promised by) the Lord. (5) For either He takes them away by misfortunes; or He forgives those who repent; or He reserves torment for the unrepentant forever. (6) For the one who is poor but without envy, giving thanks to the Lord for everything, is rich beyond all things, because he does not have the corrupting distractions of men. (7) Therefore, put away hatred from your lives, and love each other in uprightness of heart.

READING 29: Persevere in self-control and chastity (*T. Joseph* I.1—III.3; VIII.5—X.3; XVIII.1-2)

The *Testament of Joseph* is concerned with patiently enduring trials and maintaining one's self-control and chastity in the face of solicitation to indulge in illicit sexual relations. A key word is *sōphrosunē*, "sober-mindedness, decency; self-control, continence, chastity."

Cf. Gen.
48:21—49:1ff.

I.1. The copy of Joseph's testament. When he was near to death, he called his sons and his brothers and said to them: (2) My children and brothers, listen to Joseph, Israel's beloved; hearken, sons, to your father. (3) In my lifetime I have experienced envy and death, yet I did not stray from the Lord's truth.

Cf. Gen.
37—41.

Ps. 40:1-2.

Cf. Matt.
25:35-36.

4. These my brothers hated me, but the Lord loved me. They wanted to do away with me, but the God of my fathers guarded me. They lowered me into a pit, but the Most High drew me up. (5) I was sold for a slave, but the Lord set me free. I was taken into captivity, but the power of His hand helped me. I was afflicted by hunger, but the Lord Himself nourished me. (6) I was alone, and God comforted me; was sick and the Most High visited me; was in prison, and the Savior granted me favor; was in bonds, and He released me. (7) I was slandered, and He pled my cause; was the butt of Egyptians' bitter words, and He rescued me; was surrounded by envy and deceit, but He exalted me.

*Gen. 39:1,
LXX; Jub.
XXXIX.2ff.

Prov. 5:1-14; 8-9; Ps. Sol.
Sirach 9:2-4; XVI.7-8; Jub.
XXXIX.6-7.

II.1. And so Potiphar, *Pharaoh's chief baker, entrusted his household to me. (2) And I struggled against a shameless woman who continually urged me to transgress with her; but the God of my father Israel kept me from the burning flame. (3) I was imprisoned, beaten and mocked; but the Lord granted

me compassionate consideration on the part of the warden. (4)
For the Lord never abandons those who reverence Him, <small>Ps. 91:10;   Sirach 33:1;
Prov. 12:21; Ps. Sol. XV.1.</small>
neither in darkness, bonds, afflictions, nor anguish. . . . (6)
For in all places He is near at hand, and in many different ways <small>Ps. 139:7-12.</small>
He encourages, even though for a little while He withdraws to <small>Ps. 145:18-19. I Peter 1:6-7;
James 1:3.</small>
test the disposition of one's soul. (7) In ten trials He showed
me approved, and in all of them I was long-suffering; because <small>James 1:12.</small>
long-suffering is a great medicine, and patience gives one <small>Rom. 5:3-4;
I Cor. 13:4;</small>
many good things. <small>Col. 1:11;
3:12.</small>

III.1. How often did the Egyptian woman threaten me with
death! How often did she deliver me to punishments, then call
me back; and then threaten me when I was unwilling to come
together with her. She kept telling me: (2) "You will be my
master and control everything that is mine, if you will give
yourself to me, and you will be as our *lord." (3) Then I <small>*Despot,
owner.</small>
remembered the words of the fathers heard from my father
Jacob; and I entered my room and prayed to the Lord. <small>Prov.   Sirach 9:1-9;
6:20—7:27; Jub. XXXIX.6.</small>

Joseph recounts some of the ruses used by Memphia, and how he stedfastly withstood her wiles, although she vexed him sorely.

VIII.5. Now when I was in bonds, the Egyptian woman was
sick with grief; and she listened to how I kept singing to the <small>Job 35:10; Ps.
42:8; cf. Acts
16:25.</small>
Lord while in the house of darkness. In a cheerful voice I
joyfully praised my God, solely on account of being removed <small>Ps. 40:3.</small>
from the Egyptian woman's pretexts.

IX.1. Often she sent to me, saying, "Consent to fulfill my
desire, and I will release you from bonds and remove you from
the darkness." (2) Yet not so much as in thought did I incline
toward her. For God loves him who fasts in chastity in a pit of
darkness, rather than one who lives in luxury and licentiousness in royal apartments. (3) And if he who lives in chastity
also desires honor, and if the Most High knows that it is
expedient, then He bestows it on him, just as He did for
me. . . . (5b) For she was very beautiful, and she adorned
herself most attractively so as to seduce me. But the Lord kept
me from her attempts.

X.1. Observe, then, my children, what patient endurance and
prayer with fasting can accomplish. (2) As for you, therefore, <small>James 1:4, 12.</small>
if you follow the way of self-control and purity with patience
and humility of heart, the Lord will dwell among you, because <small>Cf. Ps. 146:8c;
Prov. 11:20;</small>
He loves chastity. (3) Now where the Most High dwells, even <small>15:9; 22:9.</small>
if one fall victim to envy, bondage or slander, the Lord who
dwells in him because of his self-control will not only rescue

Sirach 2:1-11; IV.23; cf. Job
Ps. Sol.   5:19; Ps. 34:6;
17; Isa. 52:13.
him out of such evils, but will also exalt and honor him, just as He did me. . . .

Ps. 84:11;
89:15-18;
128:1-6.
*Or, "into the
age (to
come)."
Prov.   I Peter 3:13.
24:28-29;
25:21-22;
Rom. 12:20.
XVIII.1. If then you also walk in the commandments of the Lord, my children, He will exalt you in this world and will bless you with good things *for ever. (2) And if anyone wants to harm you, you must pray for him and do good; and the Lord will deliver you from all harm.

READING 30: "Resist the devil" and be long-suffering (*T. Job* III.4—V.1; VII.12—VIII.3; XVI.1-2, 7; XVII.1; XIX.1-4; XXI.1-4; XXVI.1—XXVII.7)

The main theme of the *Testament of Job,* which is *not* one of the "Twelve Patriarchs," is resistance to the Adversary and stedfastness in the face of calamity and suffering. The New Testament teaching that "all who will live godly lives . . . will suffer persecution" has its roots in pre-Christian Jewish piety.

According to this testament, Job provoked Satan's wrath by demolishing an idol sanctuary. He did this at the encouragement of an angel, who also warned him of the consequences.

*Literally,
"soul."
III.4. And when I heard this, I fell down on my bed and worshiped, saying: (5) "My lord, who has come for the saving of my *life, (6) since this is the place of Satan in which men are led astray, I pray you to grant me authority to go and purify the place (7) so as to make offerings to him to cease. For who is he who can hinder me, since I rule over this country?"

Exod. 19:8;
I Sam. 3:10.

Cf. Rev.
12:9-12.

Job 1:12; 2:6.

I Peter 5:8;
I Thess. 3:4; II Tim. 3:12.

Matt. 10:22;   5:11; Rev.
James 1:12;   2:10.

*Matt.
13:39-40;   9:26. Cf. Dan.
28:20; Heb. 9:27; 12:4.

Deut. 10:17;
Rom. 2:11;
I Peter 1:17.

Job 14:14;
Dan. 12:2, 13;
Ps. Sol. II.3;
III.12.
IV.1. Then the Voice from the light replied: "You will indeed be able to purify this place. But I am going to show you all those things which the Lord commanded me to disclose to you." (2) And I said: "Everything that He whom I serve commands, I will hear and do." (3) So he spoke again: "The Lord says these things: (4) If you endeavor to cleanse the place of Satan, he will rise up against you in wrath for conflict. Only death will he be unable to bring upon you; but he will inflict many calamities upon you. (5) He will take your possessions away, and he will kill your children. (6) But if you endure, I will make your name famous among all the generations of earth until the *consummation of the age. (7) And I will restore your wealth, and will give it back to you twofold, (8) so that you may know that God is without partiality, but gives good things to everyone who obeys Him; (9) and you will be raised in the resurrection.

10. For you will be as an athlete wrestling and persevering in Eph. 6:12ff.; Job I Cor. 9:25-26; XXVII.3-7,
the struggle, and expecting the victor's wreath. (11) Then you James 1:12; T. below.
will know that the Lord is righteous and dependable and Ps. 28:7; 29:11; 138:3; I Sam. 2:4;
strong, strengthening His elect ones." Song of Azariah 3, 4.

V.1. Then, my children, I answered him in return: "I will
endure until death all the things to come upon me, for the love
of God, and will never take a step backward."

Job razes the idol's temple, then returns home and secludes himself,
forbidding anyone to be let in to see him. Satan, disguised as a beggar,
requests bread as a ruse to see Job. Job commands the servant to give him
bread, with a message for him to go away; and the servant gives Satan a loaf
which had been scorched.

VII.12. When *he heard this, he sent the servant back to say to *Satan.
me: "As this bread is a burnt offering, so will I do likewise to
your body. For in one hour will I go away and desolate you."
(13) And I answered him: "Whatever you are going to do, do.
For if you want to lay me waste, I am ready to stand up under
whatever you bring upon me." II Macc. 6:18—7:21; Phil. 3:8.

VIII.1. Now when he left me, going away under the firma- Job 1:7, LXX.
ment, (2) he made the Lord swear to grant him power over my
possessions. (3) Then, having gotten the power, he came and
took away every vestige of my wealth.

Job now describes all his wealth and recounts the good which he used to
do with it on behalf of the poor and weak. See Reading 25.

XVI.1. Now since I kept doing this during the seven years
after the angel had warned me, (2) Satan finally attacked me
unmercifully, after he had obtained the authority. . . . (7)
And they reported to me the destruction of my possessions;
yet I glorified God and did not blaspheme. Job 1:22.

XVII.1. Then when the Adversary learned of my endurance,
he plotted schemes against me.

In the guise of the king of Persia, Satan appears outside Job's city and
incites all the villains and rascals in it to attack Job's domicile and plunder
his possessions, after having slain the patriarch's children.

XIX.1. When the last messenger came and told me that my
children were destroyed, I was stricken with great agitation Job 1:18-20.
(2) and I tore my mantle and said to the one who informed me,
"How, then, were you saved?" (3) And then I understood
what had happened, and I called out: (4) "The Lord gave, the Job 1:21, LXX.
Lord took away; as it seemed good to the Lord, thus also it
happened; may the name of the Lord be praised." . . . Ps. Sol. III.3-6; V.1, 5

XXI.1. I spent seven years on the dung heap outside the city in my afflictions, so that I saw with my own eyes, (2) my children, my first wife carrying water for a certain elegant house, as a servant, so that she could get bread to bring me. (3) And I, greatly grieved, kept saying: "O, the arrogance of the rulers of this city! How they are using my wife as a slave-woman!"

Eccl. 7:8b; T.
Joseph II.7; Rom. 5:3-4 4. But later I adopted an attitude of reasonable long-suffering.

His wife, worn out by her menial toil and denied food, is finally forced to sell her hair to get enough bread for just three more days. And the bread seller who cuts off her hair is Satan in disguise! Completely disheartened by her sufferings, she finally urges Job to curse God and die.

XXVI.1. Then I answered her: "Look, I have had seven years of these plagues, submitting to the worms in my body, (2) and my soul has not been weighed down by these miseries nearly so much as by your saying, 'Speak some word against the Lord, and die.' (3) In short, are you and I enduring *these things . . . yet you are wanting us to speak something against the Lord, so as to be alienated from great riches? (4) Why do you not recall those great good things in which we once lived? If then we received the good things from the Lord's hand, can we not also endure the bad things? (5) But we should be long-suffering until the Lord has compassion and grants mercy to us. (6) Don't you then see the Adversary standing behind you and confusing your reason so that he may lead me astray? For he wants to prove you to be as one of the witless women who lead their own husbands astray from single-heartedness."

*Loss of children and possessions, etc.

Job 2:10;
Ps. Sol.
XVI.14-15.

James 5:11;
Rom. 2:7; Heb.
6:15.

II Cor. 2:11;
Rev. 12:9.

Cf. Reading
24.

XXVII.1. Then, turning now to Satan who was behind my wife, I said: "Come forward, stop hiding! Does the lion display his might in a cage? Does a bird resist, when put in a basket? Come out and struggle with me!" (2) Then he came out from behind my wife; and he stood and wept, saying: "Behold, Job, I am giving up and withdrawing from you who are in the flesh, yet I am spirit. You, indeed, are afflicted, but I am in great distress. (3) For you are like one wrestler with another, one of whom has pinned the other down. And the one on top has silenced the one underneath by filling his mouth with sand; (4) and he has broken every one of his limbs. Yet, since *he displays endurance and doesn't yield, the one on top calls him great. (5) So you, too, Job, are underneath and in affliction; yet you have overcome the skills of wrestling which I have used against you." (6) Then Satan, being put to shame, withdrew from me. (7) Therefore then,

James 4:7;
I Peter 5:8, 9.

*The one beneath.

my children, you also are to be long-suffering in everything
which happens to you, because long-suffering is better than
everything.   Cf. *T. Joseph*
                                                                         II.7, Reading
                                                                         29.

READING 31: Follow the example of a good man (*T. Benjamin* III.1—IV.5;
VIII.1-3)

III.1. So then, my children, you must love the Lord, the God of
heaven, and keep His commandments, imitating that good   *T. Zebulon*   11.1; Heb.
                                                               VIII.4-5; I Cor   13.7; I Peter
and pious man, Joseph. (2) And let your inclination be toward   2.12
the good, just as you also know me. He who has the good   Cf. Reading
                                                              32.
inclination sees everything aright. (3) Reverence the Lord and Deut. 6.5; Lev.
                                                              19.18.
love your neighbor. And if the spirits of Beliar demand you so Cf. *T. Job*
                                                              VIII.2, Reading
as to distress you harshly, yet such affliction will in no way get 30.
dominion over you, as my brother Joseph's example shows.   Readings 29
                                                              and 30; Sirach
(4) How many were the men who wanted to kill him! But God   33.1; I Peter
                                                              3.13.
protected him. For he who fears God and loves his neighbor
cannot be smitten by the spirit of the air, Beliar, since he is Cf. Eph. 2.2.
protected by godly reverence. (5) Nor can he be overcome by
the design of men or beasts, since he is aided by the love of the *T. Issachar*
                                                              VII.6-7,
Lord which he maintains toward his neighbor. (6) For Joseph   Reading 24.
also entreated our father Jacob to pray for our brothers, that
the Lord might not impute to them whatever evil they had
planned concerning him. (7) And Jacob cried out thus: "O my   Luke 23:34;
                                                              Acts 7:60;
child Joseph, you have overcome the emotions of your father   II Cor. 5:19.
Jacob!" He embraced and kissed him for two hours, and said:
(8) "By you will the prophecy of heaven be fulfilled, concerning the lamb of God and *savior of the world, that   *Possibly, but
                                                              not
                                                              necessarily, a
    a blameless one will be delivered up on behalf of the lawless, Christian
                                                              addition.
    and a sinless one will die on behalf of the ungodly

for the salvation of the Gentiles and of Israel; and he will put
Beliar and his cohorts out of business."

IV.1. Do you see, children, the outcome of the good man's life? I Peter 5:4; cf.
                                                              Ps. 8:5, Isa.
Imitate his good-heartedness with a good inclination so that 28.5.
you also may wear a crown of glory. (2) The good man does not Matt. 6:22-23.
have a dark eye; for he shows mercy to all men, even if they are *T. Zebulon*   Matt. 5:7; Luke
                                                              V.3; VIII.1-3.   6:36; Rom.
sinners. (3) Yes, even if they plot wicked things concerning Reading 25.   12:8.
him. Thus the one who does good conquers what is bad, since   Rom. 12:21.
he is protected by goodness; and he loves the righteous as his
own life. (4) If anyone is honored, he is not envious; if anyone
is rich, he is not jealous; if anyone is valiant, he praises him.
He lauds the virtuous, has pity on the poor, has sympathy for
the *weak, praises God in song. (5) And he loves as his own   *Or, "sick."
life the one who has the grace of a generous spirit. . . .   V. 5 follows
                                                              Charles
                                                              shorter text.

VIII.1. Flee then, my children, from wickedness—both envy and hatred of brethren—and cling to goodness and love. (2)
He who has an inclination cleansed by love does not look lustfully at a woman; for he has no defilement in his heart, because the spirit of God rests on him. (3) For just as the sun is not defiled by turning its rays on dung and mire, but rather dries up both and drives off the bad odor, so also the pure mind living amidst the pollutions of earth is not itself defiled.

Matt. 5:27-28

I Peter 4:14

Titus 1:15,
Phil. 4:8

5. TWO SPIRITS, TWO WAYS: CHOICE DETERMINES DESTINY

READING 32: The two "spirits" or "inclinations" (*T. Judah* XX.1-5; *T. Benjamin* VI.1-7)

Man. Disc.
III.17—IV.1,
15-18, 23b-26.

Sirach 15:14ff.

Heb. 4:13.

Cf. John 14:16;
16:13.

Sirach 14:2;
I John
3:19-20.

T. Judah XX.1. Know, then, my children, that two spirits are active in man, the one of truth and the one of error. (2) And between is that of the mind's insight, whose function is to incline as it may choose. (3) Indeed, the things of truth and those of error have been written upon the breast of the man; and the Lord is aware of each one of them. (4) And there is no time in which men can hide their works; because on their very breastbones they have been inscribed in the Lord's sight. (5) And the spirit of truth testifies about all things and makes accusation about all things; and the sinner is set afire out of his own heart, and cannot raise his face in the presence of the judge.

I Enoch XL.8;
LII.5; LIII.4;
Man. Disc.
III.24-25.

Ps. 62:10;
Sirach 29:11;
Matt. 6:19;
I John 2:15.

Ps. 15:3; Prov.   Deut. 4:19;
3:28-29;   Ezek. 18:12;
14:21; 24:28.   Job 31:1,
*   26-27.*

Cf. John 5:41,
44; I Thess.
2:6.

Phil. 4:4.

James 3:9-12.

T. Benjamin VI.1. The inclination of the good man is not in the power of Beliar, the spirit of deceit, for the angel of peace guides his soul. (2) He does not regard corruptible things with passionate desire, neither does he gather wealth to support fondness for pleasure. (3) He does not delight in sensuous pleasure; he does not grieve his neighbor, does not fill himself up on luxuries, is not led astray by lifting up his eyes.

4. The good inclination does not accept glory from men. It does not know how to engage in any guile or falsehood, strife or reviling. For the Lord dwells in it and illumines one's soul; and he rejoices for all things in every season. (5) For the good intention does not have two tongues, one of blessing and one of cursing, of insult and of honor; of grief and of joy; of quietness and of agitation; of hypocrisy and truth; of penury and of wealth; but it maintains a sincere and pure disposition regarding all men. (6) It does not have two ways of seeing or hearing. For one knows that for everything he does, whether

speaking or seeing, the Lord examines his soul. (7) So he purifies his intention so as not to be condemned by God or men. But in every work of Beliar there is duplicity: he has no sincerity. ^I Sam. 16:7; Ps. 44:20-21; Jer. 17:10.^

Comment:

Jewish pietism developed the doctrine of the two spirits, tendencies, or "inclinations" in man to explain the sinful proclivities that especially troubled the pious. Each man is given, at birth, a good or holy spirit or "inclination"—Heb., *yētser*; Gk., *dianoia* or *diaboulion*—and an inclination to evil. Each struggles for mastery in him, and it is his responsibility to choose which shall be his master. In effect, if he does not choose the good, he will be overcome by the evil inclination. Although Paul uses the term "law" or "principle," it is clear that in Romans 7 he is giving an interpretation of this doctrine on the basis of his personal experience, and is refuting the statement in Sirach that man can follow the good inclination by his own will and strength: Sirach 15:14ff. See Gal. 5:17ff. for another version, in which the language and conceptualization is closer to that of the passages above. The doctrine of the "two inclinations" leads naturally into, and is closely connected with, the doctrine of the Two Ways, which follows.

READING 33: Two Ways, and heavenly treasures (*T. Asher* I.3-9; III.1-2; V.1—VI.3; *T. Job* XXXIII.1-9)

T. Asher I.3. God has appointed two ways to the sons of men: two inclinations, two kinds of activity, two dispositions and two outcomes. (4) Therefore all things are by two, each opposing the other. (5) The ways are two: one good, one evil, in regard to which the two inclinations in our breasts make their choice. (6) Therefore, if a person wills to do good, every deed is done in righteousness; and even if he sins, he repents forthwith. (7) For by taking thought for right things and rejecting perversity, he immediately overturns wickedness and roots out sins. (8) But if the inclination leans toward evil, every deed is done in perversity. Driving away the good it accepts the bad, and is ruled over by Beliar. And even when it would do good, *he twists it about in perversity. (9) For whenever one begins to do good, Beliar forces the outcome of his action so as to accomplish something wrong, since the treasury of his inclination is filled with the poison of an evil spirit. . . .

Man. Disc. IV.2-15; Didache I—VI.

Cf. references in Reading 32.

Beliar.

Cf. Matt. 12:35b.

III.1. As for you, my children, do not have two faces like them: one of goodness and one of wickedness. But adhere only to goodness, because God is refreshed by it and men long for it.

*Or, "flee
from."

Rom. 12:21;
Titus 3:8-9.

Rom. 1:32;
Phil. 3:18-19;
Titus 1:16.

Sirach
33:14-15; 42:24-25.

I.e., evil in the
abuse of good.

*I.e., comes
after.

Amos 5:7;
II Tim. 4:4.

John 3:21.

*Literally,
"single-facedly."

Cf. Man.   I Enoch
Disc. I.9-11a; XV.11-12.
III.21-24;

Isa. 5:20; Mic.
3:2; cf. Amos 5:7.

Amos 5:14.

Cf. Ps. 119:24,
35, 165.

Ps. 16:11; cf.
Col. 3:1-2.

I John 2:17.

I Peter 1:4.

*aion, "realm,
age."

Job 12:14-15;
Isa. 50:2; Jer.
51:36; Ezek.
31:15-18.

Isa. 41:18;
44:3; Ezek.
47:1-12.

Ps. 37:35-36; 14:5ff.; 16:6;
48:4-5; Isa.   23:9.

*Cf. Ezek. 1
and 10. The
"Heavenly
Chariot"
visions led to
esoteric
speculations.

2. *Shun wickedness, answering the Adversary with your good deeds. Two-faced people do not belong to God, but they serve their cravings slavishly so as to please Beliar and men like themselves. . . .

V.1. Observe, then, children, how there are two aspects to all things, one opposite the other, and one *hidden in the other.

2. . . .All things are under the day, and righteous things are under life; wherefore eternal life *awaits death. (3) So one is not to call the truth falsehood, nor righteousness unrighteousness, because every truth is under the light, just as all things are under God.

4. All these things I tested out in my life, and was not led astray from the Lord's truth; but I searched out the commandments of the Most High, with all my strength walking *unswervingly toward the good.

VI.1. Take heed, then, children, to follow the Lord's commandments unswervingly in the truth, (2) for the two-faced are doubly punished. Hate the spirits of error which struggle against mankind. (3) Keep the Law of the Lord, and do not give heed to evil as being the good; but pay attention to the truly good and watch carefully for it in all the Lord's commandments, engaging yourselves with it and resting in it.

T. Job XXXIII.1. Elihu prolonged the mourning while the kings responded to him, so that they made a great commotion. (2) When the outcry ceased, Job said to them: "Be still! Now I will show you my throne and my glory and my dignity which are among the holy ones. (3) My throne is in the world above, and its glory and dignity is at the right hand of the Father. (4) The whole world is passing away and its glory is perishing, and those who hold on to it will share in its overthrow. (5) But my throne belongs to the holy land and its glory is in the Unchangeable *Realm.

6. The rivers will dry up and their proud waves will descend into the depths of the Abyss. (7) But the river of the land where my throne is does not dry up, neither will it disappear; but will exist for ever.

8. These kings will pass away . . . and their glory and boasting will be as a mirror's reflection. (9) But my kingdom is for ever, and its glory and dignity are in the *chariots of the Father."

6. The "last times": preparation for Messiah

READING 34: Decadence and apostasy (*T. Levi* XIV.1-6; XVI.1-3; *T. Judah* XXII.1—XXIII.2; *T. Issachar* VI:1-2a; *T. Dan* V.4-5)

T. Levi XIV.1. And now, children, I know from Enoch's writing that at the end you will act impiously against the Lord, putting forth your hands to every kind of wickedness. Your brethren will be ashamed of you, and it will become a source of mockery for all the Gentiles. . . . (3) The heaven over the earth is clean, and you are the lights of heaven, like the sun and moon. (4) If you become darkened by ungodliness, what will all the nations do for whose sake the light of the world has been given among us as a light for every man? Wanting to do away with it, teaching commandments contrary to God's ordinances, (5) you will rob the Lord's offerings. From His portions you will steal, taking the choice parts before sacrificing to the Lord, and eating with harlots *in contempt. (6) You will teach the commandments of the Lord *in covetousness. You will defile married women and virgins of Jerusalem you will violate. You will be joined with harlots and adulteresses, *purifying them with an illegal purification; and your uniting will be like Sodom and Gomorrha for ungodliness. . . .

Cf. *T. Simeon* V.4; Reading 16.

Ps. Sol. II.3-13; VIII.8-14.

I Macc. 1.10—2.12; Ant. XII.5.

Cf. Readings 2, 3, and 8.

Phil. 2.14-16.

John 1.9.

Isa. 29:13; Jer. Ezek. 22:26; 2.8; 5:31; 8.8; Mark 7:7-8. I Sam. I Macc. II Macc. 2:12-17; 1.1-14; 4:7-17.
*I.e., of the Lord or the Law.

*For gain: cf. Mic. 3:11; Isa. 1.23b; I Peter 5:2.

Zad. Doc. *I.e., ritually. V.6-12.

XVI.1. And now I know by the Book of Enoch that you will go astray for seventy *weeks: you will defile the priesthood and pollute the sacrifices; (2) you will conceal the Law and the words of prophets you will disdain; you will perversely persecute righteous men, and godly men you will hate, detesting words of truth. (3) A man who renews the Law in the power of the Highest you will call a deceiver and finally, *as you suppose, you will kill him, not perceiving his eminence, and receiving guiltless blood in wickedness upon your heads.

*Literally, "sevens"; cf. Dan. 9:24ff.

Zad. Doc. I.10ff.

*Probably a Christian gloss.

T. Judah XXII.1. Now the Lord will bring upon them divisions against each other, and continual conflicts will occur in Israel; (2) and by strangers will my kingdom be brought to an end, until the Deliverer of Israel comes, until the *appearance of the God of righteousness to bring rest to Jacob, and to all the nations, in peace. (3) And He will guard the power of my kingdom until the Age. For the Lord swore to me by an oath not to forsake my kingdom or my seed all the days, until the Age.

I Macc. 2; II Macc. 2—6; cf. Reading 8.

*Gk., parousia.

Isa. 40:9-11; Zeph. 3:14-20.

II Sam. 7:14-16; Ps. 89:19-37; 132:11; Acts 2:30.

Jer. 44:15ff.;
Ezek. 8.

XXIII.1. But I am deeply grieved, my children, because of the licentiousness, deception and idolatry which you will practice in the temple, following ventriloquists, omens and spirits of error. (2) You will make singing girls and courtesans of your daughters, and you will join in gentile abominations.

*Gk.,
haplotes; cf.
Reading 24.

T. Issachar VI.1. I know, my children, that in the last times your sons will abandon *generosity and will be joined to greediness. They will forsake guilelessness and draw near to evil-working and, abandoning the Lord's commandments, they will be joined to Beliar. (2) Forsaking agriculture, they will follow after their evil inclinations. . . .

*Apostatize.

T. Dan V.4. For I know that in the last days you will *revolt from the Lord. You will be full of wrath at Levi and will oppose Judah. Yet you will be unable to do anything against them. For the angel of the Lord will guide them both, because by them Israel shall stand. (5) And when you apostatize from the Lord, you will walk in every kind of wickedness, engaging in gentile abominations, committing fornication with *women of the lawless, while the spirit of error produces in you every kind of *vice.

*Either gentile,
or "liberated"
Jewish.

*Corrupt
practice.

READING 35: Punishment by captivity and dispersion (T. Levi XV.1-4; XVI.4-5a; T. Judah XXIII.3; T. Dan V.7-8; T. Issachar VI.2; T. Asher VII.5-6)

*Deut.
12:11-14;   *Ritual
26:2.   impurity.

Deut. 28:15,
36-37.

*Rom. 2:5, Gk.

*I.e., God's
covenant with
them.

T. Levi XV.1. Because of these things, the sanctuary *(whichever the Lord may choose) will be desolate in *uncleanness, and you will be captives among all the nations. (2) You will be an abomination among them and will receive reproach and eternal shame by the *righteous judgment of God. (3) Everyone who sees you will flee from you. (4) And were it not for *Abraham, Isaac and Jacob, our forefathers, not one of my descendants would be left upon earth. . . .

Deut.
28:15-37.

XVI.4. Therefore your holy things will be desolate, even to the pollution of the foundations. (5) And there will be no place clean for you; but you will be for a curse and a dispersion among the Gentiles.

*Cf. Reading
34.

Amos 4:6-12;
8:9-14.

*I.e., attack
dogs, or wild
dogs.

T. Judah XXIII.3. Because of *these things, the Lord will bring upon you famine and pestilence; death and sword; an avenging siege and *dogs for the rending of enemies; reproaches of friends; loss and gangrene of eyes; slaughter of children, kidnapping of wives and plundering of goods; burning of God's sanctuary, desolation of the land; and your slavery among the nations.

T. Dan V.7. And my sons will come near to Levi, and will sin with them in all things. . . . (8) Therefore you will be led away with them into captivity, and there you will *receive all the plagues of Egypt, and all the evils of the nations.

*As payment due.

T. Issachar VI.2. Leaving farm work, they will follow their evil inclinations. They will be scattered among the nations, and they will serve their enemies as slaves.

T. Asher VII.5. For I have read in the *heavenly tablets that you will disobey him. . . . (6) Because of this you will be scattered like Gad and Dan your brethren, who will become ignorant of their land, their tribe and their language.

*T. Levi V.4, Reading 15.

READING 36: Repentance and return (*T. Judah* XIII.5; *T. Issachar* VI.3-4; *T. Zebulon* IX.7-8; *T. Naphtali* IV.3; *T. Levi* XVI.5b)

T. Judah XXIII.5. Whenever you turn back to the Lord with a perfect heart, repenting and walking in all the commandments of God, then the Lord will visit you in mercy and in *love to bring you back from captivity to your enemies.

Hos. 14; Jer. 29:13-14; 30:18ff.; Ezek. 36:16-36; 39:25ff.; Deut. 30:1-10; II Chron. 15:2.

*Gk., agapē.

T. Issachar VI.3. Therefore you must tell these things to your children, so that if they sin they may quickly turn back to the Lord; (4) because He is merciful and will bring them out to return them to their own land.

T. Zebulon IX.7. After these things you will remember the Lord and repent; and He will turn you back, for He is merciful and compassionate. He does not reckon wickedness to the account of the sons of men, since they are flesh and the spirits of error deceive them on the occasion of all their acts. (8) After these things the Lord Himself, the Light of righteousness, will arise upon you with healing and compassion in His wings. *And you will return to your own land.

II Chron. 6:24-39.

Cf. Exod. 24:5-7.

Cf. Gen. 6:3; Reading 12 and Comments.

Cf. I Chron. 21:1.

Isa. 60:1-3; Mal. 4:2.

*Charles, after A.

T. Naphtali IV.3. After you have been diminished and made few, you will turn back and acknowledge the Lord your God; and He will bring you back into your land, according to His great mercy.

Deut. 4:27; 28:62; Isa. 6:11-12; Amos 5:3.

Deut. 4:30-31; 30:1ff.

T. Levi XVI.5b. . . . but you will be for a curse and a dispersion among the Gentiles, until He visits again and has compassion, and receives you in faithfulness and in water.

Deut. 28:15ff., 37.

Hos. 29:10; Zeph. 5:15—6:3; 2:7; Hos. Jer. 27:22; 2:19-20.

Ezek. 36:22-25; Man. Disc. III.6b-9.

Comments:

1. It is obvious that these "prophecies" of apostasy, punishment, repen-

tance and return depend upon the O. T. histories of the captivities and dispersions which Israel suffered, and upon the prophecies of the same in Deuteronomy and the Prophets, as noted. Each patriarch is made to prophesy those details which, in the author's judgment, would be most appropriate for him. The author is using his scriptures to interpret the times in which he lives, which have disturbing similarities to the past. By N. T. times, it is clear, a schema of the events which would precede the advent of Messiah included these elements (general apostasy, tribulation, repentance of a "remnant") and had become somewhat standardized, just as in Christian millennialism today.

2. "In water" (*T. Levi* XVI.5b, above) obviously refers to the cleansing lustration undergone by the priests according to Exod. 40:12. Cf. Zech. 13:1.

7. THE "LAST TIMES": MESSIANIC GLORIES

READING 37a: Restoration under messianic leadership (*T. Simeon* VI.1-5; VII.1-2; *T. Dan* V.9-11)

T. Simeon VI.1. Behold, I have foretold to you all things so that I may be acquitted from your sins. (2) But if you put away from you envy and all your stiffness of neck, then my bones will flower as a rose in Israel, my flesh as a lily in Jacob, and my odor will be *as the smell of Lebanon. Like cedars, saints will be multiplied from me forever, and their branches will grow very long. (3) Then the seed of Canaan will perish, there will be *no remnant of Amalek; the Cappadocians will perish, even all the Hittites will be completely destroyed. (4) The *land of Ham will fail, and all its people will perish. Then the land will rest from trouble and the whole world under heaven will cease from war. (5) Then the *sign will be glorified—for great is the Lord God of Israel—appearing upon earth *as man and saving mankind *by him. . . .

Deut. 10:16; 29:1; Gal.
Prov. 14:30; 5:26.

*Hos. 14:6.

Ps. 92:12;
Hos. 14:5b-6.

Gen. 15:12-21;
Deut. 20:17.

*Exod.
17:14-16.

Exod. 23:28;
34:11; Deut. 20:17.

*Egypt: Isa. 19
and other
oracles against
Egypt.

Isa. 2:4;   *Or,
11:6ff.   Name = God
            (Gk. *sema* for
            Heb. *shem*).

*In the   *Or, "for
Messiah; cf. himself."
Zech. 14; Isa.
35:4; Zeph.
3:17; Zech.
9:16.

VII.1. So, children, obey Levi and by Judah you will be rescued. Do not rise up against these two tribes for from them God's deliverance will arise for you. (2) For the Lord will raise up from Levi one as high priest and from Judah one as king. Thus He will deliver the nations and the race of Israel.

Deut. 4:29-31;
Lev. 26:40ff.; Jer. 3:12-14.

Isa. 51:11;   37:21-28;
Ezek.   Zech. 8:3-8.

*I.e., Messiah.

Rev. 15:2;
17:14.

T. Dan V.9. Thus, when you have turned back to the Lord you will receive mercy. He will bring you to His holy place and will grant you peace. (10) Then, out of the tribes of Judah and Levi the *Deliverance of the Lord will arise for you, and he will make war on Beliar and he will grant us victorious vengeance at last. (11) The captivity, the lives of the saints, will he take

from Beliar; he will turn disobedient hearts back to the Lord, _{Mal. 4:5-6}
and will grant eternal peace to those who call upon him. _{Joel 2:32;
Rom. 10:13}

Comment:

The connection of Levi and Judah in the military affairs of Israel may at first seem puzzling until one remembers that in the "war of the Lord," or holy war, the priests—who were of Levi's tribe—led the host to battle and sounded the shophar-horns as the signal for attack (Num. 10:8-9; 31:1-6; Josh. 6:3-5, 15-16; II Chron. 13:13-15). The *Qumran War Rule* is a detailed field manual of holy war, looking forward to the final great battle between God's people and the hosts of Belial. From Judah, of course, was to come the political ruler, the Messiah, commander-in-chief of the armies.

READING 37b: The two anointed ones ("messiahs"), and the messianic times (*T. Levi* XVIII.1-3, 6-8; *T. Judah* XXIV.1-6; *T. Levi* XVIII.4-5, 9-14; *T. Dan* V.12-13)

T. Levi XVIII.1-2. Then, after the Lord punishes *them He will raise up in the priesthood a new priest to whom all the words of the Lord will be revealed; and he will perform true justice upon the land for many days. (3) His star will arise in heaven, as of a king, shedding the light of *knowledge like the sun of the day, and he will be magnified in the world until he *is taken up. . . . (6) The heavens will open and out of the glorious sanctuary there will come upon him sanctification with the paternal voice as from Abraham, Isaac's father. (7) The glory of the Highest will be uttered over him and the spirit of understanding and of sanctification will come to rest upon him *in the water. (8) He will give the Lord's majesty to his sons in truth for ever; and there will be no successor to him for generations and generations for ever.

The corrupt priests, cf. Reading 34

Cf. Num. 24:17.

**Of the Law, of God.*

**I.e., dies. Cf. Sirach 50:5ff.*

Exod. 40:12-13, 30-34; cf. Isa. 15.   11:2; T. Levi VIII.5, Reading

**Of installation, cf. Exod. 40:12; Lev. 8:6.*

T. Judah XXIV.1. Now after these things there will arise for you a star out of Jacob in peace, even a man from my seed will rise up like the sun of righteousness, walking with the sons of men in righteousness, and *no sin will be found in him. (2) The heavens will be opened over him to pour out the blessing of the spirit of the holy Father, and He will pour out the spirit of grace upon you. (3) Then you will be His sons in truth, and will walk in His ordinances first and last. (4) This one is the branch of the Most High God, and this is the *fountain of life for all flesh. (5) Then the scepter of my kingdom will be resplendent, and from your shoot will grow a shoot; (6) and out of it a rod of righteousness for the nations will come up to judge and to deliver all who call upon the Lord.

Num. 24:17; Isa. 11:1.

Mal. 4:2.

**"no sin" = "righteousness"; Isa. 11:3-5; Ps. Sol. XVII.36.*

Isa. 11:2;   Zech. 2:10b. 42:1b; 44:3;

Hos. 1:10;   Mic. 4:1-5.

Isa. 4:2; Jer.   Zech. 3:8; 23:5; 33:15.   6:12-13.

**The Lord's   Ps. 36:9; Jer. ordinances,   2:13. the Law*

Isa. 11:1; Jer. 33:15.

Isa. 11:4; Ps.   Joel 2:32; Isa. 45:6; cf. Gen.   12:4; Zeph. 49:10   3:9.

*I.e., the new high priest.

Isa. 44:23; 49:13.

Ps. 96:11-13; Isa. 35:1ff.

Isa. 11:9.

Cf. Gen. 3:24.

Isa. 44:3; Joel 2:28.

Cf. Luke 10:19; Rev. 20:1-3.

Isa. 62:5; Zeph. 3:17.

Isa. 61:3, 10.

Isa. 65:18ff.; Amos 9:15; 60:21, Ezek. Zeph. 3:15-17; 37:26-27; Zech. 8:3.

Ps. 89:18; Isa. 12:6.

T. Levi XVIII.4. *He will shine as sun on the earth, he will take away all darkness from under heaven, and there will be peace in the whole land. (5) The heavens will exult in his days, and the land will rejoice; the clouds will make merry; and the knowledge of the Lord will be poured out upon the land, as the water of the seas; and the angels of the presence of the Lord will be glad because of him. . . . (9) Now upon the inauguration of his priesthood, all sin will leave off: the lawless will cease their wickedness, and the righteous will rest in him. (10) And he will open the gates of the Garden, and remove the sword which threatens mankind. (11) He will grant the saints the right to eat from the tree of life, and the spirit of holiness will be upon them. (12) Beliar will be bound by him, and he will give authority to his children to tread upon evil spirits. (13) The Lord will take pleasure in His children, the Lord will be delighted in His beloved ones for ever. (14) Then Abraham, Isaac and Jacob will exult; I will be glad; and all the saints will be clothed with happiness.

T. Dan V.12. Then the saints will rest in Eden, and over the new Jerusalem, which will be for the glory of God forever, the righteous will rejoice. (13) Jerusalem will endure desolation no longer, nor will Israel suffer captivity, because the Lord will be in the midst of them, even the Holy One of Israel ruling over them.

Comment:

On the theory that *T. Levi*, or much of it, belongs to the older strata of the *Testaments*, XVIII.1ff. applies either to Simon Hashmon (I Macc. 14) or to his son John Hyrcanus who, according to Josephus, enjoyed the high priesthood, kingship and the gift of prophecy (cf. *War* I.68, in the Historical Sketch above). Hence the prophecy of his star arising "as of a king," v. 3. On Charles' theory that a later Pharisaic redactor revised the text at various points, *T. Judah* XXIV.1ff. can be viewed as an instance of the technique of correction by adding or rewriting: the "Star" (from Num. 24:17) really means the Messiah, son of David, descendant of Judah.

Viewed otherwise, the passages could be expressions of the expectation of the rise of both the ideal high priest and the ideal Davidic king in the messianic age yet to come. The Qumran documents express the expectation of both "anointed ones," as well as of a prophet, i.e., the restoration of the Davidic monarchy (with king, high priest, and prophet to the throne) was expected. The stronger emphasis upon the high priest probably reflects the realities of the intertestamental period together with the bias of the author(s). Support for this theory can be found in Ezek. 40—46 and especially in Zechariah.

READING 38: Final destinies (*T. Asher* VI.4-6; *T. Job* IV.7-9; XXXIX.11—XL.4a; XLIII.4-11a; *T. Simeon* VI.6-7; *T. Judah* XXV.1-5; *T. Benjamin* X.6-10)

T. Asher VI.4. Because the *ends of men show up their right- ·I.e., deaths.
eousness, making known the (presence of the) angels of the
Lord or those of Satan. (5) For if one's soul is agitated when it
is departing, it is being tormented by the evil spirit which it
served in lusts and evil works; (6) but if (it departs) quietly
and with joy, it reveals the angel of peace inviting it into life. Luke 16:22.

T. Job IV.7. And *I will restore your wealth, and will give back ·The Lord is speaker.
to you twofold, (8) so that you may know that He is impartial,
but gives good things to everyone who obeys Him; (9) and Rom. 2:11; 10:12.
you will be raised in the resurrection. . . .

XXXIX.11. So they *started off to dig, but I hindered them, ·To find his children,
saying: "Don't trouble yourselves needlessly, (12) for you will buried in the
not find my children, since they have been taken up into ruins of their Cf. Job
heaven by their Maker the King." (13) Then they replied, home. 1:18-19.
"Who will not say that he is out of his mind and is mad—
because you say, 'My children have been taken up into
heaven'? Therefore, make the truth plain to us!"

XL.1. So I said in my turn: "Raise me up so that I can stand."
So they raised me, holding my arms on both sides to steady
me. (2) Then, as I stood, I uttered praise to the Father. (3) And Cf. Exod. 17:12.
after praying I said to them: "Lift up your eyes toward the east
and see my children, crowned, beside the glory of the
Heavenly King." (4) When my wife Sitidos saw it, she fell to
the ground and worshiped, saying: "Now I know that my
memorial is with the Lord. . . ."

XLIII.4. This is what Eliphaz said: "Our sins are taken away
from us, and our iniquities have been buried. (5) Elihu the Ps. 103:12; Isa. 38:17c;
evil one, he alone will have no memorial among the living. (6) Mic. 7:19.
But the lamp of his glory will depart from him into judgment, Prov. 13:9; cf. Job 19:8-9.
because he is of the darkness and not of the light. The door- Prov. 4:18-19; 3:19-21;
keepers of the darkness will inherit his glory and his dignity. cf. John 13:30.
(7) His kingdom has passed away, his throne has decayed,
and the honor of his tent is in Hades. (8) He loved the beauty
of the Serpent and the scales of the Dragon: its gall and its Cf. Isa. 27:1; 20:1-3; Ps.
venom will be his food. (9) For he did not take the Lord for Rev. 12:1-17; Sol. II.25.
himself nor did he fear Him; but he provoked to anger those Cf. Deut. 32:33.
precious to Him. (10) The Lord forgot him and the holy ones
abandoned him. (11) Wrath and anger will be his dwelling. . . ."

T. Levi
XVIII.9,
Reading 37b;
Luke 10:19;
Rom. 16:20.

T. Simeon VI.6. Then the spirits of error will be given over to be trampled on, and men will rule over the evil spirits. (7) Then I will arise in happiness and bless the Most High for His marvelous works. . . .

T. Judah XXV.1. After these things Abraham, Isaac and Jacob will arise to life, and I and my brothers will be chiefs of Israel's tribes. . . . (3) And you will be one people of the Lord, with

*Zeph. 3:9.

Cf. Reading 12;
Rev. 20:10.

Isa. 65:13-15;
Matt. 5:3-12.

*one language. No longer will there be any deceiving spirit of Beliar, because he will be cast into the fire for ever. (4) Those who died in grief will rise in joy. Those who were poor for the Lord's sake will be made rich; those who were hungry will become strong; and those who died for the Lord's sake will be

Cf. II Macc. 7.

Ps. 18:33; Isa.
35:6; 40:31.

Isa. 65:14.

awakened to life. (5) And the gazelles of Jacob will run exultingly; the eagles of Israel will fly joyfully; but the godless will grieve and sinners will lament; and all the people will glorify the Lord for generations.

T. Benjamin X.6. Then you will see Enoch, Noah and Shem, Abraham, Isaac and Jacob, rising on the right hand with exultation. (7) Then *we will also rise, each over his own tribe,

*Jacob's sons.

worshiping the Heavenly King. (8) Then all men will arise, some to glory, some to dishonor. And the Lord will judge

Dan. 12:2; Isa.   Reading 46;
26:19; Ps.   John 5:28-29.
Sol. II.31,

Ezek. 9:9-10;
Amos 3:1;
9:9-10.

Israel first, in regard to its wickedness. (9) Then He will reprove the nations. (10) And He will reprove Israel through the chosen ones of the nations, just as He reproved Esau by the Midianites. . . .

8. THE LAW OF THE LORD— OF DIVINE ORIGIN

READING 39a: Angels who mediated the Law to Moses kept it (*Jub.* I.26-27, 29; II.1-3, 16-19, 33; XV.24-25, 27)

*The deity
speaking.

Jub. I.26. "Write down for yourself all these things which *I declare to you on this mountain, from first to last, which will occur in all the divisions of the days in the Law and in the testimony, and in the weeks and the jubilees in perpetuity until I descend and dwell with them throughout eternity."

Cf. Luke 1:19.

(27) And He said to the Angel of the Presence, "Write for Moses from the beginning of Creation till My sanctuary has been built among them for all eternity." . . . (29) And the

Exod. 23:20ff.;
Josh. 5:13-15.

angel of the Presence who went before the camp of Israel took the tablets of the divisions of the years, from the time of Creation, of the Law and of the testimony of the weeks, of the jubilees, according to the individual years, according to all the number of the jubilees. . . .

II.1. And the angel of the Presence spoke to Moses according to the word of the Lord: "Write the complete history of Creation, how in six days the Lord God finished all His works and all that He had created, and kept Sabbath on the seventh day and hallowed it for all ages, and appointed it as a sign for all His works. (2) For on the first day He created the heavens which are above the earth and the waters and all the spirits which serve before Him: the angels of the Presence and the angels of sanctification *. . . . (3) Thereupon we saw His works and praised Him, and lauded before Him because of all His works; for He created seven great works on the first day. . . . (16) And He finished all His work on the sixth day: all that is in the heavens and on the earth, and in the seas and in the abysses, and in the light and in the darkness, and in every thing. (17) And He gave us a great sign, the Sabbath day, that we should work six days, but keep a sabbath from all work on the seventh day. (18) And all the angels of the Presence, and all the angels of sanctification—those two great classes—to us He gave order to keep Sabbath with Him in heaven and on earth. (19) And He said to us, 'Behold, I will separate for Myself a people from among all the peoples. These will keep the Sabbath day, and I will sanctify them for Myself as My people, and I will bless them. As I have sanctified the Sabbath day and do sanctify it for Myself, so I will bless them and they will be My people, and I will be their God.' . . . (33) This law and testimony was given to the children of Israel as a law in perpetuity for all their generations. . . .

*Long catalog of angels.

XV.24. And on that very day Abraham was circumcised, and all the men of his house. . . . (25) This law is for all the generations forever . . . for it is an ordinance in perpetuity, ordained and written on the heavenly tablets. . . . (27) For all the angels of the Presence and all the angels of sanctification have been *so created from the day of their creation; and before the angels of the Presence and the angels of sanctification He has sanctified Israel so that they should be with Him and His holy angels. . . ."

*I.e., circumcised.

Comment:

The argument of *Jubilees*, as of Ps. 119:89, is that the Law of Moses is of heavenly origin and divine authority. Sirach, Baruch and Wisdom of Solomon concur. The author's concern focuses on those matters of orthodox Judaism which were under attack by the hellenizing party (cf. I Macc. 1—2; II Macc. 4—5; *Ps. Sol.* II and VIII). The author's method was to rewrite Genesis to show that: (1) Moses wrote down, on Mt. Sinai, what he learned from an angel sent by God to instruct him; (2) the angel told him what had already been written down on heavenly tablets; and (3) the laws which he was to enact—those in Exodus through Deuteronomy—were the laws which either (a) were already being kept by the angels, e.g., the Sabbath, or (b) were enacted by the Patriarchs in the past, usually by angelic direction.

It now seems possible that *Jubilees* was an Essene writing. At least it is safe to say that it was a hasidic, "pietist," production. It stands in complementary relationship to the *Testaments of the Twelve Patriarchs*: it is concerned primarily with ritual and Jewish separateness, whereas the *Testaments* are more concerned with personal morality. Whether its extreme claims for the Law were promoted by the Pharisees in Jesus' day or not, no pious Jew would have disagreed with its fundamental premise concerning the binding authority of the Mosaic Law upon every son of Israel.

READING 39b: The Law written on the "heavenly tablets" before Moses' time (*Jub.* III.8-10, 30-31; V.13-14; *T. Asher* VII.5)

The Creator.

Ritual impurity following childbirth; cf. Lev. 12:2-5.

The angels.

Jub. III.8. In the first week Adam was created, also the rib, his wife. In the second week *He showed her to him. So for this reason the commandment was given, to keep women in their *defilement, for a male seven days and for a female fourteen days. (9) After Adam had completed forty days in the land where he had been created, *we brought him into the Garden of Eden to till and keep it; but they brought his wife in on the eightieth day, and after this she entered into the Garden of Eden.

Here is quoted Lev. 12:2-5.

10. For this reason, then, the commandment is written on the heavenly tablets in regard to her that gives birth.* . . .

Adam and Eve are put out of the Garden after yielding to temptation by the serpent.

Nakedness, especially of the genitals.

30. And to Adam alone, of all creatures, did God give something to cover his *shame (31). Therefore it is prescribed on the heavenly tablets as touching all who know the judgment of the Law, that they should cover their shame, and not expose themselves as Gentiles do. . . .

V.13. And the judgment of all is ordained and written on the heavenly tablets in righteousness, even of all who depart from the path in which it is ordained for them to walk: if they do not walk in it, judgment is written down for every creature and every kind. (14) . . . all their judgments are ordained and written and engraved.

T. Levi V.4; Reading 15.

T. Asher VII.5. For I have learned by the heavenly tablets that you will assuredly disobey Him and act impiously, not heeding the Law of the Lord. . . .

Jub. XXX.
Deut. 28 here
becomes
patriarchal
"prophecy."

READING 40: The Law taught by the Patriarchs before Moses (*T. Levi* IX.1-2, 5—X.1)

IX.1. And after *two days, Judah and I went with our father to see Isaac. (2) And my grandfather blessed me according to all the words of the visions which I had seen. But he would not come with us to Bethel. . . . (5) So we came to Hebron to lodge, (6) and Isaac frequently called me to remind me of the Law of the Lord, just as the angel had shown me. (7) He taught me the law of the priesthood and of the sacrifices: whole burnt-offerings, first fruits, free-will offerings, peace-offerings. (8) Day by day he instructed me, busying himself with me before the Lord. (9) And he would say: "Beware, child, of the spirit of fornication, for it will persist and, through your descendants, is going to defile the holy things. (10) Therefore, take for yourself a wife while you are young, a woman not having a blemish nor having been profaned, nor from another tribe nor a Gentile. (11) Before entering the holy place take a bath, and when you offer the sacrifice, wash; also, wash upon completing the sacrifice. (12) Of the twelve trees always having leaves, make offering to the Lord, as Abraham taught me; (13) and of every clean animal and bird, sacrifice to the Lord. (14) Of all your first ripe produce and of your wine, offer a sacrifice of first fruits; and put salt on every sacrifice.

*After his
vision, cf.
Reading 15.

Cf. Lev.
1—10,
16—17.

Cf. Readings
22, 23, 34.
Cf. Ezek. 44.

Lev. 21:13-14

Lev. 21:14

Exod. 29:4;
30:19-20; Lev.
16:4, 24.

Gen. 7:1-3;
8:20; Lev. 11.

Lev. 2:12, 14; Lev. 2:13;
23:10ff.   Ezek. 43:24.

X.1. Now, then, observe the things which I am commanding you, children, because I am disclosing to you the things which I heard from my fathers."

Comment:

According to *Jub.* XXI, Abraham gave Isaac similar instructions concerning ritual, in even greater detail. *Jub.* XXXII.1 recounts Levi's dream at Bethel in which angels invested him with the priesthood, as in *T. Levi* VIII (Reading 15), but no account is given in *Jub.* of his receiving any instructions from Isaac. However, *Jub.* XXXI tells how Isaac gave Levi and Judah the patriarchal blessing, granting Levi the place of greatest honor: at his right side.

READING 41: Moses' vision of heavenly exaltation (from the *Exodus* of Ezekiel "the Tragedian" as preserved by Eusebius)

Moses relates to his father-in-law a dream which he has had. The latter gives him an interpretation.

Exod. 24:9-18;
34:1-8.

Cf. Reading
13b, I Enoch
XIV.8ff.;
II Esdras 8:21

Moses is
granted
supreme
authority by
God.

Moses thus is
made God's
vice-regent.
Prov. 8:22-30;
Sirach 24:4-5;
he sees all the
domain of the
divine
Wisdom.

Another
symbol of
Moses'
exaltation: the
hosts of
heaven honor
him.

Deut. 33:4-5,
in KJV or ASV.
*Implies
teacher,
instructor.

*Literally,
"inhabited," or
civilized,
area."

It seemed there was on Sinai mountain's top
A mighty throne which touched the firmament,
On which sat one of light-filled countenance,
Wearing a diadem, a mighty scepter holding
In his left hand. With his right to me
He beckoned, and I took my stand before the throne.
The scepter then he handed me, on a great throne
He bade me sit; a royal diadem he gave to me,
And he himself departed from the thrones.
Then I looked on all the encircling earth,
And under earth and up above the heaven.
Then before my knees a multitude of stars
Fell down. I numbered all as they passed by
Like military ranks of warrior men.
Then, terrified, I wakened from my sleep.
   (Moses' father-in-law interprets the vision.)
O friend, God has given sign to you of good.
Oh, that I might be alive when all these things come true for
   you!
For sure, a mighty throne shall you set up,
And you yourself will be judge and *guide of men.
Since all the *human world you gazed upon,
And underneath it, and above the heaven of God,
Thus you will see things present, things of former times, and
   things still yet to come.

Comments:

1. Although preserved only through citations in the Church Fathers, this piece is usually placed in the second century B.C. It is in good Greek poetic style, and probably represents one of many attempts made to popularize Jewish beliefs among non-Jews.

2. This piece is important for the evidence it gives of the high claims which were made for Moses, and of the legendary form in which those claims were made. It embodies an early (though probably not the earliest) form of the claim that Moses was shown the whole sweep of his people's history on Mt. Sinai. *Jubilees* (cf. Readings 39a and b) makes a similar claim, but with different emphases.

3. The dream of exaltation, for which those of Joseph (Gen. 37:5-7) possibly formed the inspiration, was a way of claiming special authority for a person and his words. However, enthronement symbolized supreme authority (cf. Dan. 7 and Reading 55).

4. Deut. 33:4-5 appears to be the direct scriptural support for the notion that Moses was king. The Hebrew text can be rendered either by "There

was a king" (as some modern versions) or "He was king" (as an early targum and KJV/ASV). In effect, Moses exercised all the prerogatives of an oriental *melek* or sheikh: the people's chief leader, lawgiver and judge. Of course, the claim that he had been given a divine grant of supreme authority was, in the poet's day, tantamount to claiming as a divine revelation the supreme authority of the Mosaic Law over mankind, and especially Israel.

READING 42: Learn, teach and practice the Law (*T. Levi* XIII.1-9; *T. Judah* XXVI.1; *T. Dan* V. 1-3; *T. Asher* VI.1, 3; *T. Joseph* XVIII.1; *T. Benjamin* X.3-5)

T. Levi XIII.1. And now, my children, I charge you to reverence our Lord wholeheartedly, and to walk in *sincerity according to all His Law. (2) Teach your children *to read so that they may have understanding throughout their lives as they make constant practice of reading the Law of God; (3) since anyone who has knowledge of God's Law will be honored, and will be no stranger, anywhere he goes. (4) Indeed, he will gain many friends in place of parents, and many men will wish to serve him and hear him teach Torah.

*haplotēs, cf. Reading 24.
*Literally, Deut. 6:6-7; "letters"; cf. 11:19.
Sirach 39:6-11; Wisd. Sol. 8:10ff.; Man. Disc. VI.6-7; I Tim. 4:13.

5. My children, practice righteousness upon earth so that you may find treasure in heaven; (6) and sow good things in your souls so that you may find them in your life. For if you sow bad things, you will reap every kind of trouble and distress. (7) Acquire wisdom in the fear of God with eagerness; because even if you are taken captive and cities are destroyed, and fields and gold and silver and every possession perish, no one can take away the wisdom from the wise, except the blindness of impiety and the hardening of sin; (8) for *it will become a lamp for him when he is up against adversaries, and even in an alien land and among enemies he will find a friend. (9) If he teaches and practices these things, he will become a throne companion of a king, just as happened to our brother Joseph.

Mark 10:21; Luke 12:33.
Hos. 8:7; Gal. 6:7.
Prov. 1:7; 4:1, 5, 7.
*Godly wisdom; Prov. 4:18; 6:23.

T. Judah XXVI.1. Therefore, my children, keep all the Law of the Lord, because there is hope for all those who keep a straight course in His way.

T. Dan V.1. So, my children, keep the commandments of the Lord and be observant of His Law. Keep far away from anger and hate falsehood, so that the Lord may dwell among you and Beliar may flee from you. (2) Each one must speak truth to his neighbor; and so you will not fall into sensual pleasure and distraction, but you will be in peace, possessing the God of

Zech. 8:16; Eph. 4:25; Col. 3:9.

Eph. 4:32; Col.
3:12-14;
I Peter 1:22;
2:17.

peace; and war will not overcome you. (3) Love the Lord all through your life, and one another with a true heart.

T. Asher VI.1. Take heed then, children, to the Lord's commandments, following the truth *unhypocritically. . . . (3) Keep the Law of the Lord and do not give heed to evil as to good; but pay constant attention to what is truly good, and carefully observe it in all the Lord's commandments, living in *it and resting in *Him.

*Literally,
''single-facedly.''

*The good of   *Possibly,
the Law.   ''it.''

T. Joseph XVIII.1. If then, my children, you also walk in the commandments of the Lord, He will exalt you in this world and will bless you with good things *for ever.

*Or, ''in the
(Coming)
Age.''

T. Benjamin X.3. So then, each of you must perform truth and righteousness with his neighbor, even judgment for establishing fidelity, and keep the Law of the Lord and His commandments. (4) For I am teaching you these things in place of any inheritance. So you, then, must give them to your children for an everlasting possession. (5) For all these things *they gave us, saying: Keep the commandments of God until the Lord reveals His salvation to all the nations.

Zech. 8:16;
Isa. 42:3; LXX;
Man. Disc.
I.3-5; John
3:21; Eph.
4:25; I John
1:6.

*The
Patriarchs,
Gen. 18:19.

Isa. 40:5;
46:13; 56:1.

III. Judea Under Rome
(ca. 69 B.C.-A.D. 70)

A. Historical Sketch: from John Hyrcanus II to Herod I (selections from Josephus' Jewish War I; cf. his Antiquities of the Jews, Books XIII through XVII, for greater detail.)

1. STRUGGLE FOR CONTROL: Aristobulus II versus Hyrcanus II and Antipater the Idumean (War I.117-40)

117 (4). Alexandra now became ill and her younger son Aristobulus seized his opportunity. Aided by his followers . . . he took possession of all the fortresses and, with the money he found in them, recruited a mercenary force and proclaimed himself king. (118) Hyrcanus' complaints at these actions moved his mother's compassions, and she imprisoned Aristobulus' wife and children in *Antonia. . . . (119) But before Alexandra could move against Aristobulus for deposing his brother she died, after a reign of nine years.

*The tower fortress on the north side of the Temple area. Cf. sec. 401, below.

120 (vi.1). Hyrcanus . . . was *sole heir to the throne, but he was surpassed by Aristobulus in strength and determination. When a battle for the crown took place near Jericho, most of Hyrcanus' troops deserted him for Aristobulus. (121) With those who remained with him, Hyrcanus hastily took refuge in Antonia, securing Aristobulus' wife and children as hostages for his safety. However, before any grievous harm was done the brothers came to terms: Aristobulus to be king, and Hyrcanus to abdicate the throne but to enjoy all his other honors as the king's brother. (122) The reconciliation on these terms took place in the Temple. In the presence of the spectators they cordially embraced each other. They then exchanged residences, Aristobulus moving into the palace, Hyrcanus withdrawing to the house of Aristobulus.

*So named by Alexandra while she lived.

123 (2). When Aristobulus unexpectedly gained the advantage, fear fell on his opponents, especially on Antipater, an old and bitterly hated foe. An *Idumean by race, his ancestry, wealth and other powers gave him a *leading position in the nation. (124) He now persuaded Hyrcanus to seek refuge with Aretas, king of Arabia, with a view to recovering his kingdom. At the same time, he urged Aretas to receive Hyrcanus and to reinstate him on the throne. Defaming Aristobulus while praising Hyrcanus, he urged the appropriateness on the part of the ruler of so resplendent a realm of giving aid to one who was unjustly treated—and Hyrcanus had indeed suffered

*Edomite.

*By annexing Edom and making its populace Jews by force, John Hyrcanus I had made it possible for Idumeans to get a foothold in Judean politics.

injustice, robbed of the throne which by right of the first-born belonged to him.

125. When he had thus *prepared both parties, one night Antipater fled from the city with Hyrcanus and, traveling swiftly, safely reached Petra, the capital of the *Arabian kingdom. (126) There he put Hyrcanus in Aretas' hands. Winning him over with much talk and beguiling him with many gifts, Antipater persuaded the king to give him a force of fifty thousand, both infantry and cavalry, with which to reinstate Hyrcanus. Aristobulus was unable to resist this army: he was defeated in the first engagement. He was driven into Jerusalem (127) and would have been taken by force if Scaurus the Roman general (who intervened at just this time) had not raised the siege. . . .

128 (3). So as soon as he entered Jewish territory, deputations from the brothers arrived, each begging his assistance. Three hundred talents offered by Aristobulus took precedence over justice: having received so much, Scaurus sent a messenger to Hyrcanus and the Arabs with the threat of a visitation from the Romans and Pompey if they did not raise the siege. (129) Terrified, Aretas withdrew from Judea to *Philadelphia, and Scaurus returned to Damascus.

130. It was not enough for Aristobulus not to be defeated, however, so he assembled all his forces and pursued the enemy. He fought them in the vicinity of a place called Papyron, and killed upwards of six thousand. Among these was Phallion, Antipater's brother.

131 (4). Deprived of Arab assistance, Hyrcanus and Antipater transferred their hopes to the *Romans: when Pompey entered Syria and reached Damascus, they sought refuge with him. Coming without presents and employing those pleas for justice which they had used with Aretas, they kept urging him to indicate his hatred of Aristobulus' violence by restoring the reign to the one to whom it belonged by character and seniority. (132) Nor was Aristobulus to be outdone. Trusting in his bribery of Scaurus, he too appeared decked out in the utmost of regal style. But he felt it demeaning to play the courtier, and he could not endure serving his ends in a humbler way than his dignity demanded; so at *Dion he departed.

133 (5). Pompey was indignant at this and, urged on by the entreaties of Hyrcanus' friends, he hastened after Aristobulus with the Roman forces and many of his Syrian auxiliaries. (134) Passing Pella and Scythopolis, he came to Coreae. (Here,

*I.e., to co-operate in his schemes.

*The Nabateans, who controlled the desert fringe from Damascus to Petra in Edom.

Scaurus had been sent into Syria by Pompey. He marched southward when he got word of matters in Judea.

*Modern Amman in Jordan.

*Literally, "the opposites."

*One of the towns of Decapolis, east of the Sea of Galilee.

for one *going up into the interior, Judean territory begins.) There he heard that Aristobulus had entered Alexandreion, a most lavishly equipped fortress on a high mountain, for safety; and he sent the latter orders to come down. (135) Aristobulus had the impulse to brave the risk rather than to obey this imperious summons; but he saw that the people were fearful, and his friends advised him to reflect on the invincible power of the Romans. Persuaded by them, he came down to Pompey and, after arguing at length the rights of his claim to the throne, returned to his stronghold. (136) At his brother's invitation he came down and discussed the rights of his case, then withdrew unhindered by Pompey. . . . (137) Finally, Pompey commanded him to give up the *fortresses. Since he knew that the governors had orders to obey only those orders written in Aristobulus' own hand, he compelled Aristobulus to write each of them a notice to evacuate. Aristobulus did as ordered, but angrily withdrew to Jerusalem and prepared to fight against Pompey.

*From the Jordan; cf. maps of the area.

*Alexandreion and others held by Aristobulus partisans.

138 (6). Pompey allowed him no time for preparations, but followed him up immediately. . . . (139) At Jericho, Pompey encamped for an evening only and at daybreak went on to Jerusalem. In panic at his approach, Aristobulus met him as a suppliant. By the promise of money and of the surrender of the city and of himself, he mitigated Pompey's irritation. (140) However, none of these agreements were fulfilled; for the partisans of Aristobulus refused to admit Gabinius, who had been dispatched to receive the promised money, into the city.

2. POMPEY BESIEGES JERUSALEM AND TAKES IT (War I. 141-54)

141 (vii.1). Indignant at this affront, Pompey kept Aristobulus under guard and, advancing to the city, he carefully looked around it to see how best to attack it. He noted the stoutness of the walls and how difficult it would be to assault them; also the formidable ravine in front of them; also that *within the ravine the Temple was so stoutly walled that even were the town captured, it would be a second refuge for the defenders.

*The Kidron valley on the east, joined by the Hinnom vale coming down from the west and south of the wall; cf. a good diagram of the city for this period.

142 (2). However, while he remained undecided, dissent arose among those within the walls. Partisans of Aristobulus insisted on fighting and trying to rescue the king, while those of Hyrcanus were for opening the gates to Pompey. Fear caused by their observing Roman discipline made many of *these. (143) Aristobulus' faction, discomfited, withdrew into the Temple. They cut the bridge which connected it to the city, and got ready to hold out to the last. The others admitted the

*I.e., who sided with Hyrcanus.

*City and
palace.

Romans to the city and delivered up the palace. (144) Pompey sent Peison, an undergeneral, with troops to occupy *them. The officer posted squads about the town and, since he failed to persuade any of the refugees in the Temple to come to terms, he prepared the environs for an assault. For this, he had the willing advice and services of Hyrcanus' partisans.

145 (3). Pompey was on the north slope, filling up the moat and the whole of the ravine with materials that the troops gathered. It was most difficult to fill that limitless depth, with the Jews hindering in every way from above. (146) Indeed, the labors of the Romans would have remained endless, but that Pompey took advantage of the Sabbaths, on which the Jews refrain from all manual labor for religious reasons. He raised the earthworks, but restrained his troops from fighting, for on the Sabbaths the Jews fight only in self-defense. (147) When the ravine was filled up, he set up tall assault-towers on the earthworks, brought up the battering machines which had been conveyed from Tyre, and tried them out against the walls while catapults repulsed interference from above. However, the *towers on this side, which were unusual both in size and beauty, long withstood the blows.

Cf. I Macc.
2:41.

*Of the wall.

148 (4). While the Romans were enduring these difficulties, Pompey greatly admired the perseverance of the Jews, especially because they omitted nothing of their religious duties, though in the midst of missiles. Just as if deep peace prevailed in the city, the daily sacrifices, sin-offerings and every ritual of divine worship were performed to the letter. On the day when the Temple was taken, when they were being slain around the altar, the priests never ceased from the prescribed daily rites. . . .

152 (6). Nothing of all the calamities of that time more deeply affected the nation as that the Holy Place, formerly hidden from view, was exposed to the eyes of aliens. Pompey indeed, with his staff, went into the sanctuary (into which none but the high priest was authorized to go) and looked at what was there: the candlestick and its lamps, the table, and libation vessels and censers. There were also a large quantity of spices and about two thousand talents of sacred money. (153) However, he did not touch this or any other of the sacred treasures; but the day after the capture of the Temple, he ordered the custodians to cleanse it and to celebrate the traditional sacrifices. He proclaimed Hyrcanus as high priest again, in return for the latter's willing aid during the siege (particularly for drawing away the many in the rural areas who were

Cf. Lev. 16:1ff.

Pompey
refrains from
plundering the
Temple.

Hyrcanus
reinstated.

inclined to fight for Aristobulus). In this way . . . by good
will more than through fear, he won over the people. (154)
Aristobulus' *father-in-law . . . was among the prisoners. ·Also Aristobulus' uncle.
Pompey executed those who were principally responsible for
the conflict. . . . Both Judea and Jerusalem were placed under
tribute.

3. ANTIPATER CONSOLIDATES HIS GAINS (War I. 187-203)

Hyrcanus, directed by Antipater, assisted Pompey in subsequent military operations as a means of showing good faith. They supported Pompey's cause in his struggle with Julius Caesar. Aristobulus (who, hoping to
gain, championed Caesar from the start) was poisoned by Pompey's partisans.

187 (3). When Pompey died, Antipater changed sides again
and began to serve Caesar.

(Josephus here gives details of how Antipater assisted partisans of Julius
Caesar in an assault upon Egypt. Antipater was much praised to Caesar by
the general of the Roman forces, one Mithridates.)

193 (5). Caesar, indeed, encouraged Antipater by praises and
*expectations to further daring in his interest. In every battle ·I.e., of reward.
Antipater was the boldest of fighters. He was frequently
wounded and bore the marks of his valor on almost every part
of his body. (194) When Caesar had finally settled matters in
Egypt and returned to Syria, he bestowed on Antipater the
privilege of Roman citizenship with exemption from taxes,
and by other honors and courtesies made him an enviable
man. To please him, Caesar confirmed Hyrcanus' appointment to the high priesthood.

In about 47 B.C. Antigonus, son of the ill-fated Aristobulus II, presented
his claims before Caesar but was rebutted by Antipater, who displayed his
wounds as proof of his loyalty to Caesar (cf. above; II Cor. 11:24ff.; Gal.
6:17). He pointed out that Antigonus' father had really been an enemy of
Rome and a troublemaker, just as Antigonus now was.

199 (3). Having heard these things, Caesar pronounced Hyrcanus the more deserving of the high priesthood, and gave
Antipater a choice of *offices. Leaving it with *him who gave ·Literally, "powers." ·I.e., Caesar.
the honor to determine the measure of the honor, Antipater
was then appointed procurator of all Judea. He also obtained
the right to rebuild the walls of the city that had been destroyed. (200) Caesar sent orders to Rome that these honors be
engraved in the Capitol as a memorial of his own justice and of
Antipater's valor.

Thus empowered, Antipater made a pacification tour of Judea, urging the populace to accept Hyrcanus and refrain from supporting any attempted insurrection. He warned them Rome would not allow an appointee of Caesar to be removed without reprisals.

> 203. . . . But while he spoke thus he assumed general control of the country, since Hyrcanus was indolent and lacking the energy needed for administration. So he appointed Phasael, his eldest son, as governor of Jerusalem and its environs; and he sent his second son, Herod (though but a mere youth), with equal authority to Galilee.

4. HEROD BECOMES "KING OF THE JEWS" (War I.281-401)

Herod energetically curbed a notorious band of brigands who were harassing Galilee, and vigorously pacified the district. By such actions he increased in power. He endured several vicissitudes, including the famous power struggles of Mark Antony and Octavian against Julius Caesar's murderers, on the one hand, and the Parthian invasion of Palestine, on the other. The latter was instigated by Antigonus (cf. above). Herod's brother Phasael was killed and Hyrcanus was displaced by Antigonus, who became a puppet of the Parthians. Herod himself narrowly escaped death at their hands, making his way with difficulty to Rome.

*Masada, south on the east shore of the Dead Sea.

> 281 (3). . . . He went immediately to Antony, his father's friend. He told him the story of his own and his family's misfortunes, how he had left his nearest relatives in a besieged *fortress and sailed for help in stormy weather.

*On the occasion of the earlier invasion of Egypt; cf. sec. 187, above.

> 282 (4). Antony's compassion was moved at his change of fortune. Moved by the memory of Antipater's *hospitality, but above all by the outstanding merit of the man who stood before him, he decided on the spot to have him appointed king of the Jews—this one whom he himself had formerly appointed tetrarch. No less than the high regard he held for Herod was the strong aversion he had toward Antigonus, whom he considered seditious and Rome's enemy.

*Octavian ("Augustus").

> 283. *Caesar proved a yet more ready champion than was Antony. He recalled Antipater's hospitality and unswerving loyalty in the Egyptian campaigns as he contemplated Herod and read his energetic character. (284) So he convened the Senate to which Messala, seconded by Atratinus, presented Herod and dwelt on the services rendered by his father and his own good will towards the Roman people. At the same time they proved that Antigonus was their enemy, not only from the former quarrel which they had had with him, but

because he had also just been guilty of contempt of Rome in accepting his crown from the Parthians.

These words stirred the Senate, and when Antony came forward and said that in anticipation of war with Parthia it was expedient that Herod be king, they all voted for approval. (285) The meeting was adjourned and Antony and Caesar left the senate house. Herod walked between them . . . as they went to offer sacrifice and to lay up the decree in the Capitol. On this, the *first day of his reign, Herod was given a banquet by Antony.   •In 40 B.C.

Herod returned to Palestine and rescued his family from Masada where they had been besieged by Antigonus' forces. Then with Roman help, he finally regained control of Judea and Jerusalem. He captured Antigonus, who was sent to Antony and executed. When the Temple was taken, Herod bought off the Roman soldiers to prevent their pillaging it.

He remained loyal to Antony during the latter's struggle with Octavian, although he both despised and feared Cleopatra, who tried to ensnare him. He also subdued the Nabatean Arabs who invaded his territory for plunder following an earthquake. This was about the same time as the Battle of Actium, 31, B.C., the conclusion of which left Octavian sole ruler of the Roman Empire. The student should review the history of this period, so important for Christian beginnings, in some detail.

386 (XX.1). But once he was through *this, Herod was immediately concerned about his personal situation, since he was Antony's friend, and Antony had been defeated by Caesar at Actium. . . . (387) The *king nevertheless decided to meet the danger head-on. He sailed to Rhodes, where *Caesar was spending some time, and presented himself without a diadem, like a commoner in dress and general appearance, but with the self-confident bearing of a king.   •The war with the Arabs.   •Herod.   •Octavian.   Ca 30 B.C.

Prior to his journey, Herod found occasion to have the now aged Hyrcanus II executed on charges of conspiring with the Arabs. At Rhodes, before Octavian, Herod frankly admitted his friendship and support of Antony. He also pointed out that he had advised Antony to dispose of Cleopatra. Resting his hope of safety on his own integrity, he asked that Caesar consider not so much *whose* friend but *how loyal* he had been.

391 (2). To this Caesar replied: "On the contrary, your safety and kingship are more than ever assured. One who so stands by friendship is worthy to rule over many subjects. Only try to remain loyal to *those who have been more fortunate; for indeed, I have the most splendid hopes for your aspirations. Antony did well, however, to let Cleopatra rather than you persuade him, for we have gained you through his folly. (392) But, it seems, you have already done me a good turn; for   •I.e., himself, the Caesar.

> Quintus Didius wrote me that you sent him military assist-
> ance against the gladiators. Therefore, I am now announcing
> the confirmation of your kingship to you by decree. Later I
> shall try to confer some further benefit on you, so that you may
> not feel the loss of Antony."
>
> 393 (3). Thus Caesar treated the king in a kindly way and
> placed the diadem on his head. Then he made the conferral
> public by a decree in which he generously praised this man
> whom he had so honored.

Herod lavishly entertained Octavian and fully provisioned his troops for
their march to Egypt and back. For this, and in return for other services,
Octavian began to add to Herod's territory and rank until he became, in
effect, procurator of all Syria.

> 400. . . . But what was better to Herod than all these ad-
> vancements was that in Caesar's friendship he was next after
> *Agrippa, in Agrippa's next after Caesar. After this he forged
> ahead to the greatest prosperity; yet his purpose was to trans-
> cend it, and his magnanimity was principally exerted toward
> *works of piety.

*Caesar's chief
confidant and
assistant.

*Subsidizing   Judea and
public works in elsewhere.

> 401 (XXI.1). Thus, in the fifteenth year of his reign, he began
> to repair the Temple. *By raising new foundation walls, he
> enlarged it to double its former area. Such immense sums
> were expended on it that its opulence was never surpassed.
> For evidence were the great colonnades which were around
> the sacred area, and the fortress on the north side. Herod
> reconstructed the colonnades from the foundations up. The
> fortress he restored at lavish expense so that it was in no way
> inferior to a palace; and he called it Antonia in honor of
> Antony.

*Ca. 20-19
B.C.; cf. John
2:20.

Cf. Mark
13:1-2; Luke
21:5-6.

Cf. John
10:23.

For the rest of Herod I's reign, historical introductions to New Testament
times and literature should be consulted. Since more of this history (especially for the life of Christ) is dealt with in such introductions, the historical
sketch will conclude here. Historical notes will be inserted along the way
wherever deemed appropriate or necessary.

B. Literature of the Times (Before Jesus's Birth)

The main extant documents from the early Roman period in Palestine
prior to Jesus' birth are the collection known as the *Psalms of Solomon* (or, *of
the Pharisees*). After careful study several scholars agree in dating none of
them later than about 40 B.C., while the earlier ones reflect the times of
Pompey's capture of Jerusalem. They faithfully represent the religious
beliefs and general outlook of Judaic piety in those times, hence their
importance for New Testament studies.

1. HASMONEAN DECADENCE AND DECLINE

READING 43: The prosperity, self-confidence and secret sins of Jerusalem (*Ps. Sol.* I)

This psalm seems to have been composed as a sort of introduction to the collection and it sets the general tone. In it the "I" seems to be Jerusalem, personified.

1. I called loudly to the Lord when I was afflicted to the utmost, to God when sinners set upon me.

Cf. II Macc. 14:15; Ps. 86:7; 118:5.

2. Suddenly an outcry of conflict was heard *in my presence. "He will hear me [I said] because I am full of righteousness."

*"In front of me" = before the walls. Ps. 34:15-17.

3. I reckoned in my heart that I was full of justice, since I was thriving and had many children.

Deut. 28:2ff.

4. Their wealth was distributed throughout the land, and their honor spread from end to end of it. (5) They were exalted to the stars. They said: "We will never fall."

Ps. 30:6.

6. But they acted insolently in their prosperity, and they had no anxious cares.

Ps. 10:3ff.; 73:3-12.

7. They sinned in secret places, and I did not know about it.

II Kings 17:9ff.; Isa. 29:15; Ezek. 8:6-12; Job 24:13-17.

8. Their lawless deeds exceeded those of the nations *who preceded them: they polluted by defilement the holy things of the Lord.

*In the land. Cf. Ezek. 5:5-6; 16:46-52.

Comment:

The psalm expresses the orthodox "deuteronomic" viewpoint in regard to divine rewards and punishments. On the basis of Deut. 28:1ff. and similar passages, the prosperity of a growing populace was generally taken as evidence that Jerusalem was righteous in God's sight. However, on the basis of Deut. 28:15ff. and other prophetic teaching, the sudden sounds of war and assault were regarded as a sign that all was not really well: somebody had sinned, if not overtly, then certainly in secret. It is the same argument that the three friends used against Job.

The author(s) of this and *Ps. Sol.* II. VIII, and XVII knows who the culprits are. The "many children" of Jerusalem whose wealth and prestige were increased and widespread, and who boasted of their security, refers no doubt to the Hasmonean aristocracy and their supporters. As the following psalms make clear, the writer(s) sees little difference in the conduct of these decadent descendants of the Maccabeans and that of the hellenizing priests of pre-Maccabean and Maccabean times.

READING 44: Hypocritical perverters of justice (*Ps. Sol.* IV. 1-8)

Superscription: "Discourse of Solomon, to the men-pleasers"

*Gk.,
sunedrion = "sanhedrin."
Isa. 29:13;   Mark 7:6.

Cf. I Kings
16:2; Jer. 25:7; 44:8.

Deut. 13:8-10.

*For justice.
John 8:7;
Rom. 2:1-4.

1. Why, O profane man, do you sit in the *council of the pious while your heart stands afar from the Lord, provoking the God of Israel to anger by your iniquities? (2) Wordy and censorious, in judgment he condemns sinners harshly; (3) and, as if in *zeal, he is the first to vote against the sinner, yet he himself is guilty of all kinds of sins and incontinence.

Jer. 7:8-9;
Matt. 5:27-28.
Num. 30:2;
Zech. 8:17.

4. He eyes any and every woman lustfully; he makes contracts with perfidious oaths;

Job 24:15; Isa.
29:15; John 3:19-20.
Prov. 6:12-14.

5. he sins at night and in hidden places as if unseen; his eyes talk to every woman of evil trysts.

Cf. Deut.
28:27, 58-61.

6. O God, take away by corruption of flesh and destitution of life those who live in hypocrisy with the pious.

Cf. II Sam.
12:12.

7. Disclose, O God, the works of men-pleasers; expose their deeds to ridicule and derision.

Mal. 3:5.

8. And may the pious justify the judgment of their God when He takes sinners away from the presence of the righteous, when He removes a man-pleaser who talks about the Law with guile.

READING 45: Illegitimate and cruel rulers (*Ps. Sol.* XVII.1-20)

Superscription: "A psalm of [for] Solomon with song, concerning the King"

Ps. 29:10;
74:12; 145:1.
Ps. 34:2; 44:8;
Jer. 9:24.

1. Lord, you yourself are our King for ever and ever; so in you, O God, we will take pride.

Ps. 90:9-12;
39:4-6.
Ps. 38:15;
39:7; 42:5, 11.

2. And what is the time of a man's life on earth? According to his time, so also is his hope in it.

Ps. 106:21;
Isa. 45:15;
49:26; 60:16.

*I.e., the   Dan. 2; 7:2-18;
expected   Zeph. 2:1-15;
messianic age. 3:8.

3. Yet we hope in God our Savior, because the might of our God is for ever with mercy, and the kingdom of our God is over the nations in justice *into the Age.

II Sam. 7:8-16;
Ps. 89:3-4,
19-37; Jer.
23:5.

4. You, O Lord, chose David as king over Israel, and you swore to him forever concerning his seed, not to let his dynasty be removed from your presence.

*The
Hasmoneans:
John
Hyrcanus I
expelled the
Pharisees from
the national
council.

5. But because of our sins, sinners rose against us; *they to whom you made no promise set upon us and drove us out; they took away violently, and did not glorify your worthy Name with praise.

6. They placed a royal palace opposite their *high place: they desolated David's throne in the arrogance of this change.

*The Temple. of living. They The built a palace Hasmoneans west of the assumed royal Temple area. rank and style

7. But you, O God, will destroy them and remove their offspring from the earth by arousing against them a man *foreign to our race.

*Probably, Pompey.

8. Repay them according to their sins, O God; let them receive according to their works.

Job 34:11; Ps. Lam. 3:64. 28:4; 62:12; Prov. 11:31; 65:6-7; Rom 24:12; Isa. 2:6.

9. Show no mercy to them, O God; search out their offspring and leave not one to them.

Ps. 21:10; 34:16; 37:28; Prov. 2:22.

10. The Lord is faithful in all His judgments that He performs upon the earth.

Ps. 19:9; 36:5-6; 119:75, 137; Isa. 26:9; 49:7.

11. The*Wicked One desolated our land of its inhabitants; he destroyed youth, elders and children all.

*Possibly cruelly Alexander massacred the Janneus, who Pharisees, who was hated by resolutely the pious. He opposed him.

12. In his burning wrath he sent them away as far as *the west, and the leaders of the land he subjected to mockery, and he did not spare.

*Perhaps to Rome, as slaves.

13. In foreignness the Enemy worked insolence, and his heart was foreign to our God.

14. And everything that he did in Jerusalem was just as Gentiles do in their mighty wars.

15. And the sons of the covenant prevailed over *them, while mingling among the Gentiles. There was none among them practicing mercy and truth in Jerusalem.

*Probably, Hasmoneans Gentiles. The all had dealings Maccabean with Gentiles. brothers and the

16. Those who loved the assemblies of the pious ones fled from them; as sparrows from their nest they flew away.

Cf. I Macc. 2:29. Cf. Isa. 16:2.

17. They wandered in deserts to save themselves from harm; and precious in the eyes of a *sojourner was one of them who was saved.

Cf. Ps. 34:6; Heb. 107:4-7; Ezek. 11:38. *One of the Judea. Cf. Jewish I Peter 1:1, dispersion RV/ASV. outside of

18. Their scattering by the lawless occurred in all the land, so that heaven stopped raining on the land.

Cf. I Macc. 9:24; Deut. 11:17; Ps. Sol. II.9-10.

19. Everflowing springs out of the deep, from high mountains, were stopped because none among them practiced righteousness and justice.

Amos 4:7-8; 7:4.

20. From their rulers even to the least of the people they committed every kind of sin: the king in transgression, the judge by disobedience, the people in sin.

Zeph. 3:2-4; Jer. 5:25-28; Ezek. 22:23-27.

Comment:

Review the Historical Sketches and I Maccabees. The author writes from a partisan, probably Pharisaic, viewpoint. References to persons whom the pious oppose—or fear—are somewhat unclear. In vv. 1-10 the author leads up to the justified retribution which, in his view, will overtake (or has overtaken) rulers whom he considers illegitimate and cruel. In the verses following he reverts to earlier history to add further justification for the judgment visited upon them.

The Hasmoneans had no legitimate claim to the Davidic throne nor, really, to the high priestly office. Yet John Hyrcanus I's successors openly claimed the royal title. The author sees just retribution against them in the person of the "man foreign to our race"—probably Pompey, who deported Aristobulus II and his family to Rome. Aristobulus and leading members of his family finally met death at Roman hands (vv. 7-10; cf. the Historical Sketch, above).

In vv. 11ff., the "Wicked One" (if different from "the Enemy") may refer to Antiochus IV Epiphanes. "The Enemy" (vv. 13-14) is almost certainly Alexander Janneus, whom the pious considered no true high priest, not even a true Jew and as wicked as any of their gentile oppressors. The remaining verses characterize the whole troubled period, from the beginning of the Maccabean revolt.

READING 46a: Judgment by invasion (*Ps. Sol.* VIII.1-24)

Superscription: "For Solomon, concerning strife"

Cf. *Ps. Sol.*
I.2, Reading 43.

Cf. Jer. 4:19-21.

1. Affliction and a noise of war my ear heard, the sound of a trumpet pealing out slaughter and ruin;

Cf. Isa.
17:12-13.
Cf. Jer.
4:11-12.

2. a sound of many people as of a violent wind, as a fiery tempest rushing through a desert. (3) And I said in my heart: "Where, then, will God judge him?"

Cf. Isa. 52:1;
Matt. 4:5; Rev.
21:2.

4. I heard a noise within Jerusalem, the holy city.

Cf. Dan. 5:6;
Ezek. 7:17;
21:7; Job 4:14.
*Or, "linen
cloth."

5. My loins were afflicted at the sound, my knees were weakened, my heart became fearful, my bones were shaken like a *piece of string.

Cf. *Ps. Sol.*
I.2-3, Reading 43.
Ps. 77:12-14;
119:52; 143:5.
Ps. 18:30a;
19:9; 51:4b.

6. I said: "They will make their ways straight by righteousness." (7) I pondered the judgments of God from the creation of heaven and earth; I justified God in His judgments from ages past.

Cf. II Sam.
12:12.

8. God exposed their sins before the sun; all the earth knows the righteous judgments of God.

Cf. *Ps. Sol.*
I.7, Reading 43.
*I.e.,
sexually,
cf. Lev. 18:6ff.

9. In subterranean hide-aways they committed their iniquities in provocation of God, son *mingling with mother, and father with daughter.

10. Each committed adultery with his neighbor's wife: they made *solemn agreement with them about these matters. ^{Cf. Jer. 5:7-8; 29:23.} ^{*Literally, "with an oath."}

11. They plundered the holy things of God as if they were not the inheritance of the redeemed.

12. They trod the altar of the Lord after committing every kind of filthiness, and by menstrual blood they defiled the sacrifices, as if they were common meat. ^{Cf. II Macc. 6:3-5.} ^{Cf. Lev. 15:19ff.}

13. There was no sin which they did not do more than the Gentiles. ^{Cf. Ps. Sol. 1.8, Reading 43.}

14. For this cause, God poured out to them a spirit of erring; He made them drink a cup of strong wine to make them drunk. (15) He brought *one from the end of the earth, the one smiting powerfully. He decreed war on Jerusalem and on her land. ^{Cf. Isa. 29:10. Jer. 25:15-16; Ezek. 23:32-33; Hab. 2:16.} ^{*Pompey; "from the end [west] of the earth" = Rome.}

16. The princes of the land met him with joy. They said: "Your way is desired. Hither! Enter in peace." ^{Cf. Historical Sketch, above.}

17. They smoothed rough roads for his entrance, they opened the gates to Jerusalem, they adorned her walls.

18. He entered as a father into the house of his sons, in peace; he set his feet in great firmness.

19. He seized the towered fortresses and the wall of Jerusalem, because God led him with security against their error. (20) He destroyed their rulers and everyone wise in counsel; he poured out the blood of those inhabiting Jerusalem as unclean water. (21) He led away their sons and daughters, whom they had begotten in defilement. ^{Cf. Ps. 79:2-3. I Macc. 7:17.}

22. They did according to their unclean ways just as their fathers: they defiled Jerusalem and the things consecrated to the name of God.

23. God is vindicated in His judgments among the nations of the earth; and the saints of God are as innocent lambs among them. (24) Praised be God who judges all the earth in His righteousness!

Comments:

    1. General features of the entrance into Jerusalem by the forces of Antiochus IV Epiphanes—cf. I Macc. 1:29-37; II Macc. 5:23-26—and of that by Pompey about a century later are similar enough to make interpretation of the personal references in this psalm somewhat difficult. However, v. 15 seems to point more strongly toward Pompey.

    2. If the references are to the times of Antiochus IV, then vv. 8ff. relate to

the venal, hellenizing priesthood described in I and II Maccabees. If they are taken to be of Pompey's time, then the author is describing the later Hasmoneans as being just as guilty of the same kinds of defiance of the Mosaic Law as were those earlier priests. In any event, he believes that they have received the judgment which their violation of the levitical ordinances deserved. His viewpoint on these matters agrees with that of the Qumran Essenes.

READING 46b: The invader judged (*Ps. Sol.* II.1-4, 15-32)

The omitted verses of the psalm give some details of the desolation of Jerusalem and the reasons for it: God's judgment on the corruption of the priesthood as described in the preceding psalm and in I Maccabees 1:14-15; II Maccabees 4:13ff.; 6:3-5; and Reading 34.

Superscription: "Concerning Jerusalem"

*Cf. I Macc.
4:60.

Cf. Historical
Sketch, above.

1. When the sinner exalted himself, he cast down *strong fortifications with a battering-ram and was not hindered. (2) Alien peoples went up to your altar and trampled it arrogantly with their feet.

Cf. II Macc. 6:3-5.

Cf. Ps. Sol.
VIII.9ff., Reading 46a

Cf. Jer. 7:15;
Hos. 9:17

3. Because the sons of Jerusalem polluted the holy things of the Lord—they profaned the offerings of God by lawless deeds—(4) therefore He said: "Cast them far away from me! I have no pleasure in them." . . .

Cf. Ps. Sol.
VIII.7, Reading
46a

Ps. 28:4;
62:12; Rom.
2:6.

15. I will vindicate you, O God, in uprightness of heart, because your justice is in your judgments, O God; (16) because you requited sinners according to their works, even according to heinous sins.

Ps. 90:8; Eccl.
12:14; Jer. 16:17-18.

Ps. 9:5; 37:20, 38.

*Literally, "will
not honor
face"; Rom.
2:11.

17. You disclosed their sins so that your justice might appear. You abolished their memorial from the land. (18) God is a righteous judge, and He *is without partiality.

Cf. Ps. 79:1-7

19. The Gentiles reproached Jerusalem by trampling her down; her beauty was dragged down from her throne of glory. (20) She put on sackcloth instead of lovely garments, and a band of rushes instead of a diadem.

Reference to
the well-built
walls with
attractive
towers.

21. The handsome girdle which God put around her was stripped off; her beauty was dishonored, cast off to the ground.

Cf. Ps. 83;
106:40-47.

Cf. Lam. 1:7c;
Ezek. 22:4.

22. And I saw and I implored the Lord; and I said: "Suffice it, O Lord, for your hand to be heavy upon Jerusalem by means of the gentile invasion, (23) for they mock and spare not in wrath and hostile anger; and they will make an end of her

unless you, O Lord, rebuke them in your wrath. (24) For they act not in *zeal, but in covetousness they pour out their wrath on us by plundering us. (25) Do not delay, O God, to repay them upon their heads, to *change the arrogance of the Dragon into dishonor."

*Ps. 85:4-7; Isa. 1:9.

*I.e., for God's will or justice.

Cf. Isa. 66:6; Ezek. 11:21.

*Literally, "speak, command."

26. And I did not wait long until God showed me his insolence pierced upon the hills of Egypt, despised more than the least thing upon land or sea, (27) his body scattered upon the waves in much shame; and no one gave it burial, because God brought him to naught in dishonor.

28. He did not consider that he was only *man, and he did not reckon with what would come later.

*And not God. cf. Ezek. 28:2; Dan. 4:28-32.

29. He said: "I myself will be lord of land and sea," and he did not understand that God is great, mighty in His great power.

30. He is king above the heavens and judges kings and rulers— (31) He who *raises me to glory and who puts arrogant ones to sleep in disgrace for eternal destruction because they have not know Him.

Dan. 2:21, 37ff.; 4:24-25, 34-35.

*Also translated "resurrects."

Cf. Dan. 12:2, LXX; John 5:25-29.

32. Now behold, O great ones of the earth, the judgment of the Lord, because He is a great and righteous king, judging what is under heaven.

Comments:

1. This psalm seems less ambiguous in its references to Pompey than the preceding. Vv. 1-2 agree with the description of his siege and assault upon Jerusalem. Also, vv. 26-27 agree with accounts of how Pompey met his death in 48 B.C. Trying to escape from Julius Caesar, he was assassinated as he was about to disembark at Pelusium, Egypt.

2. The outlook of these psalms regarding foreign invaders is in agreement with that of the O. T. prophets: God sets over the nations whom He will. When His people sin, He uses these rulers and their armies to chastise the holy people. Yet, because they act from self-interest and do not acknowledge or glorify God, His judgment falls upon such invaders, too, in due time. Cf. Isa. 10:5-19; Dan. 4—5; Hab. 1—2.

2. PERSONAL PIETY AND HOPE

READING 47: The righteousness of the "pious" (Ps. Sol. III and VI)

Superscription: "Concerning the righteous"

III.1. Why are you sleeping, O soul, and not blessing the Lord? Sing a new hymn to God the Praiseworthy!

Cf. Jonah 1:6

Ps. 33:3; 18:3; 105:1-6.

*Or, "on His watch"; Col. 5:19; Col. 4:2; I Cor. 3:16. 16:13, Eph.

2. Sing psalms and keep alert *on watch for Him, for a psalm to God from a good heart is appropriate.

Ps. 19:9; 119:13, 39. *Or, "judgments."

3. The righteous ones remember the Lord always, by confession and vindication of the Lord's *decrees.

Prov. 3:11.

4. The righteous will not disregard it when disciplined by the Lord. It is his good pleasure to be in the presence of the Lord always.

Ps. 16:8-11.

Ps. 51:4.

5. When the righteous stumbles he justifies the Lord; when he falls, he ponders what God will do for him; he considers whence his salvation will come.

Ps. 37:23-24.

Ps. 121:1-2.

Ps. 108:1-6. 112:6-8.

6. The stedfastness of the righteous is from the God of their salvation: sin upon sin does not lodge in the house of a righteous person. (7) The righteous man always inspects his house so as to remove *guilt occasioned by his trespass. (8) He expiates sins of ignorance by fasting and humbling his soul; and the Lord cleanses every pious man and his house.

Sirach 5:4ff.

*Or, "offense." Cf. Lev. 4—5; Job 1:5. Ps. 19:12; cf. Num. 15:24ff. Lev. 4:2ff.; Ps. 51:7, 10.

9. When the sinner stumbles, he curses his life, the day of his birth, and his mother's birth labors.

Cf. Job 3.

10. He adds sin upon sin to his life. He falls and, since his fall is grievous, he will not be *raised.

*Verb frequently used in sense of "resurrect"; cf. v. 12.

11. The destruction of the sinner is forever; and he will not be remembered when the righteous *are visited. (12) This is the lot of sinners for ever; but those who fear the Lord shall be raised to life eternal, and their life will be in the light of the Lord, and He will never abandon them.

*i.e., by God, for reward and blessing. Ps. 34:16; 37:10, 20; Jer. 13:24-25.

Dan. 12:2-3.

Ps. 36:9.

Deut. 31:6; Isa. 41:17; Heb. 13:5.

Comments:

1. This psalm presents a contrast between the righteous and the wicked, both individually and as a class. As in the canonical Psalms, this is a favorite theme in the *Psalms of Solomon* and in the Qumran *Thanksgiving Hymns*. A major difference is the clarity with which the hope of resurrection for the pious is expressed in these intertestamental psalms.

2. The theme of keeping alert/awake, or on watch (v. 2) recurs also in the N. T. and is expressed by the same word: cf. Matt. 24:42-43; 26:41; Acts 20:31; I Cor. 16:13; Col. 4:2; I Thess. 5:6; I Peter 5:8; Rev. 3:2-3; 16:15.

3. The notion of a person's "lot" (v. 12) was a strong tenet of Pharisaic piety, combining ideas of one's "station-in-life" and one's destiny, as well as earthly rewards and punishments. Final destiny was determined by one's response to God: faith and obedience, or lack of it. Within the community of faith, one's lot or station-in-life was a matter of God's decree (*Ps. Sol.* V.4, Reading 48) and it was the wisdom of piety to accept whatever that was. This notion quite probably lies behind Paul's counsel to Chris-

tians given in I Cor. 7:24: " . . . in whatever state each was called, there let him remain with God."

Superscription: "In hope—to [for] Solomon"

VI.1. Blessed is the man whose heart is prepared to call upon the name of the Lord: by remembering the name of the Lord he shall be saved. (2) His ways will be guided aright by the Lord, and the works of his hands are protected by the Lord his God.

Ps. 40:4; 112:1.

Joel 2:32; Rom. 10:13.
Ps. 23:3; 31:3; 32:8; 73:24.
Ps. 37:23.

3. He will not be agitated by seeing evil night visions. He will not be terrified in crossing rivers or by the tossing of seas.

Ps. 4:8.

Isa. 43:2.

4. He rises from sleep and blesses the name of the Lord. For quietness of heart he sings hymns to the name of his God, (5) and he beseeches the face of the Lord concerning all of his house.
For the Lord hearkens to the prayer of everyone who prays in fear of God; (6) and the Lord will fulfill every request of one who directs his hope toward Him.

Ps. 5:3; 59:16.

Isa. 26:3, RSV.

Job 1:5.

II Chron. 7:14; Ps. 4:3.
Ps. 37:4;   Matt. 7:7-8;
84:11;   I John
145:18-19;   5:14-15.

7. Blessed be the Lord who performs kindness for those who love Him stedfastly.

Ps. 5:11-12; 32:10;
103:1ff.,
107:1ff.

READING 48: Trust in God's providence (*Ps. Sol.* V)

1. O Lord my God, I will praise your Name with exultation among those who understand your righteous judgments (2) because you are good and merciful, the refuge of the poor. When I cry out to you, do not remain silent from me. (3) For no one can take booty from a mighty man; so who can take from all of what you have made unless you give it?

Ps. 9:1-2;   107:31-32;
22:22-23;   149:1.
35:18;

Ps. 9:9; 14:6;
46:1, 7, 11;
142:5.

Ps. 27:7; 28:1;
143:1; cf.
22:1.
Isa. 49:24;
Mark 3:27.

4. For a man and his lot are before you in a balance: one may not add to increase it contrary to your decision, O God.

Job 31:6; Prov. 16:2; Dan. 5:27.

5. When we are afflicted we will call upon you for aid, and you will not turn our petition aside, because you are our God.

Ps. 9:12; 18:6;
34:15; 40:1;
118:5.

6. Do not make your hand heavy upon us, lest we sin through distress. (7) And except you turn us again, we will not obtain; but to you we will come.

Cf. Ps. 32:4;
38:2, 39:10;
Job 23:2.
Cf. Ps. 80:3, 7,
19; 85:4; Jer.
31:18-19;
Lam. 5:21.

8. For if I hunger, to you I will cry out, O God, and you will give to me.

9. You nourish the fowls and the fishes by giving rain in the wilderness for *grass to spring up. (10) You prepare pasturage

*Or, 'herbage.'

Ps. 104:14-28;
145:15-16;
147:8-9.

in the wilderness for each living thing; and if they hunger, they will lift their faces to you.

Ps. 35:10;
40:17; 68:10;
72:2ff.

11. You nourish kings and princes and people, O God; and who is the hope of the poor and needy except you, O Lord? (12) And you will give heed; for who is so generous and benign to cheer the heart of the humble by opening his hand in mercy, except yourself?

13. The generosity of man is grudging and little, and if he gives a second time without grumbling, that also is amazing. (14) But your giving is plenteous with kindness and abundance, and whoever hopes in you will not be grudged a gift.

Ps. 37:4;
103:2ff.;
145:19.

(15) Your mercy in kindness is upon the whole earth, O Lord.

Prov. 28:20.

Prov. 28:22;
Luke 12:15;
Heb. 13:5.

Prov. 10:22;
Matt. 6:20-34.
Prov. 15:16;
19:1; cf. Phil.
4:11-12.

16. Blessed is the one whom God remembers with a moderate degree of sufficiency. If a man has too much, he commits offense. (17) Sufficient is moderate means with righteousness, for in this the blessing of the Lord tends to fulness in righteousness.

*Or,
"kingdom."
Ps. 5:2; 10:16;
24:10; 44:4;
74:12, etc.

18. May those who fear the Lord rejoice in good things; and may your kindness be upon Israel in your *reign. (19) Blessed be the glory of the Lord, for He is our King!

READING 49: May God judge wickedness and have mercy on His people (*Ps. Sol.* IV.9-25 and IX)

Cf. Reading 44
for the first part
of this Psalm.
*Because
crafty and
deceptive.
Cf. Ps. 35:20;
52:2; Prov.   10:6, 11;
                 12:5b-6a.

IV.9. Like those of a serpent, his eyes are fixed on a man's household, to impair the discernment of each by *iniquitous words. (10) His words are deceptive, for he intends a deed of wicked lust. He does not withdraw until he manages to scatter

Cf. Prov. 6:12.

Job 22:13; Ps.
10:3-11;
73:11; 94:7;
Isa. 29:15;
Sirach 16:17.

them just as if by bereavement, (11) and he desolates a house for the sake of his lawless desire. He deceives himself by saying that there is no one who sees or judges.

Prov. 1:31; Ps. 36:1-4; 52:3-4
Cf. Prov. 11:9a; 24:15.
*Or, "that   arouse
excite, or   passion."

12. He gets his satisfaction by this kind of unlawful activity; so his eyes select another house to destroy with *fickle words.

Prov. 27:20;
30:15b-16a;
Hab. 2:5.
*Cf. Reading 47,
Comment 3.

13. Like Hades, he is never sated by all this.

Ps. 5:6, 10;
35:8; 55:23;
73:18-20;
145:20.

Cf. Deut.
28:28.

14. May his *lot, O Lord, be in disgrace in your sight, his going out with groanings and his coming in with cursing. (15) May his life pass in griefs and penury and want. May his sleep be disquieted, may he awaken to perplexities. (16) May sleep be denied to him by night.

17. Let his every endeavor meet with dishonorable failure, and may his house lack everything by which he might satisfy his needs. (18) Until his death, may his old age be spent in the loneliness of childlessness. [Deut. 28:29. Prov. 11:18-21.] [Cf. Wisd. Sol. 3:16-19; Sirach 16:4.]

19. May the flesh of men-pleasers be scattered by wild beasts, and may the bones of the iniquitous be *disgracefully scattered in the sight of the sun. (20) May ravens pluck out the eyes of the hypocrites, because they ravaged the houses of many men disgracefully and scattered them in covetousness. (21) They did not remember nor did they fear God in any of these things. Instead they provoked and exasperated God (22) to take them off the earth, for they beguiled the *innocents by deceitful speech. [*To be refused burial was the ultimate dishonor.] [Cf. Prov. 30:17.] [Ps. 14:1-4; 36:1-4; 55:19; Rom. 3:13-18.] [*Or, guileless ones.]

23. Blessed are those who fear the Lord in their *innocence. The Lord will rescue them from deceitful men and from sinners, and from every *occasion of iniquity. [*Or, guilelessness, harmlessness.] [*Literally, stumbling block.]

24. May God take away those who practice every kind of sin highhandedly, because our God is a Great Judge and a Mighty Lord in righteousness. (25) O Lord, may your mercy come upon all those who love you. [Num. 15:30-31.]

Comment:

The pious poor were often the prey of the unscrupulous who had the means or the skill to take advantage of them. The kind of person who is described in the psalm is one all too well known to history and to contemporary society: a lustful person who has the power and prestige to accomplish his evil desires, preying upon lower class households. Suave, clever, perhaps handsome, he seduces the marriageable daughter, perhaps even the wife, while he manages to hold the husband either in the dark, or helpless through fear of slander or of economic or physical reprisal. When he has had all he can get from this game, he casts his hapless victims aside to begin all over again with another household. He walks through life leaving a trail of human wreckage behind. One can sympathize fully with the prayer for vengeance with which the psalm closes.

Superscription: "To Solomon—for reproof"

IX.1. When Israel was led into a foreign land into exile because they apostatized from the Lord who had redeemed them, they were rejected from the inheritance which the Lord gave to them. [Cf. Ps. Sol. VIII.21. Reading 46a.] [Cf. II Kings 17:13ff.] [Cf. Lev. 18:26-30.]

2. The dispersion of Israel is in every nation in accord with the word of God, so that you may be vindicated, O God, by your [Deut. 28:15-68. Neh. 9:26ff.]

Ps 50:6; Tobit 3:5ff
51:4b; 96:13.

Cf. Ps. Sol.
IV 24, above.

Ps. 139:1ff.
Sirach
17:14-15; Ps.
Sol. IV.11,
above.

Sirach
15:11-17.

Ps. 11:4; Jer.
17:10.

Matt. 6:19-20;
cf. Rom.
2:4-5.

Ps. 32:1-5;
103:8-13.
*Literally,
"faces."

Cf. Prayer of   Apocrypha,
Manasseh,   which expands
RSV   on v. 7.

Isa. 55:6-7;   Luke 5:32,
Hos. 14:1-2;   15:7, 10;
Mark 2:17;   II Cor. 7:10.

Deut. 7:7-9;
Jer. 31:3; Hos.
11:1.

*The Gentiles
v. 9.

Deut. 4:37,
10:15.

Cf. Deut.
5:2ff.; II Sam.
7; Ps. 105:8ff.

righteousness in our wickedness, because you are a righteous Judge over all the peoples of the earth.

3. For no one who does unrighteous deeds will be hidden from your knowledge, and the righteous deeds of your pious ones are before you, O Lord. Where will any man be hidden from your knowledge, O God?

4. Our works are in our own power of choice, to do either right or wrong; and in your righteousness you examine the sons of men. (5) He who does right treasures up life for himself from the Lord; and he who does wrong treasures up guilt which leads to destruction, for the judgments of the Lord are upon a man and his house in righteousness.

6. To whom will you show kindness, O God, if not to those who call upon the Lord? You will cleanse a person from sins when he makes acknowledgment and confession; because all such things are a shame to us and to our *reputations. (7) And for whom will you forgive sins if not for those who have sinned? You will bless the righteous and not censure them concerning their sins; but your kindness is upon sinners when they repent.

8. And now, you are God and we are the people whom you love. Look and have pity, O God of Israel, for we belong to you! Do not set your mercy far from us lest *they should set upon us; (9) for you chose for yourself the seed of Abraham rather than the Gentiles, and you set your name upon us, O Lord: you will not reject us for ever.

10. In a covenant you arranged with our fathers concerning us, and we will set our hope on you in our turning back (to you).

11. May the mercy of the Lord be upon the house of Israel for ever and ever.

Comments:

1. The author speaks for the company of the pious who obviously consider themselves to be the faithful Remnant spoken of in the O. T. prophecies. Note particularly v. 10. This outlook persisted among those who formed the early Church. The student should study this outlook and its scriptural backgrounds carefully.

2. The acceptance of Israel's dispersion as a just judgment of God on a sinful nation, the Pharisaic doctrines of divine retribution, individual free will and responsibility, and of the necessity for repentance and confession in order to receive divine forgiveness of sins—all are set forth with great clarity in this psalm. And all are met with again in the New Testament in one way or another.

READING 50: Goodness in God's discipline of His elect (*Ps. Sol.* X, XVI and XIII)

X.1. Happy is the man whom the Lord remembers by way of reproof and who is *restrained from an evil way, to be purified by a scourge so as not to increase in sin.

*Literally,
"encircled",
cf. Ps. 34:7;
125:2.

2. The one who makes his back ready for scourges will be cleansed, for the Lord is good to those who endure discipline. (3) He will make straight the ways of the righteous and will not turn away from discipline; but the Lord's mercy is upon those who love Him *faithfully. (4) And the Lord will remember His servants in mercy; for the testimony is in the law of an eternal covenant, the witness of the Lord is upon the ways of men in His visitation: (5) our Lord is righteous and holy in His judgments for ever.

Prov. 3:11-12;
I Cor. 11:32;
Heb. 12:5-11.

Cf. Ps.
145:17-18.

*Literally, "in
truth."

Cf. I John 5:10.

Cf. Exod.
32:34; Ps.
89:31-32; Jer.
8:12; 10:15,
ASV.

Israel shall praise the name of the Lord in gladness; (6) and the saints will make acknowledgment in the assembly of the people. On the *poor God will bestow mercy in Israel's gladness, (7) for God is kind and merciful for ever, and the *congregations of Israel shall glorify the name of the Lord.

Cf. Ps. Sol.
IX.6, Reading
49.

*Cf. Ps. 35:10;
40:17; 70:5,
etc. Luke 6:20.

*Literally,
"synagogues."

8. May the salvation of the Lord be upon the house of Israel for eternal rejoicing.

Comments:

1. The writer of I John seems to be making a Christian rebuttal of v. 4 when he insists that the true "witness" of God was given in His Son.

2. The term "visitation," v. 4, has dropped out of modern versions. It, with the verb "visit," literally translates terms which, in the O. T.—both the original Hebrew and the Greek translation—characterize God's activity as an overseer who comes to inspect the work of servants either to reward or to punish. The term translated "poor"—or "afflicted" in some modern versions—seems to be a term which the pious adopted for themselves under the inspiration of several of the psalms.

3. Vv. 5b-8 have eschatological overtones. "Israel's gladness" can only mean, in this context, the expected messianic age when wrongs would be righted, the oppressors dispossessed, and the land would have peace.

Superscription: "A hymn for Solomon—for assistance to the pious"

XVI.1. When my soul drowsed away from the Lord for a brief time it slipped into lethargy, sleeping far from God. (2) By but a little my soul would have been poured out to death, drawing near to the gates of *Hades, together with sinners, (3) when

Cf. Ps. Sol.
III.1, Reading
47.

*Job 38:17; 107:18; Wisd.
Ps. 9:13;   Sol. 16:13.

Ps. 30:10;
37:40; 54:4;
100:5; 103:17;
118:6.

my soul was carried away from the Lord God of Israel, unless the Lord had aided me by His everlasting mercy.

*Or, "by His
watchfulness."

Ps. 106:21; 1:47; Titus 1:3;
Isa. 45:15; 3:4; Jude 25.
49:26; Luke

4. He pricked me as by the spur of a horse *to watchfulness of Him; my Savior and Helper in every season delivered me.

5. I will publicly acknowledge, O God, that you aided me to salvation and did not reckon me with sinners for destruction.

Ps. 36:10; Isa.
54:10.

(6) May your mercy not depart from me, O God, nor the remembrance of you from my heart until death.

Cf. Ps. 19:13;
91:11.

Prov. 5:3ff.;
9:13ff.; Sirach 9:2-9.

Ps. 90:17.

*Literally,   119:133; Prov.
"place." Ps.   16:9.
37:23;

7. Restrain me, O God, from corrupt sins and from every evil woman who causes the foolish to stumble, (8) and let not an attractive transgressing woman seduce me. (9) Direct the works of my hands in your *presence, and guard my steps by remembrance of you.

Ps. 34:13;
141:3; Prov.
13:3.
Eph. 4:25-27.
I Cor. 10:10;
Phil. 2:14.
Cf. Ps. Sol.
X.1-3, above;
Heb. 12:11.

10. Protect my lips by words of truth; make wrath and unreasonable anger to go far from me. (11) Put far from me grumbling and faintheartedness in tribulation. If I sin, lead me to repentance by your discipline.

Ps. 27:14;
31:24; 119:28.
Eph. 3:16; Col.
1:11.
Ps. 94:17-19. *Or, "by
              means of."
Ps. 41:3.

12. In your good pleasure graciously support me: when you strengthen me, what is given will satisfy me. (13) For if you do not strengthen, who can endure your chastening *in poverty? (14) When one is reprimanded by means of corruption, your examination is in his flesh and by affliction of poverty.

Ps. 39:10-11.

Heb. 12:7;
James 5:11.

15. When a righteous man endures in these things, he shall be granted mercy by the Lord.

Superscription: "A psalm, to Solomon—encouragement for the righteous"

XIII.1. The right hand of the Lord protected me, the Lord's right hand spared us; (2) the Lord's arm saved us from the sword that passed through, from famine and the death of sinners.

Ps. 34:6; 44:3,
7; 77:15.
Ps. 91:5-7; cf.
Isa. 51:19;
Ezek. 6:11ff.

Ezek. 5:17;
14:15-19.

3. Evil beasts ran upon them: with their teeth they tore their flesh, and with their jaw teeth they crushed their bones. (4) But out of all these things the Lord rescued us.

Ps. 41:1-2;
50:15; 54:7;
56:13.

Cf. Ps. 19:12;
139:23-24.

5. The godly is troubled because of his faults, lest he be taken away with the sinners; (6) for the overthrow of the sinner is dreadful. But none of all these things will touch the righteous person, (7) for the discipline of the righteous for sins of ignorance and the overthrow of sinners are not alike.

Marginal
references on
Ps. Sol. X and
XVI also apply
in this section.

8. The righteous man is chastened in secret lest the sinner gloat over the righteous. (9) For God will admonish the righteous man as a beloved son, and his discipline will be as that of

a first-born; (10) for the Lord will spare His pious ones and He will remove their faults by chastening.

11. For the life of the righteous ones is forever; but sinners will be taken away to destruction, and the memory of them will no longer be found. (12) But the Lord's mercy is upon the pious, even upon those who fear Him is His mercy.

Ps. 85:8-9;
103:11, 17;
115:13; cf. 4:3;
25:14; 33:18.

Comments:

1. To one whose ear is sensitive to N. T. ideas and phraseology, there is much in these psalms that sounds familiar. This is not mysterious, since they have a common basis in the O. T., especially the Psalms and Proverbs. The student will discover that the greatest N. T. concentration of these ideas concerning the life of piety will be found in the Sermon on the Mount (and Gospel parallels) and in the hortatory selections of the epistles.

2. The reference of vv. 1-4 is possibly to the unsettled times of strife that led to Pompey's invasion, ca. 63 B.C.

3. Note in v. 9 the appropriation of the terms "beloved son" and "first-born" by the pious for themselves. These terms were earlier used in the O. T. as designations for Israel's peculiar relation to God (cf. Exod. 4:22; Jer. 31:9, 20; Hos. 11:1) and for the Davidic messiah (II Sam. 7:14; Ps. 89:27). Cf. Reading 49, Comment 1 on *Ps. Sol.* IX.

4. The opening of this psalm introduces us to the leading theme of the next reading, although its own main emphasis is on the Lord's discipline.

READING 51: The Lord protects His people (*Ps. Sol.* XIV and XV)

XIV.1. The Lord is faithful to those who love Him in truth, to those who endure His discipline, (2) to those who walk in the righteousness of His commandments, in the Law which He commanded for our life.

Cf. Ps. Sol.
X.3; Reading
50.

Deut. 5:10,
11:26-27; Ps.
84:11;
103:17-18.

Deut. 5:33,
32:46-47; John
5:39ff

3. The pious ones of the Lord will live in it for ever; the paradise of the Lord, the trees of life, are His pious ones. (4) Their planting is rooted forever: they shall not be plucked up while heaven lasts, (5) because Israel is God's inheritance and portion.

Ps. 1:3,
92:12-13; Isa.
17:9

5:7; I Chron.

Isa. 60:21;
61:3b

Exod. 19:5-6;
Deut. 9:29;
I Kings 8:51;
Ps. 78:71.

6. Not so are sinners and transgressors who love a day for participation in their sins. (7) In the brevity of corruption is their lust, and they do not keep God in mind.

Cf. Ps. 1:4; Ps.
Sol. III 9-10;
Reading 47

Cf. Job 8:13;
Ps. 50:22.

8. Yet the ways of men are always known before Him, and the secrets of the heart He knows before they occur. (9) Because of this their *portion is Hades and darkness and destruction.

Ps. 139:1-4,
11:4-7; 44:21.

*Literally,
inheritance.

Ps. 9:17.
They shall not be found in the day of mercy for the righteous,
Cf. Job 20:5-8. Cf. Ps.
Ps. 37:35-36. 106:4-5.
(10) but the Lord's saints shall inherit life in gladness.

Comments:

1. The comparison of the righteous to verdant and fruitful trees occurs several times in the Psalms. The notion that Israel is the plant (tree or vine, cf. Ps. 80:14ff.) has O. T. roots, as indicated. The metaphor occurs several times in *I Enoch*, and was appropriated by those of Qumran to designate their community.

2. Observe the eschatological overtones of vv. 9-10. The notion of eternal life, or participation in the expected messianic kingdom, is strong in these psalms.

Superscription: "A psalm for Solomon, with song"

Ps. 9:9; 34:6;
46:1;
59:16-17.
XV.1. When I was afflicted I called upon the name of the Lord. I set my hope on the God of Jacob for help and was saved, because you, O God, are the hope and refuge of the poor.

Ps. 33:1-3;
40:3; 96:1.
Ps. 63:3-5;
Hos. 14:2.
Heb. 13:15; cf.
Isa. 57:19 (v.
18 in RSV).
Ps. 15:5c;
55:22; 112:6.

Isa. 43:2b; cf.
Ps. 66:12.
Cf. Zeph. 1:18; 16:35; Ezek.
Num. 11:1-3; 7:2-4; 9:5-7,
10.
Ezek. 9:4, 6.
2. For who is strong, O God, unless he acknowledge you in truth, and what is a mighty man unless he confess your Name—with a new psalm set to music in gladness of heart, (3) the fruit of the lips on the harmonious instrument of the tongue, the first fruits of the lips from a pious and upright heart? (4) The one who does these things will never be shaken by evil. The flame of fire, even wrath against the wicked, shall not touch him (5) whenever it issues forth against sinners from the Lord to destroy all their substance, (6) because the sign of the Lord is on His righteous ones for their safety.

Cf. Ezek.
6:11-12; Ps.
Sol. XIII:2, *Those
Reading 50. calamities
7. Famine and sword and death are far from the righteous, for *they will flee from the pious as those pursued by war; (8) but sinners will be hunted down and seized, and those who commit lawlessness shall not escape from the Lord's judgment. (9) As by experienced warriors will they be seized, for the mark of destruction is on their foreheads.

Cf. Rev. 14:9f.

Job 18:5-21;
Ps. 55:23;
73:18-19;
Prov. 24:20.
*Literally, "be
found by."
Ps. 34:21; Ps. 1:4-6;
37:28b, 38; 96:13; Isa.
Prov. 5:22; 59:15-20.
11:5. Cf. Isa.
Ps. 73:18-20; 26:20-21;
92:7; Amos Zeph. 23;
9:10. Zech. 13:9.
10. And the inheritance of the sinful is destruction and darkness, and their iniquities shall pursue them down to Hades. (11) Their inheritance shall not *remain to their children; for their sins make the houses of sinners desolate; (12) and they will perish forever in the day of the Lord's judgment, whenever God makes inquisition in the earth by His judgment.

13. Those who fear the Lord will be granted mercy from their God; but sinners will perish forever.

Comments:

1. The idea expressed in v. 10b, that the iniquities of sinners pursue them to Hades (Heb., *sheol*, "death, or the underworld of the dead"), seems to receive no clear statement in the O. T. In the account of Enoch's journeys through the earth and the underworld, the seer is taken to a mountain in which are four hollow places, deep and dark. It is explained to him by the interpreting angel that one of them was made for the spirits of those sinners who did not receive their just punishment in life, so they are to be kept there in torment for their sins until the great day of judgment (cf. *I Enoch* XXII.9-11).

2. The phrase "day of judgment" *per se* also is not to be found in the O. T. However, it was easily derived from other phrases of similar import—"day of the Lord's vengeance," "day of the Lord's anger/wrath," "day of recompense/retribution," and similar phrases. These include "day of the Lord," from which the preceding were probably developed. The phrase is found in several of the intertestamental works, and reappears in the N. T.

3. THE MESSIANIC HOPE

READING 52: Hopes for the messianic age, based on the covenants (*Ps. Sol.* VII.6-10; VIII.27-28; IX.8-10)

VII.6. Since your Name dwells among us, we shall be granted mercy, and no nation shall prevail over us, (7) because you are our shield and when we call upon you, you will hearken to us.

Deut. 12:11;
Ps. 9:11; 26:8;
76:1-2.
Deut. 33:29;
Ps. 33:20;
115:9-11.
Ps. 17:6;
50:15;

8. You will be compassionate to the race of Israel forever, and you will not reject us; (9) and we will be under your yoke forever, even under the scourge of your discipline.

91:14-16; Jer.
33:3.
I Sam. 12:22;
Ps. 77:7-9; 94:14.
Cf. Reading
50.

10. Guide us aright to the appointed time when you aid us, when you bestow mercy on the house of Jacob in the day about which you made promise to them.

Isa. 11; Jer.
30:3-11,
18-22;
33:14-22.

VIII.27. Turn your mercy to us, O God, and have compassion on us: (28) gather the dispersed ones of Israel with mercy and kindness, because your faithfulness is with us.

Isa. 11:12;
54:7; Jer. 23:3;
29:14;
32:37-41;
Ezek. 34:13;
36:24.

IX.8. And now, you are God and we are the people whom you love. Look and have pity, O God of Israel, for we belong to you. Do not set your mercy far from us lest *they should set upon us; (9) for you chose for yourself the seed of Abraham rather than the Gentiles, and you set your Name upon us, O Lord: you will not reject us for ever.

For this
selection cf.
marginal
references for
Ps. Sol. IX.
Reading 49.

*Gentiles.

10. In a covenant you arranged with our fathers concerning us, and we will set our hope on you in our returning to you.

Comment:

The faith that Israel was God's chosen people with whom He had made special covenants is the basis of the hope of the pious. The promises made to David and his descendants, reiterated in the Prophets and Psalms of the O. T., are the foundation of the messianic hope of the intertestamental era. The student will not be surprised to see certain ideas and phrases in these selections reappearing in the synagogue prayers which are believed to have come into use already by the New Testament period.

READING 53: The Davidic Messiah expected (*Ps. Sol.* XVII.21-46)

For earlier portion cf.
Reading 45.
Isa. 11:1-2;
Jer. 23:4-5.
Ezek. 34:23-24;
Zech. 9:9-10.

21. Behold, O Lord, and raise up for them their king, the son of David, at the time that you have chosen, O God, so that he may reign over Israel your servant.

Ps. 2:9-11;
Isa. 11:4; cf.
Zech. 12:1-9.

22. Gird him with strength so that he may shatter unrighteous rulers and purge Jerusalem from the Gentiles that are trampling her down destructively.

Cf. Prov.   101:8; Jer.
20:26; Ps.   23:5.
Ps. 2:9; cf.
110:5-6.

23. In righteous wisdom may he expel sinners from the inheritance; destroy the arrogance of the Sinner as a clay pot; (24) shatter all their substance with a rod of iron; destroy transgressing Gentiles by the word of his mouth; (25) cause Gentiles to flee from his presence by his censure; and convict sinners by the word of their hearts.

Cf. Jude 14-15;
I Enoch 1.9.

26. Then he shall gather a holy people, whom he will lead in righteousness, and he will judge the tribes of the people that has been sanctified by the Lord his God. (27) He will not allow unrighteousness to lodge among them any more; nor shall there dwell with them anyone who knows evil. For he will know them well, recognizing that they are all sons of their God; (28) and he will divide them according to their tribes upon their land. Neither sojourner nor alien shall dwell with them any more.

Ps. 45:6-7.

Ps. 45:5; Isa.
11:3-5.
Isa. 43:6-7;
Hos. 1:10; cf.
Ps. 82:6.

Isa. 52:1.

Isa. 11:1-5;
Jer. 23:5.
Ps. 2:8;
72:8-11.
Isa. 11:10;
49:22-23.

Zech. 14:20-21.

29. He shall judge peoples and nations in his righteous wisdom; (30) and he will have the heathen nations to serve under his yoke. He shall glorify the Lord as an "ensign" for all the earth; and he shall purge Jerusalem in holiness as at the first. (31) Nations will come from the ends of the earth to see his splendor, bringing as gifts her sons who had *fainted—even to see the glory of the Lord with which God has glorified *her.

Cf. Gen. 49:10;   9:22-23; Mic.
II Chro .   5:4b.
Isa. 49:22;
*Isa. 51:20.
*Jerusalem;
Isa. 60:1ff.

32. And he shall be a righteous king, instructed of God; and there shall be no unrighteousness among them in his days, for all will be holy and their king will be the Anointed of the Lord. [II Sam. 7:10-14; Ps. 2:2; 18:50]

33. For he shall not put his trust in horse and rider and bow, nor shall he amass for himself gold and silver for war, nor shall he rely on a *large army for the day of battle. (34) The Lord Himself is his King, the confidence of him who is mighty through confidence in God; and he shall be gracious to all nations who come before him in reverence, (35) for he will smite the earth with the word of his mouth forever. He will bless the people of the Lord with wisdom and gladness. [Deut. 17:16; I Kings 10:14—11:13; Ps. 20:7; Isa. 31:1-3; cf.] [*Literally, "many (people)"] [Cf. II Chron. 14:11; 16:7; 20:15ff; Ps. 110:1] [Ps. 21:7] [Isa. 45:14-15; 49:23; 60:10-14; Isa. 11:4] [Cf. Isa. 51:3; Jer. 31:7ff.]

36. And he himself will be pure from sin, so that he may rule a great people. He will rebuke rulers and remove sinners by the might of his word. (37) By relying on his God he will not become weak throughout his days, for God will make him mighty through His holy Spirit, and wise through the counsel of discernment, with strength and righteousness. (38) So the blessing of the Lord will be with him: he will be strong and will not become weak. (39) His confidence will be in the Lord: who then can prevail against him? [Cf. Prov. 16:10] [Isa. 11:2; 42:1] [Cf. Isa. 41:10] [Ps. 27:1ff.]

40. He will be mighty in his works, and strong in the fear of God. He will shepherd the flock of the Lord faithfully and righteously, and will allow none to become weak in their pasture. (41) He will lead them all in *fairness, and there will be no arrogant pride among them so that any become oppressed. [Mic. 5:4-5; 7:14; Jer. 23:4; Ezek. 34:23] [*Or, "equity"; Zeph. 3:12-13; cf. Ezek. 46:18]

42. This is the majesty of the king of Israel whom God knows: may He raise him up over the house of Israel to discipline it. (43) His words are refined more than finest gold; in the *assemblies he will judge the tribes of a sanctified people: his words are as words of *holy ones, among a sanctified people. [Cf. Ps. 45:3-4] [Cf. Ps. 45:2] [*Literally, "synagogues"] [*Cf. Ps. 89:5; Job 5:1; Ps. 82:1; 149:1]

44. Blessed are those who are alive in those days to see the good things of Israel in the time of the gathering of the tribes, things that God will do.

45. Hasten, O God, your mercy upon Israel. Rescue us from the uncleanness of defiling enemies.

46. The Lord is our King forever and ever. [Ps. 10:16; 44:4; 47:2; 6-7]

Comments:

1. Of all the intertestamental writings this is recognized as the clearest description of the Davidic Messiah expected by the pious in Israel at the dawn of the New Testament period. It will repay close study by the student

of N. T. backgrounds. The Messiah like his forefather David was to be a vigorous warrior yet a man "after God's own heart," like Solomon in his wisdom and splendor, and like Hezekiah in his faith and faithfulness.

2. As the marginal references indicate, all the ideas expressed have their basis in certain well-known passages of the O. T. Some of the principal ones are: II Sam. 7:8-17; Ps. 2; 89:19-37; 110; Isa. 11; 42:1-4; 49:1-13; 52:13-15; 60—61; Jer. 23:5-6; 33:14-17; Ezek. 34; and Zech. 9:9-10.

3. In the opening chapters of his Gospel, Luke makes it clear that such expectations were popular: cf. Luke 1:31-35; 46-55; and especially 68-79. John also emphasizes this fact by the way in which he reports the earliest disciples' confessions of faith in Jesus: cf. John 1:40-49. And all the Gospels make it clear that Jesus' final rejection was due in large part to the fact that He did not fit the kind of expectations expressed in this psalm: cf. John 12:34.

READING 54: The certainty of God's promises (*Ps. Sol.* XVIII)

Superscription: "More concerning the Lord's Anointed"

1. O Lord, your mercy is upon the works of your hands forever; your goodness with a rich gift has been bestowed upon Israel. (2) Your eyes look upon them, and none of them suffers want: your ears hearken to the hopeful petition of the poor.

Ps. 34:10;
84:11.

Ps. 4:3b;
34:15; 86:7;
145:17-19.

3. Your judgments upon the earth are tempered with mercy, and your love is toward the seed of Abraham, the sons of Israel. (4) Your chastisement of us is like that of a first-born only son, to turn back the obedient one from folly committed in ignorance.

Cf. Isa. 54:8;
Hab. 3:2; Ps.
98:1-3.
Cf. selections
of Reading 50.

5. May God cleanse Israel in anticipation of the day of His mercy by blessing us, the day in which He chooses to bring *up His Anointed.

*I.e., to the
throne. Cf. Jer.
33:14-15 and
related
references.

6. Blessed are those who live in those days to see the good things of the Lord, which He will do in the generation to come. (7) They will be under the rod of discipline of the Lord's Anointed in the fear of his God. By the spirit of wisdom, of justice and of might, (8) he will guide everyone aright in the works of righteousness in the fear of God. He will establish them in the Lord's presence (9) as a good generation in the fear of God, in the days of *His Mercy. Selah.

Isa. 11:2-9.

*God's

10. Great is our God, praised by those dwelling in the highest, who has ordained the luminaries in their paths for the set times of the hours from day to day: they do not digress from

the way that He ordained for them. (11) From the day of
creation until eternity, their way each day is in *obedience to
God; (12) and they have not strayed since the day in which He
created them: from ancient generations they did not forsake
their course, unless God commanded them by an order given
by His servants.

*Literally.
"fear."

Cf. Josh.
10:12-13.

Comments:

1. Emphasized in this short psalm is an important element in the messianic schema of the intertestamental period, viz., that the nation must
prepare for the Messiah's coming by repentance, and that God would lead
the nation through cleansing affliction. Then, a purified people would,
under a king who would enforce justice through wise policies, experience
an age in which righteousness and peace would prevail—cf. Jer. 30:7-11;
31:31-34; Ezek. 36:22-31; *Ps. Sol.* XVII.27, 32, 36, 41.

2. The point of vv. 10-12 is indicated by its background in Jer. 31:35-37;
33:19-22, 25-26. God's promise to send the Messiah is as unshakable as His
ordinance which maintains the heavenly luminaries in their courses and
the earth in its daily rotations—cf. Gen. 8:21-22.

READING 55a: Messianic times and final judgment (*I Enoch* XLV.1-6;
XLVI.4—XLVII.4; XLVIII.1, 7-9; L.1-5)

XLV.1. And this is the second similitude concerning those
who deny the name of the dwelling of the holy ones and the
Lord of Spirits.

2. Into heaven they shall not ascend, and on earth they shall
not come. Such shall be the lot of the sinners who have denied
the Name of the Lord of Spirits, who are thus preserved for the
day of suffering and tribulation.

Isa. 59:13; cf.
Josh. 24:27;
Job 31:28;
II Peter 2:1, 9;
Jude 4

3. On that day my Elect One shall sit on the throne of glory and
will try their works, and their places of rest shall be innumerable. And their souls will grow strong within them when they
see my elect ones, and those who have called upon my glorious Name.

Cf. Matt.
25:31ff.; Ps.
9:4-5.
Cf. Rev. 20:11;
4:2ff.
Cf. John
14:2-3.

4. Then will I make my Elect One to dwell among them. And I
will transform the heaven and make it an eternal blessing and
light, (5) and I will transform the earth and make it a blessing. I
will make my chosen ones dwell upon it; but sinners and
evildoers shall not set foot thereon. (6) For I have provided and
satisfied my righteous ones with peace, and have made them
to dwell in my presence.

Ezek. 34:24;
II Esdras 7:28.
Isa. 65:17ff.
Cf. Rev. 21:1,
5.
Cf. II Esdras
7:31.
Cf. Isa. 52:1;
Rev. 21:27.
Ps. 65:4;
107:9; 132:15;
Isa. 32:17-18.

Cf. Ps. 1:5-6; 7:33;
37:9; Isa. 12:32-33; Rev.
33:14; Amos 20:11ff.
9:10; II Esdras
But for sinners there is judgment impending with me, so that I shall destroy them from the face of the earth. . . .

Cf. Dan. II Esdras
7:13f.; 13:1-40.
XLVI.4. And this Son of Man whom you have seen shall

*Text: "loosen
the reins of."
remove the kings and mighty ones from their thrones, and shall *disable the strong and break the teeth of sinners, (5)

*Text: "the Dan. 4:24ff.;
kingdom"; cf. 5:18ff.
because they do not extol and praise him, nor humbly acknowledge by whom *royal authority was bestowed upon

*Text: "put 18:5-6, 18; cf.
down the Ps. 88:6;
countenance 143:3.
of"; Job 8:22;
Job 21:23-26;
Isa. 14:10-11.
them. (6) He will *destroy the prestige of the strong and fill them with shame. Darkness will be their dwelling, and worms will be their bed. And they will have no hope of rising from their beds because they do not extol the Name of the Lord of Spirits.

*Following
Charles; cf.
Reading 46.
*Text: "rests
upon their
riches."
Cf. Isa. 44:9ff.; Cf. XLV.2,
Jer. 10:1-9. above.
7. These are they who judge the stars of heaven . . . and tread down the land, *taking people captive. All their deeds exhibit unrighteousness; their power *is based in their wealth; their faith is in the gods which they have made with their hands; and they deny the Name of the Lord of Spirits.

Ps. 145:17-19;
Prov. 15:29.
Gen. 4:10; Ps.
72:14;
79:10-11;
116:15; cf.
Matt. 23:35;
Rev. 6:9-10.
*Cf. Ps. Sol.
XVII.43,
margin.
XLVII.1. And in those days the prayer of the righteous and their blood shall have ascended from the earth before the Lord of Spirits.

2. In those days the *holy ones who dwell above in the heavens shall unite with one voice and supplicate and pray . . . on behalf of the blood of the righteous that has been shed, that the prayer of the righteous may not be in vain before the Lord of Spirits, that justice may be done for them,

Cf. Rev. 6:10,
"How long?"
and that they may not have to suffer for ever.

Cf. Dan. 7:9,
13.
3. In those days I saw the Head of Days when He seated Himself on the throne of His glory, and the books of the living

Cf. Rev. 20:12.
were opened before Him; and all His host which is in heaven
Cf. I Kings
22:19; Ps.
82:1, RSV.
above and His counselors stood before Him.

4. And the hearts of the holy were filled with joy because the
*Or,
completed?
number of righteous had been *offered, the prayer of the
Cf. Rev.
16:5-6; Joel
3:20-21; Gen.
4:10; Matt.
23:35.
righteous had been heard, and the blood of the righteous had been required before the Lord of Spirits. . . .

Prov. 13:14;
14:27; Jer.
2:13—popular
metaphor for
the Torah or
teaching from
it.
XLVIII.1. And in that place I saw the fountain of righteousness which was inexhaustible, and around it were many fountains of wisdom. All the thirsty drank from them and were filled with wisdom; and their dwellings were with the righteous and the holy and elect. . . .

*Probably *The Elect One.
refers to the
messianic
scriptures.
Cf. T. Job L.1, Reading
XLIX.1 and 21.
7. Now the *wisdom of the Lord of Spirits has disclosed *him to the holy and righteous. For he has preserved the lot of the righteous because they have hated and despised this world of

unrighteousness, and have hated all its works and ways in the name of the Lord of Spirits. For in His Name they are saved, and according to His good pleasure has it been in regard to their life.

Ps. 26:5; 119:104, 128. Cf. Ps. 54:1; 116:4-6; 124:8; 138:7. Cf. I Sam. 12:22; Ps. 115:3; 135:6; 149:4.

8. In those days the kings of the earth and the strong who possess the land shall have become downcast in countenance because of the works of their hands, for on the day of their anguish and affliction they shall not be able to save themselves. (9) And I will give them over into the hands of my elect ones. As straw in the fire so shall they burn before the face of the holy, as lead in the water shall they sink before the face of the righteous, and no trace of them shall be found any more. . . .

Cf. XLVI.6, above.

Isa. 43:13; Amos 2:14-16; Hos. 5:14; 5:18-19. Cf. Isa. 10:17; Zech. 12:6. Cf. Exod. 15:10.

L.1. And in those days a change shall take place for the holy and elect, and the light of days shall abide upon them, and glory and honor shall·turn to the holy, (2) on the day of affliction on which *calamity shall have been treasured up against sinners.

Cf. Zech. 14. Isa. 52:6ff. Cf. Isa. 60:19-20.

*Text: "evil." Cf. Rom. 2:5.

And the righteous shall be victorious in the Name of the Lord of Spirits; and He will make the *others witness it that they may repent and forego the works of their hands. (3) They shall have no honor through the Name of the Lord of Spirits, yet through His Name they will be saved; and the Lord of Spirits will have compassion on them, for His compassion is great.

Cf. Ps. 20:5; Zech. 9:14-15; 12:7-8, RSV. *Those who have not actively opposed the saints.

4. He is righteous also in His judgment; and in the presence of His glory unrighteousness shall not maintain itself. At His judgment the unrepentant shall perish before Him. (5) "And from henceforth I will have no mercy on them," says the Lord of Spirits.

Cf. Isa. 33:14. Cf. Hos. 1:6.

READING 55b: The Elect One/Son of Man (*I Enoch* XLVI.1-3; XLVIII.3-6; XLIX; LI)

XLVI.1. And there I saw one who had a head of days: his head was white like wool, and with him was another whose countenance had the appearance of a man, whose face was full of graciousness like one of the holy angels. (2) And I asked the angel who went with me and showed me all the hidden things concerning that Son of Man: who he was, and from where, and why he went with the Head of Days. (3) And he replied: "This is the Son of Man who has righteousness, with whom righteousness dwells, and who reveals all the treasures of that which is hidden; for the Lord of Spirits has chosen him and

Cf. Dan. 7:9; Rev. 1:14. Cf. Ezek. 1:26; Dan. 7:13; 8:15.

Cf. Judg. 13:6.

Cf. Col. 2:3.

Isa. 49:1-2.
*Cf Reading
47, Comment
3.
his *lot has the pre-eminence before the Lord of Spirits in uprightness forever." . . .

Cf. v. 6. Note
the emphasis
on Messiah's
pre-existence.
Cf. Prov.
8:22ff.
Ps. 23:4b.

Isa. 42:6; 49:6.
XLVIII.3. Yea, before the sun and the signs were created, before the stars of heaven were made, his name was named before the Lord of Spirits. (4) He shall be a staff to the righteous whereon they may support themselves and not fall. And he shall be the light of the Gentiles, and the hope of all who are troubled in heart.

5. All who dwell on earth shall fall down and worship before him, and will praise and bless and celebrate the Lord of Spirits with song.

*God.
6. And for this reason he has been chosen and hidden before *Him, before the creation of the world and for evermore. . . .

XLIX.1. For wisdom is poured out like water, and glory never fails before him. (2) For he is mighty in all the secrets of righteousness, and unrighteousness shall disappear as a *Text:
"continuance." shadow and have no *permanence. For the Elect One stands before the Lord of Spirits, and his glory is for ever and ever, and his might to all generations.

Isa. 11:2.
3. And in him dwells the spirit of wisdom: the spirit which gives insight, the spirit of understanding and of might, the spirit of those who have fallen asleep in righteousness. (4) And he shall judge the secret things, and none shall be able to utter a lying word before him; for he is the Elect One before the Lord of Spirits, according to God's good pleasure. . . .

*The abode of
the dead = Gk.
Hades.
*Abaddon, Job
26:6; Rev.
9:11. Rev. 20:13.
*God.
LI.1. And in those days the earth shall also give back what has been entrusted to it, and *Sheol shall give back that which it has received, and *hell shall give back what it owes.

2. And *He shall choose the righteous and holy from among them, for the day has drawn near for them to be saved.

*Charles'
margin; text:
"my."
3. And the Elect One shall sit on *his throne in those days, and his mouth shall pour out all the secrets of wisdom and counsel; for the Lord of Spirits has given them to him and has glorified him.

Cf. Ps. 114:4.
Cf. Readings
37b and 38; T.
Judah XXV.

Cf. Baruch
4:36—5:9,
RSV
Apocrypha.
4. In those days the mountains shall leap like rams, and the hills also shall skip like lambs satisfied with milk, and the faces of the angels in heaven will be alight with joy. (5) For in those days the Elect One shall arise, and the earth shall rejoice and the righteous shall dwell upon it, and the elect shall walk thereon.

Comments:

1. Readings 55a and b have been adapted from the version of R. H. Charles in his *Apocrypha and Pseudepigrapha of the Old Testament in English*, Vol. II, pp. 213ff. The phraseology has been modernized—and Americanized—as appropriate. Occasionally a suggestion from the notes has been adopted when such seemed more plausible. Such adaptations are noted in the margin above. Also, in sec. LI, line *a* of v. 5 has been restored to its original order, for the sake of good sense—Charles had interposed it before v. 2. Words and lines indicated as interpolations by square brackets in his text have been deleted in this adaptation.

2. The perceptive reader will recognize ideas met with previously— particularly in Reading 53 and its O. T. background. Certain ideas from the messianic prophecies receive emphasis and embellishment:

a. Prominent in all the Enochian "Similitudes" is the fate predicted for the "kings and the mighty," those who in that time were making the lives of the pious burdensome and risky.

b. Another strong theme is the great wisdom of the Elect One or Son of Man, wisdom which he is to share with the pious when he establishes his reign of peace. In the thought of the writer, it appears that the wisdom of the Son of Man has as much to do with interpretation of scripture as it does with administration of the kingdom.

c. Finally, there is the theme of the pre-existence and hiddenness—until God brings him forth—of the Elect One. In the First Similitude, the seer saw him dwelling under the wings of the deity (I Enoch XXXIX.7). This idea may have been generated by bringing Isa. 49:2b, with the key word "shadow," into relation with passages from the Psalms which speak of the shadow of the deity's *wings*: cf. 17:8; 57:1; 61:4; 63:7; 91:1, 4. Also, in the Third Similitude it is stated that "From the beginning the Son of Man was hidden, and the Most High preserved him in the presence of His might, and revealed him to the elect" (sec. LXII.7). Such ideas may have been developed by speculating on Isa. 49:1-3 in relation to Mal. 3:1 and other passages of messianic import. The student needs to keep in mind that by this time many O. T. passages which originally had no such associations were being given messianic significance by processes of interpretation which are by no means lost to the Church today.

C. Literature of the Times (Continued into the Christian Era)

1. LEGENDS OF THE PROPHETS

The following selections are translations from the Greek text of *The Lives of the Prophets*, edited by Charles Cutler Torrey.

READING 56a: About Isaiah ("Isaiah" 1-5)

1. He was from Jerusalem. He was killed by Manasseh, by   Cf. II Chron. 33

II. Chron.
32:3-4, 30.

being sawed in two; and he was placed beneath the oak of Rogel situated by the water-channel that Hezekiah spoiled by blocking it up.

Cf. John 9:7.

2. Now God performed the sign of Siloam for the sake of the prophet. Before he died, by faith he prayed for water to drink and immediately it was sent to him from that source. Thus it was called *Siloam*, which means "Sent."

II Kings 20:20.

*Or, "baths";
cf. John 5:2,
Gk.

3. And in Hezekiah's time, before he made the reservoirs and the *pools, a little water came out in response to Isaiah's prayer so that the city, then besieged by foreigners, might not be destroyed for lack of water. (4) For the enemy were wondering where they were to drink. Having surrounded the city, some were camping near Siloam. Waters came forth, then, if Jews came to it; but not if foreigners came. Thus the waters issue suddenly even today, so that the mystery may be displayed.

*I.e., his
prayer.

5. And since this sign occurred through *Isaiah, the people buried him nearby, carefully and in great honor, for the sake of remembrance, so that through his prayers they might thus always have the benefit of the waters.

READING 56b: About Jeremiah ("Jeremiah" 1-4, 9-15)

*Heb.,   cf. Jer. 43:5-8;
Tahpanhes;   44:1ff.

*I.e., the Jews.

1. He was from Anathoth. He was killed in *Taphnes of Egypt, being stoned by the *people.

*I.e., where it
had once been.

*Cobras.

2. He lies in the place *of Pharaoh's house, for the Egyptians honored him, since they had been benefited through him: (3) for he prayed and the *asps which the Egyptians call *ephoth* left them. (4) And to this day, as many as are God's faithful ones pray in that place; and they take the dust of the place, healing with it the *sting of asps. . . .

*Or, "bite."

Cf. II Kings 25.

*Literally,   cf. II Macc.
"rock, cliff";   2:4ff.
*Ps. 47:5;   Deut.
68:15-18,   32:39-43; Jer.
32:35; cf.   25:30-31;
                        30:23-24.

9. This prophet, before the destruction of the Temple, carried away the Ark of the Law with the things that were in it. He caused a *cave to swallow them up. And he said to those present: (10) "The Lord *went up from Sinai and He will come again in power. . . ."

*Or, "unfold."
The "tablets"
are thought of
as scrolls.

11. Then he said: "No one but Aaron is going to take out this Ark; and none of the priests or prophets shall *unroll the tablets in it except Moses, God's chosen one. (12) And in the resurrection the Ark will rise first. It will go out of the rock and will be placed on Mount Sinai. And all the saints will be

gathered to it there, awaiting the Lord and fleeing the enemies who wish to make away with them."

Cf. Ps. 50:4-5;
Jer. 31:2; cf.
Rev. 12:13-14;
I Macc. 2:29ff.

13. With his finger he put the seal of God's Name on the rock, and the characters became as if carved with iron. Then a cloud shadowed the Name and no one knows the place, nor can they read the seal, since that day nor until the End. (14) The rock is in the wilderness where the Ark was at first, between the two mountains in which Moses and Aaron lie buried. By night there is a cloud, like fire, according to the ancient text that the glory of God shall never cease from His Law.

Cf. Deut.   Hor and Mt.
32:49-50; Mt. Nebo.
Cf. Isa. 42:21.

15. And God granted Jeremiah the favor of consummating this mystery, so that he might become a partner of Moses; and they are together to this day.

READING 56c: About Ezekiel ("Ezekiel" 1-3, 6-7, 16-20)

1. This prophet was from the *area of Sarira, of the priestly caste. He died in the land of the Chaldeans in the time of the *captivity, after having prophesied many things *concerning those in Judea. (2) He was put to death by the leader of the Israelites *there, whom Ezekiel rebuked for worshiping idols. (3) And they buried him in the field of Nahor, in the tomb of Shem and Arphaxad, Abraham's ancestors. . . . (6) This prophet gave a *sign to the people, namely, that they were to observe the river *Chebar closely: (7) when it should fail, to expect the scythe of desolation to the ends of the earth; and when it should overflow, the return to Jerusalem. . . .

*Literally,
"land."
Cf. Ezek. 1:3.
*Cf. Ezek.   *Or,
1:1-3; 10:15,   "against."
20.
*In Chaldea; cf.
Ezek. 14:2ff.
I Chron.   Gen. 11:10-11;
1:24-27; cf.   27-32.
*Literally,
"wonder."
*Ezek. 1:1;
10:15.
Cf. Joel 3:12ff.

16. Also, after the manner of Moses, he saw the plan of the sanctuary and the wall and the broad surrounding area, just as Daniel also said that it was to be built. (17) In Babylon he pronounced judgment on the tribes of Dan and Gad, because they acted impiously toward the Lord by harassing those who kept the Law. (18) And he performed a great wonder against them, in that snakes killed their infants and all their livestock. (19) He foretold, moreover, that because of them the people would not return to their own land, but would stay in Media until their error *was consummated.

Exod. 26:30;
Ezek. 40—42;
Dan. 9:25.

*Or, "came to
an end."

20. It was a man from among them who killed Ezekiel; for they opposed him all the days of his life.

Cf. Ezek.
12:1ff.;
33:30-32.

READING 56d: About Zechariah ben Jehoiada ("Zechariah" 1-3)

II Chron.
24:20; cf.
23:1—24:15.

Cf. Luke 11:51.

Cf. II Chron.
24:16.

1. Of Jerusalem, he was son of Jehoiada the priest. Joash, king of Judah, had him put to death near the altar: the house of David poured out his blood in the midst of the court near the vestibule. (2) And the priests took him up and buried him with his father.

*Inner shrine.
I Sam. 23:6, 9;
30:7-8.
*The Urim and
Thummim;
Num. 27:21;
I Sam. 28:6;
Ezra 2:63.

3. After that there occurred ghostly portents in the sanctuary; and the priests were unable to see visions of God's angels, to give forth oracles from the *debir, to inquire by the ephod, to answer the people by means of the *(stones) of showing, as formerly.

Comment:

This is the incident to which, according to Matt. 23:35, Jesus made reference. However, Matthew's text has "Zechariah son of Berechiah," who was a prophet of the Restoration period, companion of Haggai. One text tradition of these Lives, as Torrey points out on p. 47, note 78, had the above selection joined to an account which began with Zechariah ben Berechiah. Perhaps Matthew knew this tradition and was responsible for adding the patronymic to his report of Jesus' words. Cf. Luke 11:51, which lacks it.

READING 56e: About Elijah ("Elijah" 1-3)

*I.e.,
Trans-Jordan,
then held by
the Nabatean
Arabs.

1. He was a Tishbite from the *land of the Arabs, of the tribe of Aaron living in Gilead, because Tishbi was given to the priests.

2. After he was born, his father Sobacha saw men in shining apparel greeting him; and they swaddled him in fire and gave him a flame of fire to eat. (3) When he came and reported this in Jerusalem, the oracle told him: "Fear not; for his dwelling will be the light, and he will judge Israel by sword and fire."

Cf. Sirach
48:1, 7.

Comment:

Elijah was the subject of many legends growing out of the O. T. stories about him and the prophecy of Malachi 4:5-6. Sirach 48:1-11 stays close to the biblical accounts, but even these are of such a nature as to make easy the embellishments of later times (cf. I Kings 17—II Kings 2). His role as forerunner of the messianic age was undoubtedly much emphasized at the dawn of the Christian era. Knowledge of this background helps make more understandable such passages as Matt. 11:7-14 and Mark 8:27-28; 9:1-5.

2. LITURGICAL PRAYERS

READING 57: The *Shemoneh 'Esreh* ("Eighteen Benedictions")

The following, believed to represent an early form of this liturgical prayer, is conceded by both Jewish and Christian specialists to have been in use in some form in the synagogues of Palestine prior to the Christian era. As may be expected, the phraseology is largely drawn from the Hebrew Bible, although some of the concepts represent intertestamental developments. The archaic style has been preserved in the opening blessing and in the concluding benediction of subsequent paragraphs to highlight both its antiquity and its liturgical character.

1. Blessed art thou, O Lord our God and God of our fathers— God of Abraham, Isaac and Jacob; the great and mighty God, possessor of heaven and earth; our Shield and the Shield of our fathers, our confidence in every generation. Blessed art thou, O Lord our God, the Shield of Abraham.

Gen. 14:22.
Deut. 33:29; 33:20; cf. Ps. 18:30; Reading 1, v. 10.
Gen. 15:1.

2. You are mighty, humbling the haughty and overpowering the violent and bringing them to justice. You live forever, raising the dead and restoring the spirit. You make rain to fall, providing for the living and making dead things alive. In the twinkling of an eye, make salvation spring up for us. Blessed art thou, O Lord our God, who maketh the dead to live.

I Sam. 2:3-4; II Kings Prov. 15:25; 4:32-36; Luke Isa. 2:11, 17; 8:55. 13:11; cf. Ps. Ps. 104:13ff.; Sol. II:31-32, 147:8f.; Zech Reading 46b. 10:1. I Kings Isa. 26:19; 17:20-23. Dan. 12:2.
Isa. 45:8, 58:8 Ps. Sol. 47; Rom. 8:11. III:12, Reading I Cor. 15:52.
Matt. Isa. 6:3; Ps. 22:31-32; John 111:9; Exod. 5:25, 28-29; 20:3; Deut. II Cor. 1:9. 6:4; Isa. 44:6-8; 45:6.

3. You are holy and revered is your Name: there is no God apart from you. Blessed art thou, O Lord, the Holy God.

Isa. 6:3.

4. Favor us, our Father, with knowledge from yourself, and with understanding and enlightenment from your Torah. Blessed art thou, O Lord, who graciously giveth knowledge.

Cf. Deut. 94:10-12; 4:4-8; 8:3; 119:18, 105; 32:46; Ps. Prov. 2:3-6; 19:8; 6:23.
Dan. 2:21.

5. Turn us back, O Lord, to yourself, and we will return. Renew our days as of old. Blessed art thou, O Lord, who taketh pleasure in repentance.

Ps. 80:3, 7; Ps. Sol. 19; Joel 2:12f.; IX:10, Reading 49
Ps. 51:16-17; Zech. 1:3-4; Isa. 57:15; cf. Luke 15:7, 10; Hos. 14:1-4; Acts 17:30.

6. Forgive us, our Father, for we have sinned against you. Wipe our sins away and make our transgressions pass away from your sight, because your compassion is great. Blessed art thou, O Lord, who aboundeth in forgiveness.

Ps. 51:1-4; Ps. Ps. 51:9, 79:9. Sol. IX:6-7 103:8-12; Isa. and 38:17; Mic. references; 7:19; Luke Reading 49 11:4.
Ps. 130:4; Dan. 9:9; cf. Hos. 14:4.

7. Look upon our affliction and take up our cause; and redeem us for your Name's sake. Blessed art thou, O Lord, the Redeemer of Israel.

Ps. 35:1, 43:1; Ps. 106:8; Isa. 3:13 143:11; Jer. I Sam. 12:22. 14:7-8.
Isa. 43:14, 44:6, 48:17.

Ps. 147:3;
103:3;
II Chron. 7:14
Ps. 12:5; Isa.
35:10.
Jer. 30:17.

Exod. 15:26.

Deut. 28:1-12; V.14-18.
cf. Ps. Sol.   Reading 48.

*Or,
"consummation";
Isa. 46:13;
51:5. Cf.
petition 2; Acts
14:17.
Deut. 28:12;
Ps. 90:17;
118:25; cf. Isa.
65:22-23.

*Isa. 27:13;   Isa. 11:10, 12;
I Cor. 15:52;   Tobit 13:13;
I Thess. 4:16. 14:5.

Sirach
36:11-12;
Baruch 5:5-9;
Ps. Sol. XI,
Reading 9.

Isa. 1:26.

Ps. 89:18; Isa.
43:15; Ps.
Sol. XVII. 1-2.
Reading 45,
XVII. 46,
Reading 53.

Tobit 13:9-14;
Judith 9:8-11; Ps. Sol. IX.
Sirach   8-9, Reading
36:12ff.; Ps.   49.
79.
*Deut. 26:15.

*Or,
"Messiah";
Ps. 80:14-19;
89:19-51; Ps.
Sol. XVII. 4,
Reading 45.

Ps. 4:1, 3;
17:1, 6.
Exod. 34:6. Ps.
33:22; 69:16;
106:45.

Ps. 65:2; 3:4,
18:6; 31:22.

Ps. 9:11; 76:2.

*Or,   Ps. 29:2; 95:6;
"worship" (the 96:9; Isa.
Hebrew word is 66:23.
used with both Ps. 4:4; 33:8.
meanings).

Ps. 144—150.

Mic. 7:18-19.

*Or,   weakness) Ps.
"bending"   73:2; 18:36;
(from   56:13; 116:8.

8. Heal us, O Lord our God, from the sufferings of our heart. Make trouble and sighing pass away from us; and provide healing for our wounds.
Blessed art thou, O Lord, who healeth the sick ones of thy people Israel.

9. Bless to us, O Lord our God, this year for good with every kind of produce; and quickly bring near the year of the *end of our redemption. Give dew and rain upon the earth, and satisfy the world from the treasuries of your good things; and grant a blessing to the works of our hands.
Blessed art thou, O Lord, who blesseth the years.

10. Blow the *great trumpet for our freedom, and lift an ensign for the gathering of our exiles.
Blessed art thou, O Lord, who gatherest those who are scattered from the people of Israel.

11. Restore our judges as in former times, and our counselors as at the beginning; and may you alone reign over us.

Blessed art thou, O Lord, who loveth justice. . . .

13. Upon the proselytes of righteousness may your compassions be extended; and grant us a good reward with those who do your good pleasure.
Blessed art thou, O Lord, the support of the righteous.

14. Have mercy, O Lord our God, in your great compassion upon your people Israel; upon Jerusalem your city; upon Zion the dwelling place of your glory, even upon the Temple, *your dwelling; and upon the dynasty of the house of David your righteous *Anointed One.
Blessed art thou, O Lord God of David, who buildest Jerusalem.

15. Hear, O Lord our God, the voice of our prayer, and have compassion on us; because you are a gracious and compassionate God.
Blessed art thou, O Lord, who hearest prayer.

16. Be pleased, O Lord our God, to dwell in Zion, and let your servants *serve you in Jerusalem.
Blessed art thou, O Lord, whom we worship in reverence.

17. We praise you, you who are the Lord our God and the God of our fathers, for all the benefits of covenant faithfulness and compassion with which you have done good to us and to our fathers before us. And if we say: "Our feet are *turning

aside," your faithfulness will hold us up.
Blessed art thou, O Lord, to whom it is good to offer praise.

Ps. 147:1; 33:1; 50:23; 107:8; Ps. Sol. III. 1-2. Reading 47.

18. Establish your *peace for your people Israel, for your city and your inheritance; and bless all of us together.
Blessed art thou, O Lord, who provideth *well-being with tranquillity.

*Shalom: 85:8; 122:6; "well-being, 147:14; Isa. with 9:7; 32:17-18; tranquillity." 66:12-13; Jer. Ps. 29:11; 33:6-7.
*The best one can do in a brief phrase with shalom.

Comments:

1. Petition 12 is omitted here because it was a rather late addition to this liturgical prayer. According to St. Jerome it was phrased thus: "For apostates may there be no hope, and may the Nazarenes and the heretics suddenly perish" (cf. George F. Moore, *Judaism*, I, p. 292 and note 8). It was inserted into the *'Amidah*—another name for this prayer—at the direction of Rabban Gamaliel II and the rabbinic academy, the highest religious authority of Judaism at that time, ca. A.D. 80-90. Its recitation in synagogue services was made mandatory. The purpose of this *Birkath haminim*, as it was called, was to expose Jewish Christians and make possible their expulsion from the synagogues.

2. The *'Amidah* was, as noted in the introduction above, in use in the synagogues before the opening of the Christian era. It is replete with biblical ideas. The student should compare it in detail with the ancient litany found attached to the Hebrew text of Sirach, as given in Reading 1, and with the prayer in ch. 36 of Sirach. Further, he will be repaid by comparing the ideas of this prayer with the teachings of Jesus, particularly as given in the Sermon on the Mount and Matthew's version of the Lord's Prayer. See further discussion in the Historical Notes of Part III.

READING 58: The *'Aqedah* petition (cf. Genesis 22)

An ancient part of the synagogue liturgy for New Year's Day was prayer petitioning God to remember the offering of Isaac on his descendants' behalf.

Our God and God of our fathers, let us be remembered by you for good. Grant us a visitation of salvation and mercy from the highest heavens of *old.

*Or, "eternity"; Ps. 68:32-33; Isa. 45:8.

Remember in our regard, O Lord our God, the covenant, the covenant faithfulness and the oath which you swore to Abraham our father on Mount Moriah.

Gen. 22:15-18.

And may the *bonds with which Abraham bound his son Isaac upon the altar appear before you: for he subdued his compassion so as to accomplish your will wholeheartedly.

*Or, "binding": Gen. 22:9.

Gen. 22:12.

Exod.
32:12-13; Ps.
85:4ff.
Cf.
Shemoneh
'Esreh 14,
Reading 57.
So may your compassion overcome your anger against us: in your great goodness may the fierceness of your wrath turn aside from your people, from your city and from your inheritance.

Deut. 4:4-10;
8:3; 32:46-47.

Lev. 26:42-45.
Fulfill, O Lord our God, your word to us in which you bade us to trust in your Law given through Moses your servant, from the mouth of your Glory, as it is said: "But I will remember for their sakes the covenant of their ancestors. . . ."

O remember the binding of Isaac this day in mercy to his descendants!

Blessed art thou, O Lord, who rememberest the covenant.

Comments:

1. The preceding is an adaptation of the text as given in the *Prayer Book for the First Day of New Year*, with a revised English translation, edited by the Rev. Dr. A. Th. Philips, p. 113. Philips' translation faces the Hebrew text, page for page. The translation has been recast into modern style; and, where it was felt necessary, the Hebrew retranslated.

2. The notions that Isaac's offering (a) was actually voluntary, and (b) had atoning merit before God on behalf of Israel, and that (c) his release was comparable to resurrection from the dead, are all ancient—cf. Heb. 11:17-19. The first two, at least, are believed to have predated the Christian era. Cf. Historical Notes for further discussion.

3. MAJOR FESTIVALS, AND SABBATH-KEEPING

READING 59: Passover—the offering (M. *Pesachim* 5.1; 6.1) and the meal (M. *Pesachim* 10.1-4, 6-7, 9; M. *Zebachim* 5.8)

The Jewish religious festival which receives the most attention in the Gospels is Passover. The Gospel of John notes the activities of Jesus at two different Passover festivals prior to His death; and all the Gospels indicate not only that Jesus was put to death at Passover time, but that His death fulfilled both the meaning of Passover and details of the Passover ritual.

a. The sacrificial offering

*Or, 1:30
P.M., figuring
from 6 A.M.
Mishnah *Pesachim* 5.1: The daily burnt offering . . . was killed on the eve of the Passover at half past the *seventh hour and offered up at half past the eighth hour, whether on a weekday or on the Sabbath.

When the eve of the Passover coincided with the eve of the Sabbath, it was killed at half past the sixth hour and offered up

at half past the seventh hour. Then the Passover sacrifice was   <small>Cf. John   Mark
19:31   15:33-34; John
Matt.   19:14-16.
27:45-46;   Deut. 16:5-7.</small>
slaughtered. . . .

6.1: These matters regarding the Passover take precedence
over the Sabbath: slaughtering it, sprinkling its blood, cleans-   <small>Exod. 12:5-10;
cf. Lev. 1:3-13;
3:1-11.</small>
ing its entrails, and burning its fat. . . .

Comment:

The Jewish day, especially for ritual purposes, was counted from sundown to sundown (cf. Gen. 1:5, 8, etc.). But the daylight hours were
counted from sunrise, or about 6 A.M. If the time notices given in the
Gospel accounts are synchronized with those of the Mishnah, above, it
would seem that Jesus was crucified at the time of the daily afternoon burnt
offerings on Passover day, a Passover whose end coincided with the eve of
the Sabbath of that week. (Cf. Mark 15:42—16:2)

   b. The ritual meal at Passover (cf. Exod.12; Mark 14:12ff.)

The Passover was a solemn occasion, and it was celebrated by family
groups—either actual, or constituted for the occasion (as a rabbi and his
"sons" or disciples). For the meal, a formal *seder*, or religious service, had
been developed. It began after sundown, and its four successive segments
were each marked by the ritual use of a cup of wine.

M. *Pesachim* 10.1: On Passover eves, from about the time of
the *evening sacrifices, one must not eat until it becomes   <small>*Cf. 5.1, above.</small>
dark. . . .

10.2: They poured out for him the first cup. The School of   <small>Cf. Luke 22:17;
"him" is
whoever acts
as head of
family for the
occasion.</small>
Shammai say: "He must say the blessing for the day, then the
blessing for the wine." But the School of Hillel say: "The
blessing for the wine, then for the day."

Comment:

Shammai and Hillel were two leading rabbis who lived into the time of
Jesus' boyhood. They founded two rival schools of Torah interpretation. A
sample of their differences appears here.

After the first cup and the benedictions, the family head had to wash his
hands. Edersheim (*Life and Times of Jesus the Messiah*, Vol. II, p. 497) thinks
that it was at this point in the liturgy that Jesus washed the disciples' feet
(John 13). Following the hand-washing, the various items of Passover food
were brought before him, to be distributed and eaten in the prescribed
order.

10.3: They brought *it before him. He dipped with *lettuce   <small>*Passover   *And/or other
food.   vegetables.
*The bitter
herbs: Exod.
12:8.</small>
until the time came for the *bread condiment.

During the next stage, the Passover story was to be recited, with the
youngest son present asking the leading questions.

The wine was
mixed with
water.

10.4: They mixed for him the second cup. At this point the child questions his father, and if the child does not have enough understanding, the father instructs him. . . .Thus according to the knowledge of the child, his father instructs him. He begins with the *abasement and ends with the great improvement in fortunes. And he explains from "My ancestor was a wandering Aramean" until he concludes the whole selection.

Cf. Exod.
12:25ff.
*From descent
into Egyptian
slavery to
entrance into
Canaan.
Cf. Deut.
26:5ff.

Before the main part of the meal, the recitation or chanting of *Hallel* (praise) psalms was begun. The Hallel psalms include Psalms 111 through 118, in particular.

*The end of Ps.
113.
*The end of Ps.
114.

10.6: How far does one recite? The School of Shammai say, *"Up to 'as a joyous mother of children,' " but the School of Hillel say, *"As far as 'the flint into a fountain of water.' " And he concludes with the *Redemption* benediction.

The main meal was then eaten. Following the eating of the main dishes, including the lamb, further ritual was prescribed: the third cup of wine, the grace for concluding meals, and a hand-washing in which all participated. The ritual was concluded with the fourth cup of wine over which the rest of the *Hallel* was chanted.

Cf. Mark
14:22-23.
*With Ps.
115—118.
*The first and
second, the
second and
third. Cf. Mark
14:25.

10.7: Then they poured for him the third cup. He utters the blessing over food. Over the fourth he concludes the *Hallel*, saying the blessing over song. Between *those cups he may drink if he wishes; but between the third and the fourth he must not drink.

The meal had to terminate at midnight, after which the remains of the Passover lamb conveyed ritual impurity.

M. *Pesachim* 10.9: After midnight the Passover offering defiles the hands.

M. *Zebachim* 5.8: . . . the Passover lamb could be eaten during that night only, and only till midnight.

The time from nightfall until midnight gave ample time for a good deal of talk, if desired. Mishnah *Pesachim* 10.8 indicates that it was not uncommon for some, even all, to fall asleep during the *seder*. Thus Jesus had time to give the discourses recorded in John 13—16. The lateness of finishing the meal would readily explain the great sleepiness of the disciples (cf. Mark 14:37-41).

Comment:

The Mishnah readings above, as well as those below, have been adapted from the translations given in *The Mishnah* as translated and edited by Herbert Danby and in *Mishnayot*, second edition in seven volumes, as translated and edited by Philip Blackman. The latter also provides the pointed Hebrew text. Constant attention has been given to this text, as well as to the notes in both works as a guide to the renderings given herein.

READING 60: Booths—The willow-branch rite (M. *Sukkah* 4.1, 5), the water libation (4.9-10), the lighting ceremony (5.2-3)

For background see Leviticus 23:33-36 and Deuteronomy 16:16; 31:10-11.

Although the Synoptic Gospels ignore the Jewish festivals except for the Passover at which Jesus was crucified, John gives much attention to the events involving Jesus during the Feast of Booths (or, "Tabernacles") which preceded His last Passover: see John 7—9. It was the festival of the harvest ingathering, and was celebrated with rejoicing and elaborate ritual for seven days. During this time the celebrants had to live in booths or huts like those temporary shelters which were thrown up in the fields for those who guarded the olive and vintage harvests from both animal and human predators.

Like Passover, Booths was a major pilgrim festival in Jesus' time. Thousands of Jews from the Diaspora came up to Jerusalem to appear before the Lord, according to the Law. Details of the Temple ritual important to the understanding of certain references in John are here given.

a. The willow-branch rite

M. *Sukkah* 4.1: The **lulab* and the willow-branch rites are performed for six, sometimes seven, days; the **Hallel* and the rejoicing, eight days; the booth and the water libation, seven days. . . .

> *A bundle of palm, myrtle and willow, for waving.
> *Ps. 111—118; Deut. 16:14

4.5: How was the rite of the willow branch performed? There was a place below Jerusalem called *Motsah*. *They used to go down there and cut young willow branches; and they came and stood them all along the sides of the altar, with their tips leaning over the top of the altar.

> *Some of the priests.

Then they *blew: a long, then a quavering, and finally a long blast. Each day they proceeded around the altar a single time, chanting: "We implore thee, O Lord, *save now, we pray; we implore thee, O Lord, send prosperity, we pray!"

> *On the ram's-horn trumpets. Cf. Ps. 26:6-7.
> *Heb., *hoshiah-nah* = "hosanna." Ps. 118:25.

Comments:

1. In Jesus' time Booths, like Passover, was a festival in which expectations of the Messiah's appearance ran high. The next verse of that psalm (118:26) reads: "Blessed is he who comes (or, is to come) in the name of the

Lord," i.e., the Messiah. John accurately represents the high pitch of messianic expectation among the festival crowds, some of whom were alternately encouraged and perplexed by Jesus' words and actions.

2. The Mishnah adds: "Rabbi Judah says: '*Ani waho*! save us, we pray!'" These words were substitutes for the opening phrase of the petition, '*ana YHWH*, in order to avoid the pronunciation of the sacred divine name YHWH. Such substitutes were common practice. However, the Hebrew letters of this expression could also be read as '*ani wahu*, meaning "I and He."

There is good reason to think that John, at 8:16b, is representing Jesus as having adopted this ritual substitute for the divine name: " . . . it is not I alone that judge, but *I-and-He* who sent me" (i.e., God, who also judges). The final clause here is thus parallel to similar "but"-clauses in vv. 26 and 42. Translated into Greek by John, the phrase comes out, as in our English text, "I and He."

b. The water libation

Cf. John 9:7;
"Isaiah" 4,
Reading 56.
*On the return

*Cf. 4.5,
above.

4.9: How was the water libation performed? They filled a golden flagon holding about one and a half pints with water from the Siloam pool. When they reached the *Water Gate they blew a long, a quavering, and a long *blast. The priest went up the altar ramp and turned to his left where there were two silverbowls. . . .

Comment:

The bowls had funnellike tops. One received the water libation and the other was for wine libations.

*Because   water on the
forbidden to   Sabbath.
draw or carry

*Of the   for use when
Temple, ready needed.

4.10: Just as on a weekday, so the rite was performed on a Sabbath, except that on the eve of the Sabbath *they would fill a golden jar that had not been consecrated with water from Siloam, and put it in a *room.

John carefully, and often subtly, connects Jesus' acts and deeds with Jewish religious institutions. He refers to their biblical backgrounds, traditional developments, and current practices. It is to be noted that Jesus' proclamation of Himself as the source of living water—in contradistinction to the Jewish claim that the source was the Mosaic Law—was made at Booths, a principal ritual of which was the water libation (John 7:37-38). Moreover, the water for the libation ceremony was drawn from Siloam, which was connected in Jewish tradition with signs performed by Isaiah (cf. "Isaiah" 4, Reading 56). Thus, on what seems to be the Sabbath following the Festival of Booths, Jesus healed the blind man by having him wash in the Pool of Siloam (John 9:1ff.). This "sign" of Jesus also has symbolic connections with the ceremony of lights, another major ritual of Booths.

c. The lighting ceremony

5.2: At the close of the first day of the festival, they went into the Court of the Women where they had made an important change. Golden lampstands with four golden bowls on top and a ladder to each bowl were placed there. Four young priests tended them: they held oil pitchers containing about seven and a half gallons each, from which they poured into every bowl.

5.3: They tore the priests' worn-out trousers and sashes into strips for wicks, and lit them. And there was no courtyard in Jerusalem that was not illuminated by the light at the place of the water-drawing.

Psalm 118:27 reads: "The Lord is God, and He has given us light." Since this psalm concluded the *Hallel* which was chanted repeatedly during the festival, it would be very much in mind during this ritual. For the Jews, the light which God had given Israel was the Law, and the light ceremony was a symbol of the Law as God's light. But for John, Jesus is the Light of the World, the true fulfillment of the Law and of this light ceremony. Jesus proclaimed Himself as such during the festival (John 8:12), and afterward performed the "sign" which dramatically symbolized the reality of the claim (cf. especially John 9:5, 39-41).

READING 61: Day of Atonement—the Temple ritual (M. *Yoma* 3.8; M. *Kelim* 1.9; M. *Yoma* 5.1-7), the solemnity of the Day (M. *Yoma* 8.1, 4, 9)

For background see Leviticus 16:3-34; 23:26-32; Numbers 29:7-11.

The Day of Atonement was to be celebrated on the tenth of the seventh month, five days prior to the beginning of the Festival of Booths. It was a most solemn day. On it the high priest went into the Most Holy Place, wherein God's Presence was believed to be resident. An annual observance, it was the only time that anyone entered the Most Holy Place. It was believed that if the ceremony was not properly performed, or if God was displeased with it, the high priest would perish when he entered. It was a long and complicated ritual. Significant excerpts from the Mishnah description are here given.

a. The temple ritual

M. *Yoma* 3.8: *He came to his own bullock, which stood between the Port and the Altar, with its head to the south and its face turned toward the west. He put both *hands on it and confessed, saying, "I implore thee, O God. I have committed sin both knowingly and ignorantly, I have transgressed

*The high priest; cf. Lev. 16:11.

*Cf. Lev. 4:3ff.

against you, both I and my house. I implore thee, O God, pray forgive the iniquities, transgressions and sins which I have committed before thee, both I and my house, as it is written in the Law of Moses thy servant, 'For on this day shall atonement be made for you, to cleanse you. . . .' " And they responded after him: "Blessed be the *Name, the glory of His kingdom is for ever and ever."

Lev. 16:30.

*Of God.

Comment:

The confessional in the ancient liturgy of the Church, with its prayer for forgiveness of sins both of commission and omission, seems to have been modeled on this prayer.

*Areas previously mentioned as holy.

*Of the yom kippur sacrifices.

M. *Kelim* 1.9: . . . The Most Holy Place is holier yet than *they are, for none may enter except the high priest alone on the Day of Atonement at the time of the *service.

Originally, after the bullock was slain, the high priest took incense and some of the blood into the Most Holy Place, to sprinkle blood of atonement on the mercy seat, which was on top of the Ark of the Covenant (Lev. 16:14; cf. Exod. 25:17-22). Then the goats, one for a sin-offering for the people and one for a scapegoat, were chosen. The high priest had to sprinkle the blood of the sin-offering on the mercy seat in the same way he had the bullock's blood. In the Temple, out of necessity, first the arrangements for the incense were made, then the sacrificial blood of each animal in turn was taken in and sprinkled on the mercy seat.

*Containing incense.

*18 to 20 inches.

*Or, held back by a hook.

M. *Yoma* 5.1: . . . He took the fire-pan in his right hand and the *ladle in his left. He walked through the sanctuary until he reached the space between the two curtains that separated the sanctuary from the Most Holy Place. There was a *cubit's space between them. . . .The outer curtain was *looped up on the south side, and the inner one on the north side. . . .

With the edges of the curtains pulled back in that way, the high priest had a walkway into the Most Holy Place, which was still concealed from view from the outside. Through the walkway he carried in the incense and later the blood.

Cf. Isa. 6:4.

*The Holy Place.

*I.e., that he had died. Cf. Luke 1:21.

He heaped up the incense on the burning coals and the whole compartment was filled with smoke. He came back by the way that he went in. In the *outer compartment he prayed a brief prayer. He did not make a long prayer so as not to make the people *afraid.

*Of the bullock.

5.3: He took the *blood from him who was stirring it. He entered the place where he had been and stood where he had

stood before. Then he sprinkled some of it, one time upward   ^{Cf. Heb.}
and seven times downward. . . .He came out and set the   ^{9.3-12.}
basin down on the golden stand in the sanctuary.

Then he sprinkled the blood of the sin-offering in the same way, coming
out afterward to complete the ritual at the great altar in the sight of the
congregation.

5.7: Every act for the Day of Atonement is here stated accord-
ing to the proper order. If *he performed an act *too soon, it   *The high   *Literally,
was as if he had done nothing at all. . . .   priest.   "before its
                                                                               fellow."

                                                                  I.e., he had
And likewise also in regard to the ritual in the sanctuary and at invalidated the
the golden altar, because each of them is a separate act of   service and had
atonement.   to begin all
                                                                  over again.

Comment:

Any deviation from the prescribed pattern of actions was considered to
render the ritual invalid. Even though this attitude could be defended on
the grounds that it was so ordered in the Law of Moses, and hence was
divinely inspired, it nonetheless bordered on viewing the Temple rites as
magical acts.

   b. The solemnity of the Day and its practical meaning
The Day of Atonement was observed as a Sabbath—a day of rest, introspec-
tion and personal repentance, and fasting.

M. *Yoma* 8.1: On the Day of Atonement, eating and drinking,
*washing and anointing, putting on sandals, and sexual rela-   *For mere
tions are forbidden. . . .   cosmetic
                                                                purposes.

8.4: Children are not required to fast on the Day of Atonement; but they should give them practice in it a year or two
*before, so they may get used to the mandatory religious   *Religious
observances. . . .   adulthood
                                                               began at age
                                                               12.

8.9: The one who says, "I can sin and repent, and I can sin
again and repent," will not be *given opportunity to repent.   *I.e., by God.
Or: "I can sin and the Day of Atonement will provide atone-   Eccl. 8.11-13;
ment," then the Day of Atonement provides no atonement.   Sirach 5.4-7;
                                                               Ps. Sol. III.6,
                                                               Reading 47.

The Day of Atonement provides atonement for transgressions
of men against *God; but for transgressions between a man   *Literally, "the   Cf. Matt.
and his fellow, the Day of Atonement provides atonement   Place," a   5.23-24;
only when he has propitiated his fellow.   euphemism for   6.14-15; Mark
                                                               the divine   11.25.
                                                               name.

READING 62: Sabbath-keeping—general rules (M. *Sabbath* 2.7; 7.1-2), healing on the Sabbath (M. *Sabbath* 22.6; M. *Yoma* 8.6), penalty for profanation (M. *Sanhedrin* 7.4)

For background see Exodus 20:8-11; 31:12-17; Numbers 15:32-36.

To the pious, the Sabbath was the major religious institution of Judaism, and its sanctity was jealously guarded. Many, at different times, had honored the Sabbath at the cost of their lives (cf. I Macc. 2:29-38). The interpreters of the Law had produced a mass of rules regarding what was prescribed, what was permitted, and what was prohibited on the Sabbath. One of the main ways in which Jesus antagonized the Pharisaic interpreters of the Law was by doing what, in their view, violated the Sabbath. A few samples from the Mishnah will indicate the spirit of these regulations.

> *a. General rules*
> M. *Sabbath* 2.7: A man must say three things to those of his household toward dusk on a Sabbath eve: "Have you set aside the tithes?" "Have you prepared the *erub*?" and, "Light the lamp." If there is doubt as to whether it is dark or not, they should not take tithes from what they know certainly to be untithed, nor wash utensils, nor light the lamps. Yet they may take tithes from produce that is *in doubt, and prepare the *erub*, and cover food that is to be kept hot.

*I.e., as to whether it had been tithed before it was bought.

Comment:

Because all "profane" activities were to cease at dark with the onset of the Sabbath, all necessary preparations—including food for the following day—had to be accomplished by the time of the lighting of the sabbath lamps at nightfall. All had to be in readiness by then.

However, some provisions were made for necessary movement beyond the confines of the household, and even of one's town. A "sabbath day's journey" as mentioned in Acts 1:12 was fixed at 2,000 cubits (= about 1,000 yards, or slightly less than 3/5 mile). The *erub* mentioned above was a device which allowed the extension of these sabbath limits on walking or traveling. *Erubin*, the tractate of the Mishnah which follows *Sabbath*, is entirely devoted to its applications.

*The "sages," or earlier interpreters.

*Or, "liable for one sin-offering." Cf. Lev. 4:27ff.; 5:15ff.

7.1: *They enunciated a great general rule in regard to the Sabbath: Whoever did many acts of work on many sabbaths, in ignorance of the principle of the Sabbath, is *guilty of only one sin; but if one was cognizant of the Sabbath principle, yet did many acts of work on many sabbaths, he is liable for every sabbath. . . .he is liable for every main kind of work which he did. But if he did many acts of work of one main kind only, he is liable for one sin-offering.

*Literally, "forty less one."

7.2: There are *thirty-nine main kinds of work: sowing, plowing, reaping, binding sheaves, threshing, winnowing, cleaning, grinding, sifting, kneading, baking; shearing wool and washing, *beating or dyeing it, spinning, weaving, making two loops, weaving two threads, *separating two threads, tying or untying a knot, sewing two stitches; hunting a deer, slaughtering, flaying or salting it, or curing, scraping or cutting its hide; writing two letters, erasing so as to write two letters; building or demolishing; putting out or lighting a fire; striking with a hammer; carrying from *one domain into another. These are the thirty-nine *main kinds of work.

*Or, "carding."

*Which are crossed in the weave of the cloth.

*"Public" to "private" and vice versa

*Literally, "fathers of work."

Comment:

From these main classes of prohibited labors, the rabbis were able to deduce detailed prohibitions against other kinds of "work," so as to protect the sanctity of the Sabbath. These were in addition to those acts which, in the Law, were prohibited at any and all times. But in addition to the possibility of doing the prescribed things in the wrong way, the prohibitions were so numerous and detailed that it would be easy for a person to err through ignorance. The principle set out by the "sages," above, takes this into account. However, John 7:49 indicates that not all the religious leaders took a charitable view concerning ignorance of religious teachings and duties.

b. Healing on the Sabbath

M. *Sabbath* 22.6: They may anoint or *rub, but not knead or scrape themselves. . . .They may not use emetic preparations; nor straighten the *limb of a child; nor set a fractured limb. Should one's hand or foot be *dislocated, they may not pour cold water on it; but he may wash it according to his custom, and if it is healed, it is healed.

*Gently; some texts add "the stomach."

*If injured or deformed.

*Or, "sprained."

M. *Yoma* 8.6: . . . In addition, Mattithiah ben Heresh said: "If someone has a sore throat, they may put medicine in his mouth on the Sabbath, since it is a question whether his life is in danger." So any case in which life is in doubt takes precedence over the Sabbath (regulations).

Cf. Luke 13:10-16; John 7:22-24

Comment:

According to the Gospels, several of Jesus' controversies with the Pharisees arose because of His healings on the Sabbath. The question at issue on some of the occasions seems to have been whether life was in danger or not. If not, Jesus was guilty of forbidden work: cf. Luke 13:14.

Even the principle of allowing medical attention when life is in jeopardy seems to have gained wider acceptance only after the Gospel period. The rabbi quoted above, along with three others mentioned in the later talmudic materials as supporting this principle, belonged to a later period.

c. Penalty for Sabbath profanation

Cf. John 5:10, 18.

M. *Sanhedrin* 7.4: These are to be stoned: . . . whoever profanes the Sabbath; whoever curses his father or his mother; he

*I.e., others to idolatry or apostasy: John 10:31-33.

who lies with a betrothed maiden; whoever *beguiles or leads astray; the sorcerer; and a stubborn and rebellious son.

Comment:

Note that profanation of the Sabbath was classed with sins of the most heinous types. Those omitted above are found enumerated in Numbers 19. The others mentioned are prohibited elsewhere in the Law. The controversies of the Jewish leaders with Jesus, and their final accusations against Him, should be studied in the light of the foregoing.

4. MISCELLANEOUS RITUAL AND ORDINANCES

a. Relating to Jesus' nativity

READING 63: The priestly ministry (M. *Taanith* 4.2; M. *Tamid* 3.1; 5.2, 4; 6.3)

Cf. this section with Luke 1:8ff.

*Num. 28:1-2.

*Cf. Lev. 1:4; 3:2, 12, etc.

*Or, "early."

Cf. I Chron. 23:1ff.; Neh. 12:44-45.

*Or, "course."

Cf. Luke 1:8.   *I.e., the laymen.

Gen. 1.

M. *Taanith* 4.2: These are the orders of Standers. Since it is said: *"'Command the Israelites and say to them, 'My offering, my food,' . . . ,'" how can one's offering be offered if *he does not stand by it? The *first prophets ordained twenty-four watches; and for every watch there was a section in Jerusalem of priests, Levites and Israelites. When the time came for a *watch to go up, the priests and Levites belonging to it went up to Jerusalem, while the *Israelites of that watch gathered in their towns and read about the Creation.

Comment:

The courses of ministrant priests and Levites had been established, according to biblical tradition, in the times of David and Solomon; and they were re-established during the Restoration under Nehemiah when the second Temple was completed.

The "Standers" were laymen of Jerusalem who stood and recited the requisite prayers during the sacrificial ceremonies. They represented the laymen of the towns and villages from which the "watch" of priests and Levites had come up for service at the time appointed for them.

*In charge of the Temple services.

*The incense altar, cf. Exod. 30.

M. *Tamid* 3.1: The *officer said to them: "Come and cast lots for who is to slaughter, who is to toss the blood, who is to clean the *inner altar, who is to clean the bowls of the lampstand. . . ."

5.2: He said to them: "You who are new to the burning of the

incense, come and cast lots." And he who was worthy at-
tained the privilege. . . .   Cf. Luke 1:9.

5.4: Whoever had gained the privilege of making the incense
offering took up the ladle. It was like a large dry-measure
vessel, of gold and holding three *kabs*. Inside it was a censer   *A kab =
full of incense, covered by a lid which had a ring handle. . . .   about 1 1/6
                                                                      quart.

6.3: He who was privileged to offer incense lifted the censer
from out of the ladle, which he gave to *his friend or rela-   *Who assisted
tive. . . . He who was to offer the incense did not offer it until   him.
the officer said to him: "Offer it!" . . . When everyone had
*withdrawn, he offered the incense, bowed in worship, and   *From the
came out.   holy place
                                                                      cf. Exod.
                                                                      30:6-8;
                                                                      40:26-27.

Comment:

The Mishnah description indicates that the incense offering was a brief
ritual. This helps explain the wonder of the people when Zachariah, father
of John the Baptist, did not reappear in the expected time. Cf. Luke 1:10, 21.

READING 64a: Purification of a mother after childbirth (M. *Kelim* 1.8; M.
Keritoth 2.4)

For background see Leviticus 12:2-5.

A woman who had borne a child was ritually unclean for a prescribed
period and was prohibited from entering the sanctuary. The period was
longer if the child was a girl than if it was a boy. Purification sacrifices had
to be offered; and if it were a first-born son, a redemption price had to be
paid.

M. *Kelim* 1.8: Inside the *wall it is still more holy than *they   *Of Jerusalem. *Other towns.
are, because there they may eat the sacrifices of lesser sanctity
and the second tithe. The mount of the Temple is more holy
yet, for no men or women with a discharge, or menstruants, or
women just after childbirth may enter.

M. *Keritoth* 2.4: . . . These bring an offering according to their   Cf. Lev. 12:8;
means: one who swears a false oath; one who utters a thought-   Luke 2:24.
less oath; one who unwittingly defiles the Temple or its holy   Cf. Lev. 5:4.
things; the woman after childbirth; and the leper.   Lev. 12.

READING 64b: Redemption of the first-born; the head-tax (M. *Bechoroth*
8.7; M. *Shekalim* 1.1, 3, 6)

For background see Exodus 13:2, 13; 30:11-16.

According to Numbers 18:15-17, the first-born children and the first-born of domestic animals not used for sacrifice (e.g., donkeys) had to be redeemed: "And those from the age of a month onward you must redeem at the value of five silver shekels, of sacred shekel weight which is twenty *gerahs*" (my translation of Num. 18:16).

M. *Bechoroth* 8.7: Five *selas* (must be paid) for a son, according to *the Tyrian *maneh*. . . .

*As a standard of value.

According to Exodus 30:11-16, every male Israelite was subject to a poll tax of a half-shekel annually, beginning with his twentieth birthday. This tax supported the Tabernacle (later, the Temple) establishment.

M. *Shekalim* 1.1: On the first day of Adar they make proclamation regarding the half-shekel tax. . . .

*Of money changers. *Or, "city"; Jerusalem.
*The Temple area.
*I.e., laymen.

1.3: On the fifteenth the *tables were set up in the *province; on the twenty-fifth they set them up in the *holy place, and when they had set them up in the Temple they began to collect the tax. From whom did they take it? From Levites and *Israelites, proselytes and freed slaves; but not from women, or slaves, or minors. . . .

1.6: And these are liable to the exchange rate differential: Levites and Israelites, proselytes and freed slaves; but not priests, or women, or slaves or minors.

Comment:

Since the valuation standard of the sanctuary coinage was different from that of the common currency, moneychangers were required in the Temple precincts. Jesus knew the hardship which the Temple taxes and required offerings worked on the poor, quite without the added burden of the exchange rate differential that was collected when common money was exchanged for the sacred sanctuary coinage. It was in this way that the Sadducean hierarchy of Jerusalem profited from the sweat and blood of the poor of the land. They had made the Temple literally a "den of robbers," as Jesus charged: cf. Mark 11:17.

b. Illustrating other New Testament references

READING 65a: The "treasury" (M. *Shekalim* 6.5)

M. *Shekalim* 6.5: There were thirteen *shophar*-chests in the Temple, labeled: "new shekel dues"; "old shekel dues"; "bird offerings"; "young birds for burnt offerings"; . . . and on six of them, "free-will offerings."

Comment:

It was probably into the horn-shaped or conical mouth of one of the free-will offering chests that the widow threw her two small coins, about which Jesus commented (Mark 12:41-44). Some of the uses made of the funds thus collected are indicated in preceding paragraphs of this tractate.

READING 65b: The "corban," or dedication oath (M. *Nedarim* 4.1, 6; 5.6)

For background see Deuteronomy 23:21-23; Mark 7:10-13.

By an oath or vow of "corban" (Heb., *qorban*) a man might dedicate any possession to sacred use (thus prohibiting its secular use), or even specify persons as "corban" so far as giving to or receiving benefits from them was concerned. Extracts from *Nedarim* ("vows") will illustrate the principle.

M. *Nedarim* 4.1: Between one who is under a vow not to have any benefit from his *companion and one who has vowed not to take any food from him, the only difference concerns the *treading of the foot and the use of vessels not employed in preparing necessary food. . . .

*In a Pharisaic brotherhood.

*He must not walk through his fellow's house or grounds.

4.6: One who has vowed not to have any benefit from his companion must not lend to or borrow from him, nor give or take a loan from him, nor sell to or purchase from him. . . .

5.6: Should one under a vow not to have any benefit from his companion have nothing to eat, *he may give it to someone else. Then the first is permitted to have it.

*The companion.

Once there was in Beth Horon a man whose father was under a vow not to have any benefit from him. He made a marriage festival for his son and he said to his companion: "The court-yard and banquet are a gift to you. Yet they are not really yours, but are given only so that my father may enter and eat the banquet with us. . . ."

Cf. Mark 7:11.

Comment:

The Pharisaic rules concerning vows were strict, in the spirit of the blameless man "who swears to his own hurt and does not change" (Ps. 15:4). Vows could be made easily, and could be introduced by several words other than *qorban* (= "It is dedicated"), even by using special idioms without the introducing word. Yet, rash vows were discouraged and means were devised to nullify those which would have done harm.

However, there was the possibility of someone's using the "corban" to escape responsibility for aging parents by pronouncing his property "corban" so far as they were concerned. It was the use of such vows to escape legitimate and biblically commanded responsibilities against which Jesus lodged His protest.

READING 66a: The leper's cleansing (M. *Kelim* 1.1, 4b; M. *Negaim* 14.1)

For background see Leviticus 14:2-32; Luke 5:12-14; 17:11ff.

Leprosy, still widespread in the Orient and Africa, was one of the most dreaded of diseases known to those of Jesus' day. The ritual defilement incurred by contact with a leper was only a little less than that from a corpse. The leper was excluded from normal society regardless of his rank, and had to announce his condition whenever anyone came near him: see Leviticus 13:43-46 and II Chronicles 26:18-21. However, if the disease abated, he could be ritually cleansed. This required that he present himself to the priest for confirmation and make the proper sacrifices.

*Literally, "fathers."

Cf. Lev. 14:8ff.

M. *Kelim* 1.1: These *principal causes of uncleanness, namely, . . . one who has been in contact with a corpse, and a leper in the days of his recovery . . . make people and vessels unclean upon contact. . . .

Lev. 15:19ff.

*I.e., a house.

Cf. Num. 19:11ff.

1.4b: A leper makes unclean more than a woman with an issue, for he defiles *it upon entering. . . . More severe than them all is defilement from a corpse, because it defiles by overshadowing, which is not true of the others.

*I.e., a priest.

*From spring or stream.   *Not raised in pen or cage.

*In the leper's presence.

*All into the bloody water.

M. *Negaim* 14.1: How did they cleanse the leper? *One brought a new pottery bowl and put about one-sixth pint of *living water in it. He also brought two *free birds. He killed one of them over the vessel that contained the water, then dug a hole and buried it *in his presence. Then he took cedar wood, hyssop and scarlet wool which he tied together with the ends of a strip of wool. He brought them close to the tips of the wings and tail of the other bird, then *dipped and sprinkled seven times on the back of the leper's hand and, some say, on his forehead also.

Comment:

Lev. 14:6-7 merely prescribes that the leper is to have the blood sprinkled on him seven times, without being precise as to where it had to be applied. The live bird was then set free.

READING 66b: Capital punishment and burial (M. *Sanhedrin* 6.4; M. *Sabbath* 23.4-5)

For background see Mark 15:42ff. and John 19:38-42.

M. *Sanhedrin* 6.4: . . . All who were stoned were also hanged, according to Rabbi Eliezer. But the Sages say that none should be hanged except the blasphemer and the idolater. . . .

M. *Sanhedrin* 7.4, Reading 62, c.

Cf. Mark 14:64; Luke 22:70-71.

How did they hang a man? They put a timber in the ground with a beam *extending from it. Someone tied the two hands together to it, and thus the body was suspended. . . .And they let it down soon, for if it remained there all night a negative commandment was violated . . . : "His body shall not remain all night upon the tree, but you must bury him the same day, for a hanged man is accursed of God. . . ."

*Like an inverted L.

Deut. 21:23.

Cf. Gal. 3:13.

Comment:

The Jewish method of capital punishment was not by crucifixion, but usually by stoning. When the victim was dead, his body was briefly displayed by hanging it on a gibbet. Recall that Jesus was considered to be leading the people astray (cf. John 7:12) and was adjudged guilty of blasphemy (Mark 14:64). He was thus subject to stoning and hanging.

However, Rome reserved the right of capital punishment at that time, so the Jewish authorities had to get Pilate to order Him crucified. Crucifixion was considered analogous to hanging. When He died, Jesus' friends removed His body according to the commandment of Deut. 21:23.

M. *Sabbath* 23.4: They may await nightfall at the sabbath limit to arrange matters for a bride; or to make arrangements for a corpse, to bring a coffin or the wrappings for it. . . .

23.5: They may get ready everything necessary for the dead, anointing and washing it; only they may not move any of its limbs. . . .They may bind up the chin, not so as to raise it but to prevent its dropping lower. . . .

They may not close the eyes of a dead person on the Sabbath. . . .

Comment:

On the recognition that some types of activities were necessary on the Sabbath, the interpreters of the Law defined in greater detail than the Bible does what might be done and how. These two Mishnah passages help one to understand the Gospel accounts of how the body of Jesus was handled, especially why the women awaited the expiration of the Sabbath before attempting to prepare His body for its final burial: cf. Luke 23:54—24:1.

5. THE RABBINIC OUTLOOK

READING 67: The oral tradition from Moses to Hillel (M. *Aboth* 1.1-3, 12-15; M. *Peah* 2.6; M. *Eduyoth* 8.7)

According to Mark 7:1-8, Jesus referred adversely to the "traditions of the elders" held by the Pharisees. Also, Matthew reports that He pointed out to His disciples that the scribes and Pharisees sat in Moses' seat, so their teaching was to be respected, but their ways were not to be imitated (Matt. 23:1ff.). He was referring to the Pharisaic claim to be the recipients of an oral tradition of Torah (interpretation of scripture) which derived ultimately from Moses. According to the Pharisees an unbroken "chain of tradition," a sort of "apostolic succession," had been maintained from the time of Moses to their own time, and the interpretations of the Law which they promulgated had been passed down along this chain. The claim is set out in the first chapter of the Mishnah tractate *Aboth* ("Fathers").

Deut. 31:23;
Josh. 1:7-8.
Josh. 24:31;
Judg. 2:7.
Neh. 8:1-8,
13ff., 9:1ff.
*I.e., weigh all
the evidence.

M. *Aboth* 1.1: Moses received Torah from Sinai and delivered it to Joshua; Joshua, to the Elders; the Elders, to the prophets; and the prophets delivered it to the men of the Great Assembly. They said three things: "Be *cautious in judgment." "Raise up many disciples." And "Make a hedge for the Torah."

Cf. Sirach 50;
Ant. XII.43 (=
ii.5).

*Literally, "the
service," i.e.,
the ritual.
Cf. Mic. 6:8.

1.2: Simeon the Righteous was of the survivors of the Great Assembly. He used to say: "The world is based on three things: upon Torah, upon *worship and upon deeds of mercy."

*The Torah
tradition.

*I.e., whole-
heartedly.
Cf. Luke
17:7-10.

1.3: Antigonus of Soko *received from Simeon the Righteous. He used to say: "Do not be like slaves who serve their master to receive a gift; but be like slaves who serve their master *without expecting a gift; and let the fear of Heaven be upon you."

The next names in the "chain" are reported in pairs, known as the *Zugoth*—"yoke-fellows"—who were co-leaders of the Pharisaic community in the late pre-Christian era. They often led schools whose interpretations of the Law differed at some points. The first mentioned are Yose ben Yo'ezer of Tseredah and Yose ben Jochanan of Jerusalem. They were followed by Joshua ben Perachya and Nittai the Arbelite, Judah ben Tabbai and Simeon ben Shetach, Shemayah and Abtalyon, and finally the famous Hillel and Shammai. With them, the succession entered the Christian era.

*The preceding
zugoth.

Ps. 34:14;
I Peter 3:11.
Cf. Mal. 2:6.

1.12: Hillel and Shammai received from *them. Hillel used to say: "Be of the disciples of Aaron, loving and pursuing peace; be one who loves humankind and brings them near to the Torah."

Mark 9:35.

*In knowledge
of the Torah.

*The Torah. *Or, "waste
         away."

1.13: He used to say: "If one makes his name great his name will be destroyed; one who does not *increase will decrease; one who does not learn deserves death; and whoever uses the *Crown for his own purposes will *pass away." . . .

Comments:

1. The first saying in 1.13 is a caution against ambition. Literally, it reads: "The name stretched [extended], his name perishes." These sayings, like several others reported from Hillel, are very terse, in the manner of the Proverbs.

2. "Whoever does not learn deserves death," since in the Pharisaic view the Torah and its study conferred life; cf. John 5:39.

3. The teaching of Torah or knowledge acquired from it was not to be for material gain. A Pharisaic teacher did not teach for pay. He supported himself by a trade, or was sometimes supported by his wife or a circle of disciples, and taught for the love of God and the Torah.

1.15: Shammai used to say: "Make your *Torah a regular duty." "Say little and do much." And "Welcome every man with a pleasant countenance."

*I.e., study of it

Comment:

Shammai and those of his school were usually "strict constructionists" in the application of the Law, and Shammai himself was hostile to non-Jews. Hillel and his school tended toward greater leniency in judgment, and tried to mitigate the harshness of the Law where possible. Hillel seemed to be genuinely philanthropic in his attitude, and was eager to lead non-Jews to become proselytes.

Except for a few dicta, notably concerning divorce, the spirit of Jesus' teachings is nearer to that of Hillel. Some of His criticisms of the Pharisees reported in the Gospels may have been directed originally against the school of Shammai.

M. *Peah* 2.6: . . . Nahum the Scribe said: "I have received from Rabbi Measha who received it from his father, who received it from the *Pairs who received it from the prophets as a *halakah* from Moses at Sinai that if anyone sowed his fields with two kinds of wheat and made of them one pile for threshing, he grants one *peah*; but if he made two heaps, he must grant two."

*Cf. note after M. *Aboth* 1.3, above.

*Authoritative rule or interpretation.

*Portion set aside for the poor.

M. *Eduyoth* 8.7: Rabbi Joshua said: "I have received it from Rabban Jochanan ben Zakkai, who heard from his *teacher, who heard it from his teacher as a *halakah* of Moses from Sinai, that Elijah will not come to determine uncleanness or cleanness, nor to expel or bring near; but to expel those who were brought near by violence and to bring near those who were removed by violence. . . ."

*Presumably, Hillel.

Comment:

The preceding are samples of an appeal to the "chain of tradition" set forth above. If a decree or an interpretation could be appealed to as having

come down the chain of tradition as a *halakah* given by Moses at Sinai, i.e.,
as part of the ancient oral tradition, it had more authority than any later
interpretation or ruling.

READING 68: Study of the Law (M. *Aboth* 1.6; 2.7-8, 12, 14; M. *Kiddushin*
4.14; M. *Aboth* 1.17)

> M. *Aboth* 1.6: Joshua ben Perachya and Nittai the Arbelite
> received from them. Joshua ben Perachya used to say: "Pro-
> cure a teacher for yourself and get yourself a companion; and
> judge every man *in the scale of merit."

*I.e., Matt. 7:1; John
charitably: 7:24.

Comment:

Since the study of the Law involved mastery of the oral tradition, one who
was serious about it needed a teacher who was himself well versed in the
tradition. Also, he needed a companion with whom to discuss regularly the
meaning of the scriptures, who would also encourage him to persevere both
in study and in the practice of righteousness. Like the Qumran Essenes, the
serious Pharisee believed that the truly blessed man was he who meditated
on God's Law day and night (cf. Ps. 1:2).

*Hillel.
Deut.
32:46-47; Isa. 32:17,
Prov. 1:1-6. James 3:18.
Prov. 2:1;
Sirach 41:12.

Cf. John 5:39.

> 2.7: . . . *He used to say: "The more Torah, the more life;
> more study, more wisdom; more counsel, more understand-
> ing; more righteousness, more peace. He who gains a good
> name gains it for himself; he who has gained for himself
> words of Torah has gained for himself the life of the Coming
> Age."

Cf. Eph. 2:10.

> 2.8: Rabban Jochanan ben Zakkai received from Hillel and
> from Shammai. He used to say: "If you have learned much
> Torah, do not take credit to yourself, for to this end were you
> created." . . .

*Disciple of I Tim. 4:7,
Jochanan ben 13ff.; II Tim.
Zakkai. 2:15.

Cf. Col. 3:17.

> 2.12: *Rabbi Yose said: ". . . .Prepare yourself to study the
> Law, since it does not become yours by inheritance." And
> "Let all that you do be done for the sake of Heaven." . . .

*Disciple of
Jochanan ben
Zakkai.
*Literally, cf. I Peter
"epicurean"; 3:15.
Matt. 6:4;
I Cor. 15:58;
Heb. 6:10.

> 2.14: *Rabbi Elazar said: "Be diligent to learn Torah." "Know
> what answer to give an *unbeliever." And "Know in whose
> presence you labor, and that your Employer, who will give
> you the wages due your work, is faithful."

*Or, "inter *Or, "world
est on it."

> M. *Kiddushin* 4.14: . . . Rabbi Nehorai says: "I would put
> aside all the occupations in the world and teach my son Torah
> only; for one enjoys the *reward of it in this *age, and yet the
> principal remains for the age to come. . . .it guards him from

*evil in his youth, and grants him a future and hope in his old age."

*Both moral evil and misfortune. Cf. Ps. 19:11; M. Aboth 2.7, above.

M. *Aboth* 1.17: Simeon *his son said: "All my days I grew up as a son of the Sages, and I have not found anything better for a man than silence." And "The principal thing is not expounding but practice; and whoever multiplies words occasions sin."

*Either of Hillel, or of Gamaliel I.

Cf. M. Aboth 1.15, Reading 67; Sirach 9:15-16, Prov. 10:19; James 1:22-25.

Comment:

There was a practical need for the study of the Law, so as to be able to apply it to the on-going and changing demands of daily life. However, *Torah* meant more than the legal aspect of the scriptures and the tradition. It meant interpretation for devotional and homiletic purposes as well. And there were many, like Rabbi Nehorai above, for whom Torah study became an end in itself, a phenomenon which has modern parallels in Christianity. It was against this tendency that Simeon reacted, just as James reacted against the similar tendency in the early Church.

READING 69: Rabbinic interpretation and reasoning (M. *Aboth* 1.5; M. *Sabbath* 9.1; M. *Pesachim* 5.5; 6.1-2)

M. *Aboth* 1.5: Yose ben Jochanan of Jerusalem used to say: " . . . Do not talk much with the wife." *They said: "If concerning one's own wife, how much more does it apply to the wife of one's companion!" Hence the Sages say: "One who talks much with a woman occasions evil to himself: he desists from the study of Torah, and at last will inherit Gehenna."

*Who discussed his meaning.

Cf. John 4:27.

Eccl. 7:26; Sirach 9:1-9.

Comment:

This illustrates the *Kal wa-Homer* argument or form of reasoning, i.e., reasoning from a minor case to a major conclusion or instance, or vice versa. The "how much more" is characteristic of this argument, which is the first of the seven principles of interpretation enumerated by Hillel. It was also a favorite form of argument with the apostle Paul: cf. Rom. 5:9, 18; 8:32.

M. *Sabbath* 9.1: Rabbi Akiba said: "How do we know concerning an idol that, when carried, it imparts defilement like a menstruant? Because *it says, 'You will *cast them away as a menstruant; you will say to it: Begone!' Just as a menstruant imparts defilement by being carried, so does an idol."

*Isa. 30:22

*Literally, "scatter, fling out."

Comment:

Idols were an abomination to pious Jews. Here rules concerning ritual defilement are extended to idols on the basis of a passage in Isaiah which metaphorically likens the treatment to be given to idols to the treatment of the menstruant. Akiba argues that if the menstruant woman conveys defilement when carried, so must an idol, because it has been declared in scripture to be like her.

M. *Pesachim* 5.5: The Passover lambs were slain by three *groups, as it is said: "And all the assembly of the congregation of Israel"—assembly, congregation, Israel. When the first group had been let in, the *court was filled, and they closed the doors of the court. . . . (And the ritual began.)

*Of those coming to the Temple. Cf. Exod. 12:6.

*Of the Temple.

Comment:

The three groups went through the ritual of the Passover sacrifice in turn. The practice was probably established out of necessity, so as to accommodate the large number of pilgrims who came for the festival. Yet, since the scripture verse uses three synonymous terms for the people, the rabbis have their desired scriptural sanction for the practice.

6.1: These things relating to the Paschal sacrifice take precedence over the Sabbath: killing it, sprinkling its blood, removing fat from its viscera and offering the fat; but roasting it and washing its insides do not *override the Sabbath. Nor does *driving it, nor bringing it in from beyond the Sabbath limit, nor cutting off a blemish.

Cf. Lev. 3:3-4
*Or, "take precedence over."
*To the Temple.

But Rabbi Eliezer says: "These do take precedence over it."

Comment:

The first four actions were obligatory, and had to be done at the Temple, Sabbath or not, in preparation for Passover. The next two actions could be postponed, if necessary, until the end of the Sabbath, since the Passover meal was eaten after sundown, at the beginning of a new day. The last three could be done before the Sabbath began. Yet Rabbi Eliezer held that all the actions enumerated overrode the rule of Sabbath rest, hence the following argument.

6.2: Rabbi Eliezer said: "Is that not the deduction? If slaughtering, in the category of 'work,' overrides the Sabbath, may not these in the category of *'rest' override it?" Rabbi Joshua replied: "A festival day refutes this, for on it *they permitted acts of 'work' and *forbade acts of the category 'rest.' " Rabbi Eliezer answered him: "How so, Joshua? What proof is a voluntary act for an obligatory act?"

Cf. M.
Sabbath 7.2, Reading 62.
*By rabbinic, not biblical, decree.
*Earlier teachers.
*Literally, "loosed and bound"; cf. Matt. 16:19.

(The argument continues, until finally settled by Rabbi Akiba. Eliezer's argument begins with a *Kal wa-Homer* form, in this instance from a major case to applicability in a minor one. When Joshua offers his refutation, Eliezer charges him with having misapplied the *Gezerah Shawah* norm [drawing a conclusion by comparison of equals]. Joshua's classes of actions are not equal, hence his argument is not valid. Finally, Akiba offers a case which satisfies Eliezer's demands. When Eliezer persists in his contention, Akiba challenges him to find specific scriptural warrant to support it. Apparently Eliezer cannot, for the argument is presented as settled.

Further discussion of rabbinic interpretation is given in the Extended Notes, Part III.)

PART THREE

Extended Notes

A. Literary-Historical Notes

1. Bibliographic: The Author's Use of the Texts

Complete bibliographical data concerning the texts on which the Readings are based appear in the Bibliography, yet it is felt that some account as to how these texts were handled should be given. In honesty, it cannot be said that every one of these selections has been translated word for word. Yet they do not represent in any instance a mere copying of an already extant translation.

The *Psalms of Solomon* are a revision of a translation I made earlier from Rahlf's edition of the Septuagint. Selections from Judith, Wisdom of Solomon, Sirach, and I and II Maccabees are from the same base. Readings in the *Testaments of the Twelve Patriarchs* are based on the Greek text edited by M. de Jonge for the Brill series *Pseudepigrapha Veteris Testamenti Graece* (1964). The excerpts from the *Testament of Job* are from my translation of the entire testament, as edited by S. P. Brock in this same series (Vol. II). The sections from *I Enoch* in the earlier Readings (11-13b) were translated from the text given in Swete's edition of the Septuagint, with reference to Matthew Black's edition in the Brill series (Vol. III). Moses' vision of exaltation by Ezekiel "the Tragedian" was translated from A.-M. Denis' edition in the same volume. The excerpts from the *Lives of the Prophets* are from C. C. Torrey's edition. Other text editions have been consulted as available.

As for the Hebrew texts, the selections from the *Zadokite*, or *Damascus*, *Document/Rule* are based on the edition of E. Lohse, with reference to the edition of Schechter (recently reissued by Joseph A. Fitzmyer) and to the text and notes of Rabin. The readings from the *Manual of Discipline/Community Rule* and the *Thanksgiving Hymns* are from Lohse's edition, with reference to that of Mansoor. The *Shemoneh 'Esreh* is from the text published by I. Elbogen, and the *'Aqedah* petition is from the text given by A. Th. Philips' edition of the liturgy for the first day of New Year. Readings from the Mishnah are from the text as given in the seven-volume edition by Philip Blackman. The litany from the Hebrew version of Sirach is from the edition of Israel Levi, with reference to Oesterley's commentary.

In a number of these publications, translations appear along with the original texts; and for others, translations exist separately. It would have been foolish to ignore them, since most of them have been done by competent scholars. However, as stated above, an attempt has been made to make the English phrasing of these selections indicate an understanding based on personal study. The results do not reflect every need for change that may exist in the way in which given passages have already been translated. If a Greek or Hebrew word means "tree" or "run," one would best translate by "tree" or "run" in English, without seeking erudite, and awkward, synonyms. In the case of Josephus, particularly, the result usually has been little more than modernizing the vocabulary and Americanizing the phraseology. Only rarely do I differ from the original translator's understanding of Josephus' meaning. A similar comment would apply to several of the Mishnah passages.

Only two excerpts have no basis in a Greek or Hebrew text: those in Readings 39a and b and in 55a and b, since these materials in *Jubilees* and *I Enoch* are not extant in either Greek or Hebrew. For these, I have revised into modern idiom the translations found in the editions of R. H. Charles. Care has been taken to avoid changing the essential meaning in the process of modernizing the phraseology. Finally, for all the texts I have generally tried to express the meanings of the originals in simple, direct, current language. Only occasionally, for considerations of style, have older patterns of phraseology been consciously adopted.

2. PROVENANCE OF THE TESTAMENTS OF THE TWELVE PATRIARCHS

Selections from the *Testaments* have been given in the Readings to illustrate pre-Christian Jewish thought, on the assumption that they originated in the last century B.C. Is this assumption justified? The origin and date of these testaments have been in dispute since at least the eighteenth century. Were they written by Jewish authors between about 150 and 30 B.C., and then later retouched by both Jewish and Christian editors for their own purposes? Or did a Judeo-Christian author develop the entire series around a small nucleus of old Jewish materials some time in the first two Christian centuries? Both theories, with variations, are held.

R. H. Charles and others, early in this century, held the former view, and it has been dominant until lately. They were originally a pre-Christian work of Jewish authorship. They were edited, true; but this was by a Jewish editor whose outlook differed from the original writer(s) mainly in that he was not a supporter of the Hasmonean dynasty. Internal evidence seems to support this view. Christians, by whom these writings have been preserved, made christological additions to them in various places. When a relatively small number of obviously Christian interpolations have been removed, the essentially Jewish, pre-Christian work remains.[1]

Yet, the second view has appeared again, advanced by M. de Jonge, editor of the Greek text from which the Readings have been translated. He has been followed by J. T. Milik, among others.[2] De Jonge, in particular,

---

1. Cf. H. T. Andrews, *An Introduction to the Apocryphal Books,* second edition revised by Charles F. Pfeiffer (Grand Rapids: Baker Book House, 1964), pp. 69ff.

2. J. T. Milik, *Ten Years of Discovery in the Wilderness of Judaea* (Naperville, Ill.: Alec R. Allenson, Inc., 1959), pp. 34-35.

thinks that the text has been so christianized that it is scarcely possible to identify Christian interpolations and excise them.[3]

A *Testament of Levi* in Aramaic and a *Testament of Naphtali* in Hebrew were found, in 1910, in the old Cairo synagogue genizah along with the *Zadokite Document*. Fragments of the same testaments were found in the Qumran caves. Partly for this reason Milik seems to feel that they formed the nucleus of, or inspiration for, the testaments now extant in Greek, to which he ascribes Christian authorship.

Yet it is far from clear whether Qumran was the origin of any of the testaments. As I and II Maccabees and Josephus testify, there were hasidim scattered throughout all Jewry in Palestine; and the theology and ethics of the *Testaments* reflect this pietistic outlook. It does not noticeably differ from that found in the biblical Proverbs and Psalms or from that found in Tobit, Judith, Sirach and other writings of the Apocrypha. It is patently absurd to suppose that the Qumran scribes were the only Jews to produce literature of this kind.

Several have argued for Christian authorship mainly on the basis of the terminology, theology and ethics of the *Testaments*. Commenting on N. Messel's argument for Christian authorship, Marc Philonenko hit the sensitive spot: "Refusing to recognize in the *Testaments* a type of Jewish piety which had been nearer to Christianity than that of Judaism up to then known, he viewed it anew as a Christian work."[4] Many Continental scholars since have been reluctant to recognize the debt of the New Testament writers to the Judaism of their day, out of which they all came originally. When dealings with Jewish-Christian relationships, literary or otherwise, at the beginnings of Christianity, a distinct anti-Jewish bias tends to affect the arguments and conclusions of many Christians scholars, and the student of the history and the literature has to learn to detect it.

Several eminent Jewish scholars, competent in the ancient literature of their people, have readily accepted the *Testaments* as genuine products of pre-Christian Judaism. In addition, they have been able to cite direct references to these testaments in later, but still ancient, Jewish texts. Concerning them, J. Klausner commented that "all these show plainly that the book is basically from a purely Jewish (and not Nazarene) source, and was originally written in Hebrew. . . ."[5] Moses Gaster, who shared in the

---

3. M. de Jonge, *The Testaments of the Twelve Patriarchs: A Study of Their Text, Composition and Origin* (Assen, Neth.: Van Gorcum & Comp. N.V., 1952), especially p. 36.

4. Marc Philonenko, *Les interpolations chrétiennes des Testaments des Douze Patriarchs et les manuscrits de Qoumran* (Paris: Presses Universitaires de France, 1960), p. 3. Comparing the so-called Christian interpolations with the relevant Qumran documents, he shows that most of them could have applied to the Teacher of Righteousness. He thus reduces the number of passages that remain to be regarded as Christian to a mere handful.

5. Joseph Klausner, *The Messianic Idea in Israel*, third edition, tr. W. F. Stinespring (New York: The Macmillan Co., 1955), p. 310. ("Nazarene" = Christian)

discovery of the old Cairo genizah materials, took a similar position.[6] So did Kaufmann Kohler.[7] Elias Bickerman, on grounds other than those taken by the preceding, dated the *Testaments* in their original edition to the first quarter of the second pre-Christian century. He stated categorically: "The Testaments were written by a contemporary of Jesus, the son of Sirach, the author of Ecclesiasticus."[8] The knowledge and opinions of such scholars should be respected.

In the last analysis, it was not ethics nor even, basically, theology that distinguished the early Church from Judaism. The first Christians were nearly all Jews and, as the New Testament clearly indicates, they brought their theology and ethics bodily into the Christian movement with them. What would be more natural? The basic scriptures of Judaism were also the scriptures of the early Church.

No, ethics is not the touchstone of the difference, and cannot be made the criterion either for dating or for distinguishing Judaic from early Christian literature. The point of separation is the uniqueness that the Christians attributed to Jesus, and the distinctive doctrines that expressed that uniqueness. Clear expressions of those doctrines in the *Testaments* or similar literature of originally Jewish provenance should be regarded as Christian additions. The remainder has to be dealt with on other grounds.

3. Apocalyptic: Form and Substance

Apocalyptic (= "revelatory") literature was a characteristic phenomenon of the intertestamental period. It had its roots in the Hebrew canon: Ezekiel 1—11, Daniel 7—12, and Zechariah 1—6 are good examples. Pre-eminent in the extrabiblical writings are *I Enoch* (a collection in itself), *II Esdras/IV Ezra* (cf. RSV Apocrypha), the *Book of the Secrets of Enoch* (or, *Slavonic Enoch*), and the *Syriac Baruch*. The Revelation to John is the only canonical New Testament example; yet Paul is probably drawing on Christians adaptations of the older apocalyptic in such passages as I Corinthians 15:51ff., I Thessalonians 4:13-18, and II Thessalonians 2:3-12. A number of short apocalypses were produced by both Jews and Christians, the latest of them in the early second century A.D.

A major concern of the apocalyptic writings is with eschatology, the End Time and the Last Things: the Messianic Age, final judgment, and the rewards of the righteous and punishment of the wicked. But eschatological

6. Moses Gaster, "The Hebrew Text of One of the Testaments of the Twelve Patriarchs," in *Studies and Texts in Folklore, Magic, etc.* (New York: Ktav Publishing House, Inc., 1971), pp. 70-77.

7. Kaufmann Kohler, "The Pre-Talmudic Haggadah," *JQR* V (1893), pp. 399-419, especially pp. 400-01; "The Testaments of the Twelve Patriarchs," in *The Jewish Encyclopedia*, Vol. XII, pp. 113-18.

8. Elias Bickerman, "The Date of the Testaments of the Twelve Patriarchs," *JBL* 69 (1950), pp. 245-60, especially p. 260.

concern alone does not characterize a writing as an example of the apocalyptic type. Thus, Isaiah 24 (some would include 25—27), Zechariah 9—14, and Mark 13 are all eschatological passages but, even though they are popularly so called, they are not properly designated "apocalyptic."

Several major characteristics are shared by literature of the apocalyptic type. First, the tract is the literary production of a *seer*, a man who has been granted special visions. Second, in at least one of his visions (often, but not always, the first reported), he is given divine authority to be God's spokesman. Often the vision is of the glory of God, of the divine dwelling or throne, or of an archangel; and with the vision he is given his commission (cf. Isa. 6; Ezek. 1—2; *I Enoch* XIV—XV, Reading 13b). Third, the seer is granted an initiation into heavenly mysteries normally inaccessible to ordinary mortals. Fourth, the visions, particularly those concerning future events, are often replete with symbolism (cf. Dan. 7—8; Zech. 1—6; *T. Joseph* XIX, Reading 14). An angel is sent to interpret to the seer the meaning of the symbolism (cf. also II Esdras 4:1; 7:1; 11—13), or to give him a message for others.

The message usually has to do with eschatological events: the coming Messianic Age, the resurrection, the Last Judgment. Then, on the basis of what has been revealed to him, the seer engages in *paraenesis*, or exhortation: to the wicked to repent, to the righteous to maintain their faith and hope. Or, sometimes the message is one of unremitting doom for the wicked, but assurances of the final welfare of the righteous (as in the Enochian "Similitudes," secs. XXXVIIff.).

Finally, these works are marked by pseudonymity: The seer is usually a great worthy of Israel's past: Adam, Enoch, Abraham, Moses, Isaiah, Ezra. Whether this is consciously adopted pseudonymity, or whether the materials used have already been traditionally connected with these great personages is a moot question. It has been observed, however, that the central concerns of an apocalypse bearing a certain name are those which could, most naturally, be conceived to have been concerns of that particular patriarch.

These are the principal hallmarks of the apocalyptic style. In addition, most of the apocalyptic literature is permeated by mythological motifs. Not a little of this may be due to the influence of the popular hellenism. Much more of, however, reflects ancient mythological traditions which appear in the biblical Prophets and Psalms, expressions of a world view that was common to the Near East before the Greek period. A flourishing angelology and demonology, adapted to Jewish theological perspective, may reflect influences from the periods of Babylonian and Persian domination. But, as indicated by such works as the *Testaments of the Twelve Patriarchs, Jubilees,* and Tobit (in the Apocrypha), this mythology was part of the popular religion and not restricted to apocalyptic.

As noted in the General Introduction, apocalyptic served a prophetic function in the troubled times from the late Restoration Period right on through the Maccabean conflict and Hasmonean decline into the times of the early Church. There are hints that prophecy, in its Old Testament mode, was beginning to fall into disrepute after the times of Zerubbabel and the prophets Haggai and Zechariah. And Ezra's religious reconstruction, with a renewed emphasis on the Law, gave greater importance in the national life to the Torah interpreters. (Cf. the following note.)

But the calm reasoning of the scribe and sage, exemplified by a Jesus (Joshua) ben Sirach, could not lay hold of the popular imagination as could the "revelations" of an Enoch, especially in times when men were wondering if the God of the Patriarchs, of Moses, and Isaiah was dead or not. When foreign customs, philosophy, and religion are beguiling the young, and laments like Psalm 74 are going up from an oppressed and tormented people, a strong message of assurance and hope is called for. This the apocalyptists supplied.

When the glittering wrappings of the apocalyptic style are laid aside, the substance of the apocalyptic message stands clear. Basically, it is a message of assurance that God cares and is in command of history, that He will see to the fulfilment of the promises given through the ancient prophets, and that evil and those who are its agents will get their just punishments, while those who persevere in righteousness will be fully recompensed according to their merit and the greatness of God's mercy.

But that is not all. Certain of the elements characteristic of apocalyptic have their own purpose in relation to the basic message. From at least 250 B.C. onward, hellenism was perceived as the great enemy of Judaism by the leaders of the pious. In its popular forms, intellectual, material, and religious, its attraction was strong and its advance insidious. The author of Zechariah 9 might think the principal danger a military one (cf. vv. 13-14), but the authors of the early apocalyptic tracts knew better. The real dangers were intellectual, moral, and spiritual; and hellenism must be countered on those levels.

Did the Babylonians have Ishtar, the Greeks their Heracles, and the Romans Aeneas, all of whom had made journeys through the underworld? Then Judaism had Enoch who lived long before those heroes. He had been taken not only through the underworld but through the celestial realms also, and had acquired information on those things of which even Job was ignorant (cf. Job 38 ff.). More than that, he and Abraham and Moses had been granted to see the future of Israel and of the world down to the Last Judgment, and had transmitted this knowledge to select teachers for Israel's sake.

Did the Greek, Egyptian, and Syrian religions (the latter an amalgam of elements from ancient Canaanite, Assyro-Babylonian and other religions) have their mysteries? The apocalyptic seers were granted to learn greater mysteries. They had been transported through the heavenly spheres into the presence of the living God (cf. II Cor. 12:2-4), and had been made privy to divine secrets mediated through angelic beings.

Were there Greek philosophers who had some answers to the problems of human existence? Never mind. Judaism had its Lawgiver, and its great seers who had been actually granted to see, in spirit, the final outcome of the troubles which the pious were now suffering. Enoch's and Daniel's wisdom matched, even surpassed, that of the Greek philosophers: they had some revealed answers to the problem of the mystery of evil, while the pagan philosophers could only speculate.

These were tracts for their times. They were adapted to the sensibilities of their intended readers, encouraging to faith, hope, and loyalty to the ancestral religion, even to the point of death if need be. That Judaism survived and thrived during its most troubled decades is due in large measure to the influence of this kind of literature and its teachings.

For Further Reading

Glasson, T. Francis. *The Greek Influence in Jewish Eschatology*. London: S. P. C. K., 1961. Paper.

Morris, Leon. *Apocalyptic*. Grand Rapids: Wm. B. Eerdmans Publishing Co., 1972. Paper.

Rowley, H. H. *The Relevance of Apocalyptic*. New and revised edition. New York: Association Press, 1963.

Russell, D. S. *Between the Testaments*. Philadelphia: Fortress Press, 1960. Paper. (Especially, Part Two)

_____. *The Method and Message of Jewish Apocalyptic*. Philadelphia: West-minster Press, 1964.

Schmithals, Walter. *The Apocalyptic Movement: Introduction & Interpretation*. Trans. John E. Steely. Nashville: Abingdon Press, 1975.

4. FROM PROPHECY TO TORAH

The prophetic books Haggai and Zechariah (especially chs. 1—8) testify to the struggle that the leaders of the people had to promote the rebuilding of the Temple following the Jews' return from Babylon. Ezra 1—6 gives the background, and records the completion and dedication of the Temple in the sixth year of Darius I, about 515 B.C. Nehemiah came from the Persian court in about 445 B.C. and led in the restoration of the walls of Jerusalem. This work completed, he returned to the Persian court for about a decade. After about 433 B.C. he returned to Jerusalem to initiate certain reforms (Neh. 13:4ff.). About a generation later, Ezra led up a large contingent of immigrants from Babylon. A priest of the lineage of Aaron's son Eleazar and a scribe well versed in the Law and its interpretation, Ezra took care to see that his company included numbers of priests, Levites, various orders of Temple servants, and Torah teachers in addition to families of lay people ("Israelites"—cf. Ezra 7—8). It was his intention to teach the people of Judea the proper interpretation and practice of the Law of God as given through Moses.

During the times of Haggai and Zechariah, it appears that a wave of revolts broke out among the subject peoples of the Persian Empire. With Zerubbabel, a prince of the house of David, at their head (as governor under Persian authority) and the Temple in construction, it seemed an appropriate time for the Jews to bid for independence. Apparently the two prophets were instrumental in promoting a freedom movement. From Zechariah 1—6, carefully studied in the light of what can be learned of Persian history at that time, the prophet's message seems to have been: (1) the present troubles of the Empire are of divine providence—now is the time when God is going to fulfill the promises of the former prophets; (2) now is the time to assert independence from Persia, to restore the Davidic monarchy with Zerrubbabel as king and Joshua as high priest. Zechariah would, presumably, become the court prophet, according to the old Davidic pattern.

In Zechariah 6:9ff., an account is given of the fashioning of a crown that is inexplicably, put on the head of Joshua the high priest. He is addressed as "the man whose name is the Branch" (cf. also 3:8-9), but this title is used in the pre-exilic prophets for the messianic *king*. He is to build the Temple, to bear the majesty (of royalty), and to sit and rule upon his throne accompanied by a priest (cf. 4:13-14; 6:13). These are the prerogatives of a Davidic messiah. Finally, and astonishingly, the crown is to be placed in the Temple as a "reminder" (v. 14).

Of what? Since Zerubbabel seems suddenly to disappear from the scene, it is not difficult to infer that, as with the others, the Persians also nipped this budding bid for independence and deposed or recalled Zerubbabel. As partial confirmation of this inference is the message of Zechariah 8, in which the prophet seems to be trying to persuade the people that, in spite of a temporary setback, God will still fulfill the earlier prophetic promises. At any rate, from that time the high priest was established as both civil and religious leader of the Jewish province, an arrangement that was maintained during the ensuing Greek and Roman periods.

These events undoubtedly played their part in the decline of the prophetic office and in the increasing importance of Torah scribes in the religious life of the Jews. It may have been in part due to the failure of Zechariah's messianic propaganda; but in any case, public prophecy does seem to have fallen into disrepute. The passage in Zechariah 13:2-6, from a later time, is unmistakable testimony. By the Maccabean period, no recognized prophet was available to give a word from the Lord on matters of public importance (I Macc. 4:42-46; 14:38-41). I Maccabees 9:24-27 mentions a severe famine and a great tribulation in Israel "such as had not occurred since the time when no prophet appeared to them." What this time may have been is suggested by a tradition found in the *Tosephta* ("supplement" to the Mishnah): "From the time of the destruction of the former house [i.e., the first Temple], the dynasty of David ceased; also Urim and Thummim ceased . . . . From the death of Haggai, Zechariah and Malachi, the last prophets, the holy spirit ceased from Israel . . . " (tractate *Sotah* 13.2). The phrase, "the holy spirit ceased," is usually interpreted to mean the cessation of the prophetic inspiration. (Cf. also Ps. 74:9.)

With the priestly hierarchy in effective control of the national life and, following the reforms of Ezra, the Torah and its interpretation given central place as the authoritative basis and guide for both civil and religious aspects of that life, the role of the priestly teacher and hasidic scribe was enhanced while that of the prophet diminished. The process was far advanced in the time of Joshua ben Sira', who wrote his book before the Maccabean revolt. Both Sirach 24 and Baruch 3:9—4:4 indicate the esteem in which the Law was held in Israel. Its teachers and interpreters enjoyed comparable prestige. And this was the situation in Jesus' day, when scribes and Pharisees sat in Moses' seat (Matt. 23:2).

Yet, although public prophecy was rare, virtually under the ban as it were, literary prophesying was not. Ethical and hortatory tracts often contained revelatory and predictive material as well as ethical exhortation. These testaments and apocalypses were produced by the spiritual leaders of the pious as a form of prophetic activity. They all support adherence to the Law, often employing explanations developed by the interpreters of the Torah—among whom the authors of some of these tracts were also numbered. But the long twilight of public prophecy was the somber background against which the message and ministries of John the Baptist and Jesus flared like lightning, to startle some with the fear of the Judgment and to thrill others with the hope of the Coming Age.

For Further Reading

Bickerman, Elias. *From Ezra to the Last of the Maccabees*. New York: Schocken Books, 1962. Paper.

Foerster, Werner. *From the Exile to Christ*. Trans. Gordon E. Harris. Philadelphia: Fortress Press, 1964. (Especially the Introduction)

Pfeiffer, Charles F. *Between the Testaments*. Grand Rapids: Baker Book House, 1959.

Snaith, Norman H. *The Jews from Cyrus to Herod*. New York: Abingdon Press, n.d.

Snell, Heber C. *Ancient Israel—Its Story and Meaning*. Third edition, revised. Salt Lake City: University of Utah Press, 1963.

Also

"Introductions and notes to the books 2 Chronicles, Ezra, Nehemiah, Haggai and Zechariah," in *The Oxford Annotated Bible*, Revised Standard Edition, ed. Herbert G. May and Bruce M. Metzger. New York: Oxford University Press, 1962.

Thomas, D. Winton. "Introduction and Exegesis of the Books of Haggai and Zechariah," in *The Interpreter's Bible*, Vol. 6. New York: Abingdon Press, 1956.

5. TRADITION AND INTERPRETATION

The recognition has finally become widespread among Christian scholars that *tradition* had an important role in the growth of the biblical scriptures into their canonical forms. It was a fact taken for granted from the earliest days by Jewish biblical scholars. The *Aboth*, quoted above, testifies to the authority of tradition when handed down through recognized channels. This authority was invoked by Paul as well. To the Romans he said: "But thanks be to God that . . . you became obedient from the heart to that form of teaching to which you were delivered" (6:17); and he later advised them to avoid those who teach contrary to what they had learned (16:17; cf. II Tim. 1:13-14). Further, he regularly used the technical terms by which the rabbis customarily designated the reception and transmission of authoritative tradition: "receive," "deliver," or "transmit," and related terms (cf. I Cor. 11:2, 23; 15:1, 3).

In the Hebrew Bible itself there is evidence not only of the early oral transmission of traditional materials until they were given a fixed written form, but also of the later re-use and reinterpretation of older materials. This would be expected in the case of legal materials; but it is true also of the narrative and other nonlegal materials, as well as of the Gospel materials in the New Testament. And once an interpretation became accepted as part of the tradition, it became the basis for later application and interpretation. The intertestamental documents, along with the Bible translations made in that period (the Septuagint, or the translation into Greek, and the Aramaic *targums* = "translations, interpretations"), witness to the truth of what is implied in *Aboth* 1.1 ff., namely, that, initially stimulated by Ezra, his school and his successors, considerable hermeneutical activity occurred in that period.

Biblical hermeneutics included two major types of activity: (1) interpretation for the purpose of deriving legal precepts (*halakah*) for the regulation of daily life; and (2) the use of Scripture for edifying purposes (devotional or homiletic), the result of which was called *haggadah*. Basic methods included *peshat*, or determining and applying the plain meaning of the text, somewhat like the modern grammatico-historical method; and *derash* ("searching, investigating"), or the application of various devices to derive legal conclusions or edifying meanings which the *peshat* would not supply directly. The results of such activities were called *midrash*, of which a voluminous collection exists today. *Jubilees*, the *Testaments of the Twelve Patriarchs*, and the *Testament of Job* are early exemplars of haggadistic midrashim.

By the time of Hillel, seven main principles of legal interpretation were recognized. (1) Inference from a minor premise or case to a major conclusion, or vice versa (cf. Num. 12:14; Matt. 6:30), was one very commonly used. (2) Inference based on a comparison of equal cases or categories (Paul's "comparing spiritual things with spiritual," I Cor. 2:13), or on the use of the same word or phrase in two different passages, was another widely used principle. Then there were (3) the generalization of a principle embodied in a particular law to apply to analogous cases and (4) the generalization of a principle embodied in two different laws to apply to analogous cases (e.g., Exod. 21:26 with 27 is the basis for the ruling that a slave must be freed if his master mutilates him in any way). (5) A general class was in application restricted by particular instances named in the same context (cf. Lev. 5:2), a principle from which several derivatives were obtained. Finally, there were (6) the exposition of the meaning of a passage by analogy to a similar passage which was more readily understood and (7) explanation from the context. (For a somewhat more detailed explanation of these principles, cf. the *Universal Jewish Encyclopedia*, Vol. 5, p. 324.) They were reasonably sober principles, and they tended to be applied soberly, in the main, by the Jewish scribes of the Law.

However, greater freedom was used in haggadic interpretation. From a study of the earlier literature a medieval rabbi collected thirty-two norms or rules for interpreting the nonlegal parts of the Bible. Some are extensions or special applications of the seven legal principles set out by Hillel. But others include the applications of the skills of the "wise" or the "sages," such as the use of parables and allegory, wordplays and puns and double meanings, among others (cf. Prov. 1:5-6; Sirach 39:1-3).

In addition, three special devices were used: (1) *gematria*, or the computation of the numerical value of a word (possible because letters were also used as numerals) so as to arrive at a hidden meaning in the text or to convey a cryptic identification (e.g., Rev. 13:18 contains a numerical cryptogram for Nero Caesar). (2) Also used was *notaricon*, or treating the letters of a word as an acrostic (the reverse of the modern tendency to make acronyms from the names of business firms, social agencies, etc.). *Notaricon* also included the practice of breaking a word into two parts, if it would yield two intelligible words, or using its letters as an anagram. Finally, (3) there was the *Athbash*: a sliding alphabet, or reciprocal cipher. An unmistakable biblical example of this occurs in Jeremiah 51:1 (cf. ASV, where it is transliterated). *"Leb-kamai"* is an *athbash* cipher for the Hebrew word *kasdim* (= Chaldeans, or Babylonians).

According to the Gospel traditions, Jesus used many of these devices in His expositions and discourses. Prominent, of course, are parables, wordplays, the use of words and phrases with double meanings, the inference from minor to major; but examples of other forms can be found in His words. It is clear from Paul's epistles that he was well versed in both halakic and haggadic forms of interpretation. Among other things, the author of the letter "To the Hebrews" was skilled in allegory and typology; and the other New Testament writers illustrate their knowledge of midrashic techniques as well. The inference to be drawn from this is that the Bible student who is ignorant of the major ways in which the transmitters and interpreters of the biblical materials, including Jesus and the apostles, interpreted *their* scriptures is not fully competent to be a good interpreter of his Bible as he has it today.

For Further Reading

Finkel, Asher. *The Pharisees and the Teacher of Nazareth*. Leiden: E. J. Brill, 1964. (Especially Part A.4 and Part C)

Finkelstein, Louis. *The Pharisees*. Two volumes. Philadelphia: Jewish Publication Society of America, 1940.

Lieberman, Saul. *Hellenism in Jewish Palestine*. New York: Jewish Theological Seminary of America, 1962. (Especially pp. 53-82)

Mielziner, M. *Introduction to the Talmud*. Third edition. New York: Bloch Publishing Co., 1925. (Especially pp. 130ff.)

Strack, Hermann L. *Introduction to the Talmud and Midrash*. Translated from the fifth German edition, revised. Cleveland: The World Publishing Co., 1959. Paper. (Especially pp. 93ff.)

Vermes, Geza. *Scripture and Tradition in Judaism*. Leiden: E. J. Brill, 1961. (Especially the Introduction, pp. 1-10)

B. Messianic – Christological Notes

1. JUDAIC WISDOM AND WISDOM CHRISTOLOGY

Along with studies of how the Qumran materials relate to the New Testament, an older line of studies has been reopened and carried forward by scholars in the last several decades. This concerns the relations of the "wisdom" notions of the Hebrew Bible, along with those in the intertestamental writings, and certain christological ideas in the New Testament. For instance, Paul calls Christ the "Wisdom of God" for Christians, applying to Christ notions which have already appeared in the Old Testament or intertestamental writings (cf. below); and John, particularly, presents Jesus as the incarnation of God's pre-existent Word.

The Judaic wisdom tradition had its rootage in the antiquity of Near Eastern civilization, with a long history of development in biblical times. The movement in Israel is clearly traceable from the times of Solomon, who was apparently a patron of the sages. The movement paralleled, even intertwined with, the prophetic movement, and continued as a force in Judaic religious thought after the prophetic movement waned. Its products are represented in the Hebrew canon by Job, Proverbs, and Ecclesiastes, especially, with Daniel representing its apocalyptic form. In the intertestamental period its chief representatives are Sirach and Wisdom of Solomon, and *I Enoch* (apocalyptic).

In its broadest sense, the Hebrew term *hokmah* included everything from special skills or crafts to understanding and insight. With the sages, however, the latter usage predominates and *hokmah* is frequently found in passages clustered with synonymous defining terms: understanding, discernment, judgment, prudence (cf. Prov. 1:1-6; 2:1-11; 5:1-2; 8:5, 12-14). To the pious, wisdom was a gift from God. He was the ultimate source of all wisdom (Prov. 2:6ff.), and the divine wisdom was especially manifested in His creative and providential activities. In Proverbs 8:22ff., wisdom is personified as being the first of God's creatures and accompanying its Creator in the acts of creation as His master craftsman.

According to Genesis 1, God spoke the creation into being; but God's utterance of His effective word was but the expression of His infinite wisdom (cf. Ps. 104:24; Prov. 3:19-20; Isa. 40:12-14; Jer. 10:12-13; Wisd. Sol. 9:1-2). Thus God's wisdom and His word became linked in later thought. But since, by the time of intertestamental sages, God's word had become fixed in the scriptures, His wisdom was equated with Torah (the Law and its interpretations: cf. Sirach 24; Baruch 3:9—4:4).

Finally, wisdom was imparted by God's spirit and was spirit (cf. especially Wisd. Sol. 7:7ff.; 8:21—9:10ff.). In the prophetic view, the messianic descendant of David would (somewhat like Solomon, cf. I Kings 3:7-9, 12) receive a special anointing or endowment of God's spirit (cf. Isa. 11:1ff.; 42:1; 61:1; this is also implied in the title "Wonderful Counselor" in 9:6). We find this idea elaborated in *Psalm of Solomon* XVII (cf. Reading 53, especially v. 37). It is also emphasized in the so-called "Similitudes" sections of *I Enoch* (XXXVII—LXXI). The Son of Man, God's Elect One, is the source of wisdom for the righteous. Truth and righteousness lodge with him, and he "reveals all the treasures of that which is hidden" to the saints (XLVI.2). He is also God's agent of judgment, pronouncing doom on the wicked, but vindicating and rewarding the righteous, just as in *Psalm of Solomon* XVII. These characteristics are drawn principally from Isaiah 11:1ff., but "Enoch" has also made use of the idea of Wisdom's pre-existence (Prov. 8:22ff.). Thus, already in the intertestamental period the ideas of pre-existence (in some sense) and a special anointing with wisdom were being predicated of the expected Messiah. He would be the "Wonderful Counselor" who would embody God's truth, righteousness and justice in a special way.

Divine origin, pre-existence, creative power and agent of creation, revealer of God and illuminator of the faithful, and God's agent for promoting righteousness and for judgment—all these motifs appear clearly in the christology of the New Testament. For Paul, Jesus was the son of David according to the flesh (Rom. 1:3); but the resurrected Jesus was also the pre-existent Christ in whom dwelt "all the treasures of wisdom and knowledge" and "all the fulness of the Godhead" (Col. 2:3, 9). If Wisdom was the first of God's creations and His agent in the creation of the universe, so Christ was the "first-born of the entire creation," by whom "all things were created" and in whom "all things cohere" (Col. 1:15-17). In the Wisdom of Solomon, the divine Wisdom is said to be "a reflection of eternal light . . . an image of His goodness" (7:26, RSV). For Paul, Christ is "the image of the invisible God" (Col. 1:15), and in His countenance is seen the "light of the knowledge of God's glory" (II Cor. 4:6). In short, Christ has been appointed for the Church as God's Wisdom, which includes "righteousness, sanctification and redemption" (I Cor. 1:30). Christ is the "end of the Law" (both the goal toward which the Law pointed as well as its termination) concerning righteousness for those who believe in Him, for He is God's new Torah (Rom. 10:4). Finally, Christ is God's agent of judgment, before whom all will stand for condemnation or reward (cf. II Cor. 5:10).

Similar concepts are found in the other epistles. In Hebrews 1:2-3, notably, phraseology reminiscent of Wisdom of Solomon 7:25 is applied to Christ. In the Gospels, Jesus appears as the true Son of Man, whose words and works of power are manifestations of God's creating and judging wisdom. Matthew, for example, presents Jesus as the legitimate son of David and Spirit-anointed Messiah who is the author of the new Torah for the Church. For John, Jesus is the incarnation of the pre-existent Word-Wisdom of God who came to pitch His tent in Israel (cf. Sirach 24:8ff.). His word has creative power as well as authority for judgment and the establishment of righteousness (cf. John 5—6; 8—9). For John, too, Jesus is God's new Torah, superseding the old Torah that was based on Moses and was claimed to be the quintessence of God's wisdom for Israel. This idea is emphasized by His words: "I am the Way, the Truth, and the Life" (John 14:6). These claims, along with the claim to be the exclusive way of approach to God, had all been previously asserted of the Mosaic Torah. The intertestamental developments in the biblical ideas concerning "wisdom" and the Messiah made it possible for the leaders of early Christian thought to see how Jesus was the supreme embodiment of these characteristics.

For Further Reading

Davies, W. D. *Paul and Rabbinic Judaism*. London: S. P. C. K., 1962. Paper (Especially ch. 7)

Grant, Frederick C. *An Introduction to New Testament Thought*. Nashville: Abingdon Press, 1950. (See remarks on pp. 109f.; 120; 264ff.)

Noth, M., and Thomas, D. Winton, eds. *Wisdom in Israel and the Ancient Near East*. Leiden: E. J. Brill, 1955. (Especially the chapters by J. Lindblom and Norman W. Porteous)

Richardson, Alan. *An Introduction to the Theology of the New Testament*. New York: Harper & Row Publishers, 1958. (Especially ch. 7)

Rylaarsdam, J. Coert. *Revelation in Jewish Wisdom Literature*. Chicago: University of Chicago Press, 1946.

Scott, R. B. Y. *The Way of Wisdom in the Old Testament*. New York: The Macmillan Co., 1971.

Also

Bourke, Joseph "The Wonderful Counselor: An Aspect of Christian Messianism," *Catholic Biblical Quarterly* XXII (1960), pp. 123-43.

Moeller, Henry, "Wisdom Motifs and John's Gospel," *Bulletin of the Evangelical Theological Society* 6 (1963), pp. 92-100.

2. "LAMB" AS VICTOR SYMBOL (re John 1:29, 36)

To those acquainted with biblical symbolism, "lamb" is usually associated with sacrifice, especially when applied to Christ (cf. I Peter 1:18-19). The historical question concerning John 1:29, 36 is: Was that the symbolism intended by John the Baptist *at that time* when he pointed Jesus out to his disciples as "the Lamb of God"? If so, it is the one historically discordant note in the whole of John 1:19-51. That section intends to show how Jesus' early disciples expressed their belief in Jesus' messianic character *in the currently popular understanding* of the Messiah's role.

In John's account, the Baptist has seen the Spirit descend and remain (or, rest) on Jesus, and has declared Him to be the "Son of God" (vv. 31-34). The event fulfills Isaiah 11:1-2, the title coming from the Davidic covenant (II Sam. 7:14; Ps. 2:7, 12; 89:26-27). If *Psalm of Solomon* XVII along with Luke 1:67-79 and Mark 8:27-33 is any indication, no Jew of that time was looking for a Messiah who was to be sacrificed. Nor must it be overlooked that, according to the tradition common to Luke and Matthew, even John came to doubt that Jesus was the Messiah, possibly because He did not set up the messianic kingdom as expected (Luke 7:18ff.). What, then, could the Baptist have meant by his announcement?

The question has proved difficult for a number of competent scholars. Several of the best recent commentaries in English overlook, or brush aside, materials which seem valuable for providing an answer (specifically, the commentaries by Barrett, Raymond Brown, Dodd and Schnackenburg). One of the points which puzzles these scholars is how to understand "takes away the sin of the world." What seems to be a reasonable solution is available from the biblical and intertestamental sources. This solution is much easier to see if one does not assume from the outset that the Evangelist, in spite of his fondness for double meanings and ironies, is always reading back his theology and his post-resurrection situation into his accounts of supposedly historical happenings and situations.

A common biblical symbol for Israel is the flock. Often the shepherd symbolizes a national leader (Ezek. 34; Zech. 9:16; 10:3; 11:4ff.). But a flock has its natural leaders, too: the most vigorous rams, as those used to the ways of sheep and goats know. If one wished to keep his imagery all on one level, what would be more natural than to let the lead ram symbolize the national leader? Micah 2:12-13 seems to be an example of this usage. Israel's regathering in peace and safety is symbolized in the imagery of flock and fold. Although not usually so treated by commentators, it seems appropriate to understand the "He who opens the breach" (RSV) as the lead ram who is first out of the fold in the morning at the head of the flock. In the last half of this stanza, the "breach-maker who will go up before them" (13a) is parallel to and identified with "their king who will pass on before them"

(13b), that is, the lead ram stands for the king. Then "the Lord [YHWH] at their head" will be the shepherd of the entire people as the flock. Such imagery is often used elsewhere (Ps. 23:1; 80:1; Jer. 31:10; Ezek. 34:11ff.).

In intertestamental literature, the first significant use of the lamb symbol occurs in the "Dream Visions" of *I Enoch* (LXXXIX—XC). In theriomorphic symbolism, Israel's history is summarized from the time of the Patriarchs to the period of the Maccabean struggle, then is carried into the New Age. The Israelites are symbolized by sheep and their leaders by white bulls, rams or lambs, usually the last. Saul, for example, is introduced as a ram, while Samuel and David are lambs. Then David is exalted to "a ram and leader of the sheep" (LXXXIX.45); and Solomon is spoken of as a little sheep who "became a ram in its stead, and became prince and leader of those sheep" (v. 46).

In scenes usually thought to symbolize the Maccabean conflict, a great horn sprouts on one of the sheep; and he and the rest of the sheep and lambs conquer the wild beasts (Gentiles) who have been attacking them (XC.9; cf. I Macc. 1—5). The scene then shifts to the final judgment. After the sinning angels (Gen. 6) and the oppressing Gentiles have been condemned to the abyss of fire, the Lord builds a new house (temple) for His people. The restored sheep, now white and clean (the righteous Remnant), along with those of the Gentiles who worship the Lord, are assembled in it (cf. Isa. 2; Zech. 14:16ff.; *Ps. Sol.* XVII.26ff.).

Finally, a white bull that is honored by all the people appears and is changed into a lamb. He grows into a great animal that "had great black horns on its head; and the Lord of the sheep rejoiced over it and over the oxen" (XC.38). This lamb apparently symbolizes the Messiah who, according to standard messianic expectations, was to take his power and throne following the judgment of the nations and the regathering of the people Israel. The great horns of the vision symbolize his great power.

Likewise, *Testament of Joseph* XIX (Reading 14) reads like a very condensed version of this vision. Similar imagery is employed. In verse 8, the reference seems to be either to one of the Maccabeans, possibly Juda, or to the coming messianic deliverer. He is a lamb who fights against the wild beasts and reptiles, with a lion at his right side to help (cf. Gen. 49:9; II Esdras 12:31ff.; Rev. 5:5). He is victorious, to the great rejoicing of the oxen (the Israelite tribes). Whether the lamb is supposed to symbolize Juda Maccabeus (or, John Hyrcanus?) or the coming Messiah, the point to observe is that "lamb" in these passages symbolizes a victorious, conquering Israelite leader.

In the commonly accepted messianic schema based on the prophets, Messiah was to "take away/remove" sin from Israel by a process of judgment and religious reform, just as the "good" kings of Israel's past had done (cf. II Chron. 29—31; Isa. 11:1-5; *Ps. Sol.* XVII.21ff.). The "Similitudes" of *I Enoch* reiterate this notion insistently. There is nothing in this conception about Messiah's "taking away" sin by an atoning self-sacrifice.

The use of the lamb (or, young male sheep) as a victorious leader symbol is thus as old as the Maccabean and post-Maccabean periods, and was known in the time of Jesus and John the Baptist. The symbol would be understood in this way by those attuned to the apocalyptic vocabulary. In this light, the Baptist's declaration is in harmony with current Jewish expectations in general, as well as with the rest of John 1:19-51. Also, John the Evangelist (who often has greater respect for historical verisimilitude than his critics realize) is here consistent in his presentation with the other Gospels.

However, John knew very well that by the time he recorded those events there were different interpretations of the lamb symbol. How Jesus fulfilled the messianic expectations of His time while transmuting them, and how He finally did "take away" sin, is the theme of all the Gospels (also cf. I John 3:5). The following note will deal with special aspects of "lamb" as sacrifice.

For Further Reading

Brown, Raymond E. *The Gospel According to John.* Two volumes. Garden City, N.Y.: Doubleday and Co., Inc., 1966. (Especially Vol. 1, pp. 58-63)

Dodd, C. H. *The Interpretation of the Fourth Gospel.* Cambridge: The University Press, 1960. (Especially pp. 230-38)

Sanders, J. N. *The Gospel According to St. John*, ed. B. A. Mastin. New York: Harper & Row Publishers, 1968. (Especially pp. 93-96)

Ward, A. M. "The Fourth Gospel in Recent Study," *Expository Times* 81 (1970), pp. 68-72.

Sanders is the only recent commentary which accepts the possibility that "lamb" in this context has its apocalyptic value as a victor symbol. Studies on this topic which are both recent and easily available to students are rare.

3. THE "BINDING OF ISAAC" AND JESUS' SELF-OFFERING

Another line of tradition involving "lamb" symbolism (and more) was extant in Jesus' day. It is one of which Christian interpreters have made little use, even though Jewish scholars have drawn attention to it in recent times. The tradition has to do with the *aqedah* ("Binding") or sacrifice of Isaac, which was important for Judaic and apostolic religious thought. It can be traced back from the Prayer Book of contemporary synagogue use into pre-Christian times.

a. Background in Genesis 22

To appreciate the development of the significant events of the Isaac tradition, the biblical account of Abraham's offering of Isaac must be analyzed. The important elements are:

(1) As the son of promise and the divinely designated heir, Isaac is called

Abraham's "only son" (Heb. *yahîd*, "only, unique") insofar as inheritance and covenant are concerned (Gen. 12; 17; 21:1-12; 22:2, 12, 16).

(2) God orders Abraham to offer Isaac "your son, your only son, whom you love" on a mountain in Moriah (Gen. 22:2). Abraham complies; and to Isaac's question about a lamb for an offering, he replies: "God will provide [literally, see] for himself a lamb for a burnt-offering" (v. 8).

(3) For his obedience, Abraham is promised that he will have a numerous progeny through Isaac and will be the medium of divine blessing to all mankind (vv. 15-18; cf. 12:1-3). Each of these points received hermeneutical treatment in the intertestamental period and later.

b. Significant elements in development

(1) The "beloved/first-born" son. In the text, Isaac is referred to three times as Abraham's "only son" (Gen. 22:2, 12, 16, Heb.), and once as the object of Abraham's special love (v.2). The Greek translation (Septuagint) regularly renders the Hebrew *yahîd* by *agapētos* ("beloved"). *Jubilees* (second century B.C.) reads "beloved" son in the first and last references, but "first-born" in the second. Philo of Alexandria speaks of him as the "beloved and only" (*On Abraham* XXXII.168), while Josephus refers to him as "best-loved" and "only/unique" (*monogenēs: Ant.* I.222). Like the Hebrew *yahîd,* the Greek *monogenēs* was used of the son who was the father's principal heir.

(2) The "servant of the Lord." In ancient Near Eastern religious idiom, a devotee of a deity was known as, and called himself, the servant of that deity. Thus, Eliezer (Abraham's chief steward) in prayer mentions Isaac as "Thy servant" (Gen. 24:14). Later, Moses in prayer mentions Isaac, along with Abraham and Jacob, as "Thy servants" (Exod. 32:13; Deut. 9:27). So, in the apocryphal Prayer of Azariah we read: "Abraham thy beloved . . . Isaac thy servant . . . and Israel thy holy one" (v. 12, RSV Apocrypha). Finally, according to Geza Vermes, Job 3:19 ("and the slave is free from his master," RSV) reads in the Targum: "Isaac the servant of the Lord, who was delivered from bonds by his Master." This is such an obvious allusion to the binding of Isaac that it must now be considered.

(3) The beloved son offered in sacrifice. The Church Fathers saw in Isaac's being offered by his father a type of Jesus' atoning death. Barnabas, for example, indicates that Jesus' death was the fulfilment of "the type established in Isaac" (*Epistle of Barnabas* VII.3). Clement of Alexandria made a similar comparison, likening Jesus' resurrection to Isaac's release from sacrifice (*The Instructor* I.v). The latter could have been inspired quite directly by Hebrews 11:19. But was the notion that Isaac's release was comparable to resurrection *original* with the writer of "To the Hebrews" (who was certainly a Christian of Jewish background)?

According to H. J. Schoeps, Paul also made use of the sacrifice-of-Isaac typology as a basis for interpreting Jesus' death as an atonement for sin. Likewise, Nils A. Dahl finds Paul applying the motifs of the binding of

Isaac to the work of Christ, especially in Romans 8:32 and Galatians 3:13-14. Was this his own special hermeneutics, or was Paul adapting traditional interpretations already available? The latter seems likely.

c. Emphases in the Aqedah interpretations

According to Isidore Lévi, the *aqedah* interpretations were part of the New Year liturgy (cf. Reading 58) which was in existence at least in the first century A.D. (cf. Abrahams, below). The emphases include:

(1) The offering of Isaac was a *voluntary self-offering*, as indicated by Josephus (*Ant.* I.228-32). Vermes points out that the Fragmentary Targum (Yerushalmi 2) XXI.8-10 and a talmudic text mention Isaac's willingness to be sacrificed. The same idea is found in Pseudo-Philo's *Biblical Antiquities* XXXII.3-4 (cf. section *d*, below).

(2) Even though not completed, it was a real sacrifice *in intent*. A talmudic text cited by Montefiore and Loewe (*Rabbinic Anthology*, item 784) says that the earlier rabbis taught that God accepted Isaac's willingness to die as a real death. In *Biblical Antiquities* XVIII.5, God answers the angels who criticize Him for favoring Abraham that "since he did not contradict but made an offering acceptable in My sight, in place of his blood I chose those [i.e., the people Israel]."

(3) The offering *secured atonement* for the sins of his descendants. *IV Maccabees* (late first century B.C.) expresses in a number of passages the belief that the martyrdom of the righteous has atoning merit. Eleazar prays God to make his blood an expiation for his people and to take his life as a ransom for theirs (6:27-29), and he explicitly likens his death to that of Isaac (7:14). The seven martyred brothers encourage each other by the example of Isaac (13:12; cf. II Macc. 7), and their mother speaks to them of Isaac as the prototype of all Jewish martyrs (16:20; 18:11). Montefiore and Loewe cite later texts which testify to belief in the atoning value of the sacrifice of Isaac for the people Israel (cf. items #587 and 612 in their anthology). Thus it appears this doctrine was given impetus by the martyrdoms suffered by pious Jews under Antiochus IV Epiphanes (ca. 168-65 B.C.). The sources indicate that a belief in the atoning value of Isaac's sacrifice (cf. Reading 58), *viewed as voluntary and real*, developed in the pre-Christian era.

d. Relation of Isaac to the "Suffering Servant"

The tenor of Isaac's speech as given in *Biblical Antiquities* XXXII.2-4 indicates that Isaiah 52:13—53:12 was brought into relationship with Genesis 22. He is represented as saying that his blessing will be a superior one because he is making a unique self-offering (cf. Isa. 52:13; 53:11-12). He then says that a posterity will be proclaimed in him (cf. Isa. 53:10b) and that the people will be made to understand through him (cf. Isa. 52:15b), since God has especially dignified the human soul by his sacrifice. The language indicates that Pseudo-Philo in good haggadic fashion is using the "Suffering Servant" passage to interpret the sacrifice of Isaac. In reverse, it should be noted that Isaiah 53:10b ("he shall see his seed, he shall prolong his days") probably owes its original emphasis and inspiration to the tradition in Genesis 22.

But Isaiah 53:10b speaks of the Servant as "an offering for sin." The original account (Gen. 22) does not suggest this. It is a new element. Is this, then, the origin of the tradition of interpreting Isaac's offering as voluntary and atoning? It is possible, especially in view of the well-attested Jewish custom of interpreting one passage by another which seems to have some common elements.

In common between Isaiah 53 and Genesis 22 are: (1) the lamblike obedience of the two victims; (2) the idea that it is God who ultimately causes the offering to be made; and (3) the release of the victims from death with a promise of posterity and honor. Without a prototype for the prophet's picture of the Servant nearer in historical time, what would be more natural than to refer it to Isaac—the "beloved son" above all others, who was offered yet preserved to fulfill God's purpose?

What seems almost assured is that it was this line of tradition that provided the Church with its basis for interpreting the death of Jesus as that of the obedient Servant-Son, the suffering Righteous One of whom the biblical Isaac and the Servant of Isaiah 53 were the prophetic types. His death was, ultimately, voluntary (cf. John 10:18) and atoning. His resurrection made possible His "seeing a posterity" (i.e., of believers, the spiritual children of His Father). And His appearance as the victorious, conquering Lamb would occur at His future Parousia. For John of the Revelation, Jesus crucified and risen is the Lion of the Tribe of Judah (Rev. 5:5; cf. Gen. 49:9; II Esdras 12:31ff.) as well as the Lamb sacrificed and risen (Rev. 5:6)—and so has He been to the Church ever since.

For Further Reading

Abrahams, Israel. *Studies in Pharisaism and the Gospels*. Second Series. Cambridge: The University Press, 1924. (Cf. Note 6, pp. 162-64.)

Lake, Kirsopp, ed. and tr. *The Apostolic Fathers*. Two volumes. New York: G. P. Putnam's Sons, 1930. (*Epistle of Barnabas* VII.3: cf. p. 365.)

Montefiore, C. G., and Loewe, H., eds. *A Rabbinic Anthology*. Cleveland: The World Publishing Co., 1963. Paper (a Meridian book).

Richardson, Alan. *An Introduction to the Theology of the New Testament*. New York: Harper and Row Publishers, 1958. (Especially pp. 180; 228-29)

Schoeps, H. J. *Paul*. Trans. Harold Knight. Philadelphia: Westminster Press, 1961. (Especially ch. 4, sec. 3)

Vermes, Geza. *Scripture and Tradition in Judaism*. Leiden: E. J. Brill, 1961. (Especially ch. VIII)

Also

Dahl, Nils A. "The Atonement—An Adequate Reward for the Akedah? (Rom. 8:32)," in E. Earle Ellis and Max Wilcox, eds., *Neotestamentica et Semitica: Studies in Honor of Matthew Black*. Edinburgh: T. & T. Clark, 1969.

Rosenberg, Roy A. "Jesus, Isaac, and the 'Suffering Servant,' " *Journal of Biblical Literature* 84 (1965), pp. 381-88.

Select Bibliography

Texts and Translations

Source Texts

Barthélemy, D., and Milik, J. T., eds. *Discoveries in the Judaean Desert I: Qumran Cave I.* Oxford: The Clarendon Press, 1955.

Blackman, Philip, ed. *Mishnayot.* Seven volumes. Second edition revised. New York: The Judaica Press, Inc., 1964.

Brock, S. P., ed. *Testamentum Jobi* (in Vol. II of A.-M. Denis and M. de Jonge, eds., *Pseudepigrapha Veteris Testamenti Graece*). Leiden: E. J. Brill, 1967.

Charles, R. H., ed. *The Greek Versions of the Testaments of the Twelve Patriarchs.* New York: Oxford University Press, 1960. (Reprint of 1908 edition)

De Jonge, M., ed. *Testamentum XII Patriarchum* (Vol. I of A.-M. Denis and M. de Jonge, eds., *Pseudepigrapha Veteris Testamenti Graece*). Leiden: E. J. Brill, 1964.

Denis, Albert-Marie, ed. *Fragmenta Pseudepigraphorum quae Supersunt Graece* (in Vol. III of A.-M. Denis and M. de Jonge, eds., *Pseudepigrapha Veteris Testamenti Graece*). Leiden: E. J. Brill, 1970.

Elbogen, Ismar. *Der jüdische Gottesdienst in seiner geschichtlichen Entwicklung.* Fourth edition. Hildesheim: Georg Olms Verlagsbuchhandlung, 1962. (Hebrew text of *Shemoneh Esreh*, p. 517).

Feldman, Louis H., ed. JOSEPHUS, Vol. IX: *Jewish Antiquities,* Books XVIII—XX. Cambridge, Mass.: Harvard University Press, 1965.

Hadas, Moses, ed. *The Third and Fourth Books of Maccabees.* New York: Harper and Brothers, 1953.

Herford, R. Travers. *Pirke Aboth—The Ethics of the Talmud: Sayings of the Fathers.* New York: Schocken Books, 1962.

Kisch, Guido, ed. *Pseudo-Philo's Liber Antiquitatum Biblicarum.* Notre Dame, Ind.: University of Notre Dame, 1949.

Kohler, Kaufmann. "The Testament of Job—An Essene Midrash on the Book of Job," in George A. Kohut, ed., *Semitic Studies in Memory of Rev. Dr. Alexander Kohut.* Berlin: S. Calvary & Co., 1897.

Levi, Israel, ed. *The Hebrew Text of the Book of Ecclesiasticus.* Leiden: E. J. Brill, 1951.

Lohse, Eduard, ed. *Die Texte aus Qumran: Hebräisch und Deutsch.* München: Kösel-Verlag, 1964.

Marcus, Ralph, ed. JOSEPHUS, Vol. VII: *Jewish Antiquities,* Books XII—XIV. Cambridge, Mass.: Harvard University Press, 1943.

Philips, A. Th., ed. *Prayer Book for the First Day of New Year.* New York: Hebrew Publishing Co., 1926.

Rabin, Chaim. *The Zadokite Documents.* Second revised edition. Oxford: The Clarendon Press, 1958.

Rahlfs, Alfred, ed. *Septuaginta: id est Vetus Testamentum Graece iuxta LXX interpres.* Sixth edition. New York: American Bible Society, n.d.

Schechter, Solomon, ed. *Documents of Jewish Sectaries.* New York: Ktav Publishing House, Inc., 1970.

Strugnell, J. "The angelic liturgy at Qumran, 4Q Serek Šîrôt ʿOlat Haš-šabāt," in *Supplements to Vetus Testamentum VII: Congress Volume, Oxford 1959.* Leiden: E. J. Brill, 1960.

Swete, Henry Barclay, ed. *The Old Testament in Greek According to the Septuagint,* Vol. III. Cambridge: The University Press, 1905.

Taylor, Charles, ed. and tr. *Sayings of the Jewish Fathers.* Second edition. New York: Ktav Publishing House, Inc., 1969.

Thackeray, H. St. John, ed. and tr. JOSEPHUS, Vol. II: *The Jewish War,* Books I—III. New York: G. P. Putnam's Sons, 1927.

Torrey, C. C., ed. and tr. *The Lives of the Prophets: Greek Text and Translation.* Philadelphia: Society of Biblical Literature and Exegesis, 1946.

Zuckermandel, M. S., ed., *TOSEPHTA: Based on the Erfurt and Vienna Codices,* with parallels and variants. Jerusalem: Wahrmann Books, 1963.

Translations of Sources (usually with introductions and notes)

Charles, R. H., et al., eds. *The Apocrypha and Pseudepigrapha of the Old Testament in English.* Two volumes. Oxford: The Clarendon Press, 1913.

————. *The Book of Enoch.* London: S. P. C. K., 1925. Reprint 1960.

————. *The Book of Jubilees, or The Little Genesis.* London: Adam and Charles Black, 1902.

————. *The Testaments of the Twelve Patriarchs.* London: S. P. C. K., 1917.

Danby, Herbert. *The Mishnah: Translated from the Hebrew, with Introduction and Brief Explanatory Notes.* London: Oxford University Press, 1933.

Gaster, Theodore H. *The Dead Sea Scriptures in English Translation.* Garden City, N.Y.: Doubleday & Co., Inc., 1957. Anchor paperback.

Harris, J. Rendel. *The Odes and Psalms of Solomon* (Published from the Syriac Version). Second edition revised. Cambridge: The University Press, 1911.

James, Montague Rhodes, ed. and tr. *The Biblical Antiquities of Philo.* New York: The Macmillan Co., 1917.

Mansoor, Menahem, ed. *The Thanksgiving Hymns.* Grand Rapids: Wm. B. Eerdmans Publishing Co., 1961.

Metzger, Bruce M., ed. *The Apocrypha of the Old Testament: Revised Standard Version.* Annotated edition. New York: Oxford University Press, 1965.

Oesterley, W. O. E., ed. *The Wisdom of Jesus the Son of Sirach, or Ecclesiasticus, in the Revised Version.* Cambridge: The University Press, 1912.

Vermes, Geza. *The Dead Sea Scrolls in English.* Baltimore: Penguin Books, 1962.

Wernberg-Møller, P., ed. *The Manual of Discipline.* Grand Rapids: Wm. B. Eerdmans Publishing Co., 1957.

Introductions and Discussions

General Introductions to Intertestamental Literature

Andrews, H. T. *An Introduction to the Apocryphal Books of the Old and New Testaments.* Second edition, revised by Charles F. Pfeiffer. Grand Rapids: Baker Book House, 1964.

Denis, Albert-Marie. *Introduction aux Pseudepigraphes Grecs d'Ancien Testament.* Leiden: E. J. Brill, 1970.

Metzger, Bruce M. *An Introduction to the Apocrypha.* New York: Oxford University Press, 1957.

Oesterley, W. O. E. *An Introduction to the Books of the Apocrypha.* London: S. P. C. K., 1958.

Pfeiffer, Robert H. *History of New Testament Times, with an Introduction to the Apocrypha.* New York: Harper & Brothers Publishers, 1949.

Torrey C. C. *The Apocryphal Literature: A Brief Introduction.* New Haven, Conn.: Yale University Press, 1945.

Discussions

Bowker, John. *The Targums and Rabbinic Literature: An Introduction to Jewish Interpretations of Scripture.* Cambridge: The University Press, 1969.

Burkitt, F. Crawford. *Jewish and Christian Apocalypses.* London: Oxford University Press, 1914.

DiLella, Alexander A. *The Hebrew Text of Sirach.* The Hague: Mouton & Co., 1966.

Edersheim, Alfred. *The Life and Times of Jesus the Messiah.* Two volumes. New American Edition. New York: E. R. Herrick & Co., n.d.

Gaster, Moses, ed. *Studies and Texts in Folklore, Magic, Mediaeval Romance, Hebrew Apocrypha and Samaritan Archaeology.* Three volumes. New York: Ktav Publishing House, Inc., 1971.

Grant, Frederick C. *Ancient Judaism and the New Testament.* New York: The Macmillan Co., 1959.

Meeks, Wayne A. *The Prophet-King: Moses Traditions and the Johannine Christology.* Leiden: E. J. Brill, 1967.

Moore, George Foot. *Judaism in the First Centuries of the Christian Era.* Three volumes. Cambridge, Mass.: Harvard University Press, 1932-40.

Rosenblatt, Samuel. *The Interpretation of the Bible in the Mishnah.* Baltimore: The Johns Hopkins Press, 1935.

Vermes, Geza. *Scripture and Tradition in Judaism.* Leiden: E. J. Brill, 1961.

For other discussions, see the suggestions for further reading in the Extended Notes.